Professionals today, whether managers, engineers, entrepreneurs, or scientists, need to maximize their effectiveness. To accomplish this, skill and motivation are not enough. The process of innovative problem solving is crucial to managing complex enterprises, but until now has been poorly understood. *Thinking Strategically* illuminates this process in the context of real world achievement. Four key components – strategic creativity, innovation, generation and elaboration, strategic problem solving, and reality checks – are integrated into a coherent framework for generating innovation and managing complexity. Specific conceptual tools are presented for classifying problem-solving style, for identification of opportunities via recognition of anomalies and contradictions, for analysis of problems, for generation of solutions, and for turning innovations into finished products.

Thinking Strategically provides the necessary power tools for dissecting complex problems and creating innovative solutions. This ground-breaking book will prove essential for all professionals who are serious about increasing their creativity, productivity, and effectiveness.

Thinking Strategically

Power Tools for Personal and Professional Advancement

Thinking Strategically

Power Tools for Personal and Professional Advancement

CRAIG LOEHLE, PhD

Argonne National Laboratory

CAMBRIDGE
UNIVERSITY PRESS

PUBLISHED BY THE PRESS SYNDICATE OF THE UNIVERSITY OF CAMBRIDGE
The Pitt Building, Trumpington Street, Cambridge CB2 1RP, United Kingdom

CAMBRIDGE UNIVERSITY PRESS
The Edinburgh Building, Cambridge CB2 2RU, United Kingdom
40 West 20th Street, New York, NY 10011–4211, USA
10 Stamford Road, Oakleigh, Melbourne 3166, Australia

First published 1996
Reprinted 1996

Printed in the United Kingdom at the University Press, Cambridge

Typeset in Monotype Ehrhardt 9/12pt

A catalogue record for this book is available from the British Library

Library of Congress Cataloguing in Publication data

Loehle, Craig.
    Strategic thinking for innovation, discovery, and problem solving/Craig Loehle.
        p.   cm.
    Includes bibliographical references and index.
    ISBN 0 521 56058 6 (hardcover). – ISBN 0 521 56841 2 (pbk.)
    1. Creative thinking.   2. Creative ability.   3. Creation (Literary artistic, etc.)
    4. Problem solving.   I. Title.
    BF408.L753   1996
    153.4′2–dc20   96–795 CIP

ISBN 0 521 56058 6 hardback
ISBN 0 521 56841 2 paperback

Dedicated to my dear wife Neda, the light of my life and my inspiration, and to my children Sholeh, Gloria, and Niki, who bring me unbounded joy

Contents

Acknowledgements

Thanks to Tim Benton and several anonymous reviewers for helpful comments on the entire book. Drafts of various chapters were reviewed by Egolfs Bakuzis, Henry H. Bauer, Dan Herms, Rolfe Leary, D. Bengston, J. Cairns, I. J. Good, D. Orth, M. C. Rauscher, J. Schear, D. Schlesinger, D. K. Simonton, R. J. Sternberg, J. Weiner, and R. Michael Miller. Their assistance is greatly appreciated. Various chapters and portions of this book are revised from the following sources and used by permission: Loehle, C. 1990. A guide to increased creativity in research. *BioScience* **40**:123–9. © American Institute of Biological Sciences. Loehle, C. 1994. A critical path analysis. *Journal of Creative Behavior*, **28**:33. © The Creative Education Foundation. Loehle, C. 1994. Discovery as a process. *Journal of Creative Behavior*, **28**:239. © The Creative Education Foundation. Loehle, C. 1994. Creativity the divine gift. In *On the Shoulders of Giants*, pp. 68–91. George Ronald, Oxford. Pencil sketches and the drawing of Charles Darwin are by Richard Loehle. Helpful editorial assistance was provided by Sandi Irvine.

Introduction

Professionals today face complexity at every turn. Whether it is managing a matrix organization or reengineering a factory, whether setting up a distributed computing network or writing a proposal, the level of complexity and extent of interrelations between causal factors have increased to almost a bewildering level. Higher education does not provide adequate preparation for making decisions in such a context because it focuses largely on procedural knowledge and the solution of well-defined problems. In school, every problem has a fixed answer, but in the real world, every new technology, every change in the markets, every customer design specification calls for a novel response. Our economic survival (individually and collectively) depends on our mastery of the complex and rapidly changing world we have created. What is required is strategic thinking, which is a process of reasoning about complex problems or systems to achieve a goal. Strategic thinking is exhibited by the general who wages a brilliant campaign, by the business manager who makes a complex enterprise run smoothly, by the scientist who always picks a fruitful problem and finds a clever way to solve it. The author believes that these successful people utilize skills and techniques that can be shared, and sets out to teach the component skills essential to strategic thinking.

In certain types of problem solving, special skills are learned and are then applied repeatedly. For example, in accounting one learns certain procedures for keeping books and doing computations, but the component skills are very specific to a well-defined domain – accounting. In contrast, strategic thinking involves the integration of several types of mental skills and techniques, as well as certain habits and attitudes, in the context of defining the problem to be solved from an initially ambiguous sea of unconnected data, and then solving it. There is an element of risk in strategic problem solving because complexity causes uncertainty. The acquisition of the skills presented in this book, and their integration, will help to reduce risk and increase problem solving success in complex domains.

While there have been many books about creativity and problem solving, they are mostly about problem-solving minutia, such as the use of analogy, visualization, generation of novelty, brainstorming, lateral thinking, and free association. We may say that these component skills are like the ability to saw, the ability to hammer a nail, and the ability to use a drill, without any skill in reading blueprints or any understanding of how an entire house fits together. While a collection of low level skills will enable one to build a bird house, they do not allow one to erect an office building. To make another comparison, brainstorming may help one to come up with a name for a new product or an advertising campaign slogan, but it will not help one to compose a symphony or build a space shuttle. This book goes beyond brainstorming and describes the tools needed both for generating new ideas and for carrying them through to a completed product.

Gardner (1983) proposes that there are discrete dimensions of intelligence, such as linguistic, musical, mathematical, and spatial mental abilities, that are relatively independent of one another and that are not necessarily measured by a general intelligence quotient (IQ). He points out that IQ measures mainly linguistic and logical/mathematical abilities. Musical aptitude is clearly not tested by IQ measures. I believe there is also a dimension of strategic intelligence. This dimension of intelligence comprises a flair for planning ahead and finding the best route or scenario to obtain an advantageous outcome. A person high on this dimension is good at planning a trip and does not often forget to pack something in his or her luggage. Such people are probably good at board games and poker (though such games may not motivate them because the outcome seems too trivial), and are also likely to be good at making career moves. The person low on this dimension goes to the laundry without soap, goes into the shower without a towel, and goes to the store or supermarket without a list. Such a person finds a job but has no concept of a career path. It is really best not to go camping with such people, because they will end up sleeping in your tent, since they did not bring any tent pegs. They usually do not think ahead and are always surprised by outcomes that do not surprise others. Such people go to pieces when faced with logistics problems such as organizing their desk, packing for a trip, or reordering the garage. I believe this dimension is independent of other dimensions of intelligence because I have known otherwise intelligent people who are absolutely incapable of planning ahead or anticipating the consequences of actions. This aspect of intelligence is not amenable to pencil-and-paper diagnostic test, which is why I believe it has not been identified and studied previously.

This book explores the strategic dimension of mental reasoning and problem solving. Specifically involved in this are the identification of the mind's strengths and weaknesses, understanding how cognitive processes operate, and learning how one can obtain reliable information and solve complex problems, how new ideas are generated and tested, and how real world complexity may be dealt with. This book also provides training for the strategic dimension of intellectual reasoning, a key dimension for success but one largely overlooked by educational systems. This book is not an academic treatise, but rather is a guide to developing strategic thinking skills.

The importance of strategic thinking can be demonstrated as follows. When the frontal lobes of the brain are damaged or removed, the IQ of the person remains unaffected and he or she may even remain at genius level if they scored this high before the removal. However, the person loses all initiative and the ability to solve novel problems. He or she will score as well as before in IQ tests, can do crossword puzzles and math problems, etc., but lack the ability to set goals or be creative. This is exactly the set of symptoms that describes mindless government officials or corporate drones: they have college degrees and appear smart but they are unable to take the initiative and withdraw in fear from novelty. These people have not had an actual lobotomy, but they have been trained and rewarded in such a way that initiative has been squashed. It is not hard to create a drone – merely scoff at all new ideas, have complex procedures that must be followed to the letter, punish mistakes severely, reward conformance, and require approval for every action. The drone can solve simple problems such as accounting problems, arranging meetings, writing a descriptive report, and doing defined technical tasks, as long as the work is defined for them, but they cannot create novelty, overcome outdated methods of operating, identify problems with existing systems, or create new concepts or products. For such tasks strategic thinking is required. Technical proficiency and the possession of a college degree is no more a guarantee of strategic thinking than is the IQ score of the lobotomy patient an indicator of their ability to function.

We may further note that the types of problem used both in IQ tests and in most creativity training are contrived and largely involve the linguistic and logical dimensions of intelligence. The problems typically involve short linguistic riddles (x is to y as z is to what?), comparisons, exclusions, analogies, etc. and simple logical operations (short computations). Training in problem solving usually involves simple puzzles such as word problems (a train leaves city P at 10:00 am and . . .). It has been shown, however, that while such tests predict success in school, there is no correlation with success later in life (Gardner, 1983). That is to say, one can do quite well on standarized tests and get good grades in school, but be incapable of innovation or of dealing with complexity. This is because real life and the production of products of real value requires strategic thinking and creativity, neither of which is either tested by IQ tests or fully developed by current schooling practices, nor is real creativity equivalent to the pure generation of novel responses.

The potential benefit from the application of the information presented in this book is enormous. Gilbert (1978), for example, has documented the huge range of observed productivities among workers. Whether we are looking at academic productivity (publications), computer programming (lines of correct code), artistic output, sales, or any other endeavor, the most productive individual within a job category is often at least 10-fold as productive as the average worker, and sometimes as much as 30-fold. Whereas in the realm of creative output some hold quality up in contrast to quantity, there is actually more often a correlation between the two: the most innovative individuals often produce the most (Simonton, 1988). This is because the same skills that enable truly innovative work to be done also enhance productivity. The success of the individual professional certainly depends on the frequent production of innovative work. Whereas most artists produce a few to a dozen paintings a year, Andy Worhol and Pablo Picasso filled warehouses with their work. While most academics write one or two papers per year (or less), some write a book each year. The same range applies to inventors, architects, software designers, or any other profession. This difference in productivity is equivalent to that produced by the industrial revolution or the introduction of computers. Might it not be that such high levels of output could be more generally achievable with the right training? In sports, coaching and training regimes have become a science, with the consequence that performance can now only be doubled at most (for example, in professional baseball the record for home runs is only twice that of the average major league player). The range of performance between the average and exceptional practitioner in the (nonsport) professions, being so wide, means that huge improvements in productivity are possible in these fields. The time spent fixing prior mistakes, spinning one's wheels, doing tasks inefficiently, and doing the wrong task add up to an easy potential doubling of productivity for almost anyone doing any type of nonroutine work. When the quality of the finished product is considered, there is room for further improvement, making an overall increase in value of an order of magnitude within reach for any professional.

Why do we think that basketball players or tennis players need a coach but no one else does? That intensive training in technique can lead to a top gymnastic performance we do not doubt, but it never seems to occur to us that a top artistic or programming or inventing performance can similarly benefit from coaching. And yet, sadly, today one cannot count on one's corporation to provide such training and productivity enhancement. In the name of keeping costs down, companies have rejected the idea that individuals should be groomed for rapid advancement by providing guidance, feedback, and special work experience and training. Instead, the idea has become popular that large numbers of employees should be just kept in the job for which they were hired. Many colleges today, for example, use part-time outside instructors for as much as one-third of their classes. Such individuals do not receive any career guidance, have no time devoted to research or professional development, do not have laboratory space, cannot have graduate students, cannot get promoted, and are not funded to attend conferences; i.e., they are in a dead end job. The same is true in many corporations today, where opportunities for advancement have become few and far between. This style of management makes perfect sense from the short-term bottom line perspective, but the consequences of the rejection of the concept of training people for advancement is that the entire process of increasing personnel productivity is becoming neglected. In the typical professional career, supervisors will rarely, if ever, come into the office to ask how the work is going or to offer a single tip on how to be more productive, creative, or effective. The sole feedback is usually at the annual review where one is often told that one is doing just fine and to keep it up. Even if completely true, and not just a cop-out from a boss who wants to avoid the performance appraisal process, such feedback is not very helpful for doing better in the future. Many supervisors actually have a disincentive to providing good career advice: if they increase the productivity of their employees, then the employees will expect a raise or even a promotion, which they have been told will not be provided. In this climate, if the employee (i.e., a reader of this book) is to get ahead, he or she must become noticeably more proficient, talented, productive, and creative so as to stand out from the crowd. To do this, he or she needs a coach. This book can be your personal coach in creativity, problem-solving technique, work habits, and productivity.

There are three pillars of professional productivity: skill, motivation, and strategic use of time and effort. Skill is what one acquires in school and what one polishes with practice. This includes mastery of facts, manual skills such as mixing of paints for a painter and soldering for an electrician, and technological mastery of such tools as spreadsheets and databases. Skill alone only guarantees one a job doing work for someone else as a cog in the machine of a large organization, but does not guarantee high quality work or outstanding performance. Motivation is a key component of success that is generally not taught in school. Few have succeeded without significant motivation, because success requires sustained and substantial effort. Many motivational books by successful business leaders have been written, and these books can be very helpful for increasing motivation, perseverance, and effort. However, motivation alone is not enough because many unimaginative people put in very long hours doing pointless tasks and producing little of value, and companies full of executives putting in 12 hour days have nevertheless gone bankrupt. The third pillar, strategic use of time and effort, is the ultimate key to success, though it depends on the first two being firmly in place. The strategic dimension is what allows one to choose the right problem to solve, to solve it in a cost-effective way, to use resources efficiently, and to be innovative and productive. The strategic dimension, not merely effort, is what accounts for the huge productivity differences noted by Gilbert (1978). In the absence of a concept of strategic use of time, many organizations reward effort rather than output, with the result being that people put in long hours to impress the boss, while being very ineffective in their use of time and perhaps without even producing anything tangible. The combination of skill, motivation, and strategic use of effort can lead to astonishing levels of productivity. This book is based on these three pillars and aims to point the way to such levels of productivity.

One may ask whether strategic thinking alone is sufficient. Of course not. In a world full of downsizing and changing technologies, there is no guarantee of success or of permanent employment. Nor is one always in a position that one's ideas can be carried out. Just because one invents a new product does not mean that one's company will develop it. However, it is especially under these conditions of uncertainty, where every professional has become a consultant, that optimal output of innovative, high quality work has become most imperative. A number of other issues impact on the success of a professional, including corporate culture, relations with bosses and subordinates, concepts of teaming,

Putting in long hours does not necessarily lead to high quality products.

and project management. While many of these issues are touched on in this book, the focus is on the performance of the individual: what can you, as a professional, do to become more effective, more innovative, and more productive.

It is useful to contrast this book with Tom Peters' works (e.g., *A Passion for Excellence*; Peters and Austin, 1985). Peters identifies organizational structures and management strategies that have been proven by the test of time (i.e., these companies make money). If you are fortunate enough to work for one of Peters' high performing companies, you will find that the work style promoted in this book will probably be encouraged and the enhanced productivity engendered by these techniques will be rewarded. If you are working for a loser, a company with a bad attitude and a cramped style, then you are probably facing downsizing and need to hone your strategic faculties to leave before you are laid off. If you are a consultant or entrepreneur, then you need this book for your very survival. While Peters' book helps one to understand the behavior of the company one works for, most professionals are not in a high enough position to alter the corporate culture. However, one is in complete control of one's own performance. In whatever setting, it is personally better to be creative and productive, even if in the short term it does not seem like this will be rewarded.

PART 1 Component skills of strategic thinking

Because strategic thinking is inherently about open-ended, complex problems, it is not possible to apply a "cookbook" approach. Rather, one must have a general approach to problem solving that is effective. For those who are not born strategists, this involves tuning up one's thinking machinery specifically for this type of problem. In particular, there are three steps to creating successful novel products. First, one must be capable of generating novel (but useful) ideas, of overcoming routine ways of functioning, and of putting together information in new ways. Without this capacity, one is limited to solving problems defined by others (my definition of a drone). Second, one must be able to use this creative capacity to discover/invent something new. This can be, for example, a new style of art, a new computer algorithm, a new building design, an improvement to a video recorder, or a new type of restaurant. Third, one must understand how to structure work to bring a new creation to fruition. Without this third step, one is just daydreaming.

In this section I show how one enhances the creative process, how one goes about making discoveries, how one puts together the solution to a complex problem, how one tests the solution one obtains, and how one enhances internal mental states for optimal performance. What is most noteworthy is that the conventional wisdom in all of these domains fails in the face of complexity. How one goes about achieving insights on simple problems does not provide a reliable guide to the solution of complex ones. Insights on simple problems can easily be "all-of-a-piece, aha!" experiences, matching the standard preparation → incubation → illumination model; but complex problems require structuring, planning, scheduling, tinkering, and iterative improvements and are almost never solvable in a single flash. The type of creativity measured by typical tests is essentially the generation of novel responses and is unrelated to true creativity, which can be assessed only in ambiguous and complex problem domains. The relationship between intelligence and creativity has traditionally been unclear (i.e., little relationship has been found when a strong one should be expected) but this can be explained when the entire problem-solving process is analyzed. A critical step, almost ignored in the creativity literature, is reality testing of a new idea or product. Finally, the attitudinal dimension has rarely been explored, but in fact turns out to be crucial and can explain many great failures of problem solving, such as military disasters and engineering fiascoes. Therefore, in this part I explore the mental operations and overall processes of strategic problem solving. The second part of the book covers strategic problem solving in practice, covering problem-solving tools and approaches and discussing general principles such as perspective, information transmission, paradox, and bottlenecks.

1 Strategic creativity

An essential component of strategic thinking is strategic creativity. Because strategic thinking deals essentially with complex problems, uncertainty, and ambiguity, and involves finding solutions that others have overlooked, it is essential that the practitioner be creative in approach. The standard view of creativity, however, is seriously flawed for application to strategic problem solving. A typical picture of the creative person is the artist or musician, who may have a wild lifestyle and dress in a bizarre fashion. This represents a confusion between the person with a novel lifestyle or a person with flair and someone who is genuinely innovative. Thomas Edison did not wear tie-dye T-shirts. Whereas a wild lifestyle may help or not hinder (though this is debatable) an artist's expression of ideas, this is not the case in the creative application of strategic thinking. In technical and management professions, one needs to be able to think extremely clearly, to be organized, to plan ahead, and to meet deadlines. Wild, magical, and fuzzy thinking are deadly in this context. This in no way means, however, that creativity must be excluded. Far from it. Those professionals who are technically competent but not creative are limited to doing what everyone else already knows how to do. They can run an organization that is already running smoothly, but will not encourage or even allow innovation. They are the managers and technocrats who very competently run a large organization right off a cliff because they either fail to see change or cannot find creative solutions to changing conditions (e.g., IBM was caught short as it failed to see the trends away from mainframe computers).

Creativity as it is commonly studied and assessed by psychologists usually involves first order creativity only. The types of measure commonly used include the generation of novel responses, use of analogy, ability to incorporate rich imagery into a story, etc. While such measures of creativity may be directly applicable to the artist, especially a modern artist, because novelty per se is a key component of success, such first-order creative responses are almost irrelevant to strategic creativity. The schizophrenic produces highly divergent responses in drawing or word association, but they are usually bizarre and not useful. For solving real world strategic problems, one must find not merely novelty, but novelty in the context of constraints, tradeoffs, and uncertainty, and the novel solution must be useful. Because of the complexity of the problems, what is required is not just the generation of innovative responses and the habit of creative expression, but rather that one takes a creative approach to the thinking process itself. That is to say, the strategic thinker must be creative in the use of mental faculties. This is strategic creativity.

Innovative entrepreneurs, academics, engineers, and inventors are held in high regard, but the means by which they achieve innovation are not spelled out in any manual. Courses on the scientific method do not cover innovation. MBA programs offer no courses on creativity, innovation, or problem-solving techniques. Philosophers of science are more concerned with formal theory structure, proof, logic, and epistemology. Popper (1963), for example, invokes the generation of alternative hypotheses but says nothing about where one is to get them. The type of creativity studied by psychologists is generally more applicable to the arts, where any type of novelty is interesting and need not conform to limitations such as feasibility or cost.

The pressures on professionals today oppose truly creative thinking. Pressures on academics to write grant applications, teach, and publish leave little time for undirected thinking. Industrial laboratories today are far more directed than in the past, particularly where product development costs are high (e.g., in drug development). Therefore one must actively counter these anticreative forces to be a successful innovator.

In this chapter, I describe the characteristics of strategic creativity and provide some guidelines for enhancing it. The capacity to generate new ideas is almost universal, but needs to be enhanced to become a significant problem-solving asset. This chapter shows how to identify problems worth working on, how to overcome barriers to the generation of new ideas, how to listen to new ideas when they arise, and how to arrange work schedules so as to enhance creative thought. This provides a basis for generating the ideas crucial to the overall strategic problem-solving process. The following chapters build on this material with a discussion of the processes of discovery and invention, which are at the heart of innovation, and of generating finished products. An appreciation of both the dimensions of creativity and the process of discovery is the key to creating results that are both novel and useful.

Choosing a problem

Perhaps the most important single step in the problem-solving process is choosing a question to investigate. In contrast to school settings, in the real world one's problems are rarely presented as already well defined. What most distinguishes those innovators noted by posterity is not their technical skill, but that they chose interesting problems. How they do so has not been entirely obvious. Here some guidance is given in this regard.

☞ Picking fights

Professional work is supposed to be an objective, dispassionate business. After all, one is dealing with numbers and facts and schedules, with machines, networks and systems. Sometimes, however, one observes something that is infuriating. This anger is an indication that at some level you recognize that here is a problem that needs resolution. The gut feeling that the other person is wrong, or that there is a better way to do it, or that a competitor's product is ugly or unwieldy, is a good guide to choosing an interesting topic for yourself.

Setting out with irrational determination to prove someone wrong provides a drive that can allow you to break out of your preconceptions. Such base emotions can be a strong creative force, causing you to dig deep and work intensely. The effort to refute someone can even lead to evidence supporting them or to a different topic altogether. Intense rivalries, as in the race to discover DNA (Watson, 1968), can also provide this essential concentration. So, whereas the finished product may appear dispassionate, truly creative work is often driven by strong passions.

☞ Where there's smoke . . .

A good strategy for finding an interesting problem is to follow the fire fighters, because "Where there's smoke there's fire." When there is intense debate on a topic, inconclusive or contradictory data, or terminological confusion, then the situation is probably ripe for a creative redefinition of the problem or application of a new method. If, however, one's tendency is just to choose sides, then one is merely more kindling and should stay away from the fire. A creative redefinition comes about from recognizing how it is that both sides in a debate could have come to their given conclusions. Once one can see clearly how the two sides could come to opposite conclusions from the same facts, then one is in a position to redefine the problem and create a resolution to it. Adler (1985) gives a beautiful illustration of this technique in his analysis of where Western philosophy has gone astray. He shows that modern philosophy has become irrelevant to the common (or even educated) person, which was not previously the case. Whereas philosophy in principle should be a useful guide to how to think about issues, about how to live and our place in the world, and about how to discover, its modern incarnation is none of these and is not even of much help in science. Adler identifies the crucial mistakes of thinkers such as Kant, Hume, and Locke, and how those mistakes created a mistaken path down which subsequent philosophers blindly followed. Once the initial mistake is uncovered, the subsequent elaboration of philosophical systems that lead to absurd conclusions (e.g., the relativistic view that scientific knowledge is purely a human construct, as though airplanes remain in the air by popular consensus) can be clearly seen and more coherent philosophies (which interestingly do provide guidance to the everyday person) can be developed (see Adler, 1985).

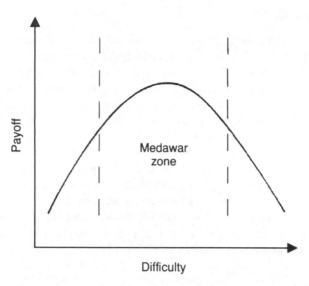

Figure 1.   Relationship between degree of difficulty and payoff from solving a problem. Solving
problems that are too easy does not advance science, whereas those that are too difficult
may be impossible for other scientists to understand, i.e., they are premature. The
Medawar zone refers to Medawar's (1967) reference to science as "the art of the
soluble."

☞ The Medawar zone

There is a general parabolic relationship between the difficulty of a problem and
its likely payoff (Figure 1). Solving an easy problem has a low payoff, because it is
well within reach and does not represent a real advance. Solving a very difficult
problem may have a high payoff, but frequently will not pay at all because one is
more likely to fail and because it may be difficult to take advantage of success. For
example, designs for a tunnel under the English Channel were proposed nearly
200 years ago, but costs were prohibitive. The Greeks had an atomic theory over
2500 years ago, but had no way to test it. Many problems are difficult because the
associated tools and technology are not advanced enough. For example, one may
do a brilliant experiment but current theory may not be able to explain it or,
conversely, a theory may remain untestable for many years. This is the case with
much of atomic physics at the moment. The region of optimal benefit lies at an
intermediate level of complexity, what I call the Medawar zone in reference to Sir
Peter Medawar's (1967) characterization of science as the "art of the soluble."
These intermediate level problems have the highest benefit per unit of effort
because they are neither too difficult to solve nor so simple that their solution is
trivial.

The issue of what is interesting and what is solvable lies at the heart of great discoveries and what we call genius. What is notable about great innovators is that they have an instinct for identifying this type of problem, and even when they are wrong, they are wrong in an interesting way and on an interesting topic. Some who choose to grapple with the big questions fail because they address problems not ripe for solution. The more common problem afflicts the average person who shies away from really interesting problems in favor of easier ones. In science, a focus on the easier, routine problems is a characteristic of Kuhn's (1970) "normal science."

Working on too-easy problems is disadvantageous both because no one may notice your results (yawn!) and because "easy" or small problems often turn out to be merely pieces of a larger puzzle and only soluble in that context. For example, in the first X-ray pictures of DNA (Watson, 1968) two forms (A and B, differing by water content of the sample) of diffraction pattern were evident. James Watson and Francis Crick did not focus on explaining or interpreting this difference, but rather they focused on the more difficult problem of the DNA structure. When that puzzle was solved, the A and B patterns were easily interpreted.

When someone succeeds in frequently hitting the target (the Medawar zone), that person will often appear to be more intelligent than a pure IQ test would indicate. To an extent, the feel for interesting problems can be transmitted by contact, which explains why the institution of graduate-student-as-apprentice is so successful and why certain laboratories ferment with new ideas. Such laboratories are often observed to fade away or return to what is considered normal after the death or departure of the person or persons who provided the creative spark.

The creative spark is not easily obtainable through the formal textbook portion of professional training, and it may not arise spontaneously. For example, Feynman (1984) recounts his experience as a visiting faculty member in Brazil in the 1960s. Physics in Brazil was just getting started. To outward appearances, the faculty knew the facts. Library and laboratory facilities were adequate. The students did very well on tests. Yet there was almost a complete lack of comprehension of the process of innovation and discovery. Science was a textbook exercise of learning definitions rather than one of discovery. For example, in a physics class that Feynman was teaching, the students could define the properties of light polarization resulting from light striking flat surfaces at extreme angles, but could not give a single example from nature, even though they were overlooking the changing color of the sky's reflection from the ocean's surface. That is to say, they were unable to relate the definitions to the real world. Even in the USA today, entire departments or disciplines sometimes become stuck in such a listless or out of touch state.

Releasing creativity

Most people can learn to be far more creative. School systems tend to emphasize single correct answers and provide few opportunities for exploratory learning, problem solving, or innovation. Suddenly, when one becomes a graduate student or professional, however, it is expected that one is automatically an independent thinker and a creative problem solver. To a significant extent, creative responses are a matter of orientation and perception rather than a special skill or a dimension of personality. We may characterize the givers of noncreative responses as being stuck with a limited vision, an inability to see things in a novel way, a conventionality rut. I therefore focus next on ways of encouraging creative approaches and reducing blocks to creativity. This aspect of creativity addresses only the ability to develop novel ideas or approaches. Other aspects of creativity involve the full elaboration and development of a novel idea into a finished product, a topic addressed in Chapters 2 and 3.

☛ Barriers to navigation

In the early fifteenth century, Prince Henry the Navigator of Portugal sent his sailors to explore Africa and open it to Portuguese trade (account in Boorstin, 1983). Portuguese expeditions began to work their way down the western coast, always within sight of land. Upon reaching Cape Bojador, a rocky stretch of desolate coast with treacherous currents, the Portuguese sailors would inevitably turn back, convinced that this was the end of land and that no ship would ever pass it. Prince Henry sent out 15 expeditions between 1424 and 1434 until finally one succeeded by sailing a few kilometers out to sea and going south for a few kilometers, thereby passing the dangerous rocks and currents.

As a navigation feat, this maneuver was trivial. While it is true that their ships were not strong and their navigation tools were primitive, the major barrier was not technological but the fear of losing sight of land. We can say that the feat of Christopher Columbus was far more difficult technically (not to get lost), but he too faced a major barrier of fear, both in his sponsors and in his crew. Once the Atlantic was crossed, this fear was swept away and only the reasonable fears of shipwreck, scurvy, and sea serpents remained. Many barriers are of this type. An item becomes fixed in the mental landscape, immutable. What lies beyond the barrier becomes not merely unknown, but unimaginable. Major enhancements in creativity can be achieved by developing the courage to recognize and overcome mental barriers, just as the Portuguese and Spanish sailors did.

A simple test for creativity involves giving test subjects a set of objects and a goal, to see whether they can use ordinary objects in unusual ways (e.g., a rock as a hammer). Noncreative individuals are often stumped by these tests. In the professions, too, objects become fixed in meaning. In many cases, an assumption comes to have the rock hardness and permanence of a fact.

My children had been playing with some yarn for months, calling it spaghetti for their toy kitchen. When my four-year-old daughter started twirling it around to the music, one piece in each hand like the Olympic gymnasts, my five-year-old daughter became upset because "You do not twirl spaghetti around and dance with it." Similarly, it is often observed that young scientists or scientists venturing in to new fields often make the most revolutionary breaks with tradition: they are able to ask, "Is this really spaghetti?"

Those whom we note as outstandingly creative have often been described as possessing a childlike innocence or sense of wonder, and they ask seemingly naive questions. Albert Einstein asking what would happen if you rode on a rocket at the speed of light and looked at a mirror held in front of you (he concluded that you would not be able to see your reflection) sounds like the ultimate naive question, like the silly questions children ask, but it turned out to be one with profound consequences. This attitude contributes to creativity by keeping the mind flexible. Ambiguity and the unknown, however, make many people nervous. It was not until the late fifteenth century that European map makers would leave sections of their maps empty. Before this period, they had filled the empty spaces of their maps with the Garden of Eden, the kingdoms of Gog and Magog, and imaginary peoples and geography (Boorstin, 1983). Neither do we easily suffer blank spaces on our mental maps.

A major obstacle to discovery is not ignorance but knowledge. Because Aristotle was so comprehensive, logical, and brilliant, his writings became the ultimate standard of truth for 2000 years. A major portion of Galileo's works was devoted to disproving Aristotle so that the reader would be able to grasp his arguments. The difficulty was that a single authority (Aristotle) was held in such high regard that alternative views could not get a hearing. In more recent times the work of Sigmund Freud has had a similar effect. Freud's system of analysis posited certain mental constructs *a priori* such that it was very difficult to amend or improve his theories. It also focused on motivation (sexual drives) to the exclusion of process (how does one solve problems or process information), as noted by Arieti (1976). The result was that some psychoanalysts remained Freudians but many psychologists began to ignore Freud altogether in order to make progress in their work. B. F. Skinner's "behaviorism" provided another classic barrier to knowledge. By defining behavior totally in terms of stimulus and response, and claiming that the mind was inherently unknowable, Skinner created a barrier to any understanding of phenomena such as emotions, memory, and cognition, subjects which in fact we are able to learn quite a bit about.

Another type of mental barrier is the definition by the professional community of what is a serious problem and what is not. Until the late 1970s, physicists regarded turbulence as largely beyond the *terra firma* of well-behaved phenomena subject to "real" scientific study. The discovery of the mathematics and physics of chaos (strange attractors, universality, relations to fractals, and all the rest) is rightly called a revolution (Gleick, 1987a) because it brought within the realm of

Aristotle's writings were so authoritative that they inhibited discovery over succeeding centuries.

orderly study an entire class of phenomena previously classified as "void, and without form."

In the case of chaos, there was a well-defined phenomenon, turbulence, that was deemed intractable. Another common situation is when a topic is initially not even recognized as such. Benoit Mandelbrot's breakthrough in the "discovery" of fractals was in recognizing a common set of properties in what were previously unconnected mathematical oddities. When Charles Darwin found earthworms interesting enough to write a book about them (Darwin, 1881), the world of science was quite surprised. Recognizing problems that others do not even see can be considered a prime characteristic of the truly innovative.

Barriers to recognizing a phenomenon or problem are many, including concreteness, visualizability, and complexity. Before Georg Riemann, the geometry of Euclid was identified with the three dimensions and properties of our sensory world. The axioms therefore were too concrete for anyone to conceive of altering them. Breaking this concreteness barrier led to many forms of non-Euclidean geometry, a result that was later instrumental in the development of relativity.

Visualizability can also be a limiting factor. Once Poincaré sections of the orbits of strange attractors were published, it became evident to everyone that there was some kind of regularity to turbulent (chaotic) phenomena. Formal proofs of this fact were far less influential to the general scientific community because they are much less accessible (Gleick, 1987a).

Complexity and heterogeneity are also major barriers to recognizing problems. One innovation of Isaac Newton was in recognizing that a ball thrown in the air and a planet circling the sun are "the same" with respect to gravity. He made the further crucial abstraction of treating his objects as point masses, reducing complexity to a minimum. These abstractions and simplifications of Newton are, in reality, simple, but only after the fact.

It is characteristic of mental barriers that once overcome they are never given a second thought. The Spanish navigators never considered the Atlantic a serious problem once it was crossed. Of course, many scientific achievements really are complex. The mathematics necessary to grasp quantum mechanics is quite difficult and is not just a mental barrier. Nevertheless, one must always be alert for barriers that can be circumvented.

A significant barrier to "navigation" is the set of structures we have erected to facilitate our work: namely, academic departments. The current system seeks to fill all the square holes with square pegs. The biology department wants one geneticist, one physiologist, and one ecologist, but they do not want three generalists who work in all three areas. In what specialty would one put Darwin: genetics, geology, taxonomy, or ecology? Darwin considered himself a geologist, but the world remembers largely his biology. Should Goethe be in the literature, biology, physics, or philosophy department? He actually was most proud of his work on optics, though that work was largely flawed. Would Newton or Ronald Fisher find comfortable academic niches today? The current rigid departmental system is confining to the truly creative person and discourages the vitally important cross-fertilization of models, data, techniques, and concepts between disciplines.

☛ Don't be an expert

All graduate students are taught that it is essential to become an expert. As a short-term goal this is, of course, valid. Academic search committees are also looking for experts. As a lifestyle, however, becoming an expert can inhibit creativity.

Why is this? After all, it seems that an expert has more tools at his or her disposal for solving problems. The problem revolves around our mental constructs. In learning a subject, one creates a network of facts, assumptions, and models. Once one thinks one understands something, it is linked up to an explanation and supporting ideas. This construct may not be true, but it comes to seem real nevertheless. As one becomes more of an expert, a larger and more complex network of facts and explanations accumulates and solidifies, making it difficult to entertain radical alternative ideas or to recognize new problems.

The expert is in danger of developing the small cage habit. Zoo animals, when moved to a larger cage, may continue to pace about an area the size and shape of their old smaller cage (Biondi, 1980). An Aristotle or a Freud may create a set of bars within which most people pace rigidly, never noticing clues from outside the cage. The danger in becoming an expert is that one tends to build one's own cage out of the certainties and facts which one gradually comes to know. Dogmatism builds cages in which the dogmatic then lives and expects everyone else to live also.

How does one not become an expert? Astronomer Subrahmanyan Chandrasekhar gave a remarkable television interview a few years ago. He led a scientific career notable for a rate of productivity that did not slow down at all into his 70s. When asked how he avoided the drop in creativity and productivity that plagues many scientists, he replied that approximately every seven years he takes up a new topic. He found that he would run out of new ideas after working in an area for too long. This pattern led him to tackle such topics as the dynamics of stellar systems, white dwarfs, relativity, and radiative transfer. Although all these subjects are in astrophysics, they are different enough to present unique problems.

We need only turn to Darwin to find a truly remarkable example of the value of changing topics. He wrote books on the origin of coral atolls, the geology of South America, pollination of orchids, ecology of earthworms, evolution, human emotions, the taxonomy of the world's barnacles, and movement in plants. Although most of this work in some sense related to or led toward his grand project (evolution), they were all quite different in themselves. When he decided that a topic was interesting, he would delve into it in depth for a period of years, write up his results, and move on. After his early books on geology, he returned to the topic only a few times during the remainder of his career. In today's atmosphere, he would have been encouraged to follow up on his early study of corals or geology for the rest of his career. Imagine him in a modern geology department telling his department head that he planned to spend the next 20 years working on evolution, earthworms, and orchids (see Figure 2).

It is easy to protest that learning a new subject is too hard and takes too long. I am not suggesting that everyone can or should strive for the diverse interests of Darwin. Taking up new subjects within a discipline or linking up with related disciplines appears more difficult, however, than in fact it is. It is much less difficult than the original university experience, because the mature professional has an arsenal of tools, terms, and techniques that are transferable between topics. I assert that the value of cross-fertilization far outweighs the cost of learning new skills and facts. Studies have shown that a wide spectrum of interests is typical of

---

Proposal of C. Darwin

This proposal is for the PI, a geologist by training, to solve the problem of speciation.

Method: Collect every possible fact and formulate an all-inclusive theory.

Duration: 20 years.

Proposal of A. Einstein

This proposal is for the study of the nature of space and time.

Method: Conduct thought experiments in armchair, supported by abstract mathematics.

Duration: 1 lifetime.

Figure 2. What would have happened if Darwin and Einstein as young men had needed to apply for government support? Their probability of getting past the grant reviewers would be similar to a snowball surviving in hell. PI, principal investigator.

highly creative scientists and helps to account for their creativity (Simonton, 1988).

Practical problems, however, beset the brave soul who eschews the expert label. Getting grants for research in a new area will be difficult. Department heads will frown. Within many corporations one may place one's career at risk. Exploring new territory inevitably evokes the Columbus response: shaking of heads and muttering as you disappear over the horizon and a hero's welcome when (if) you return. A strategy some researchers employ is to maintain a home base of expertise in a narrow area to keep department heads and deans happy, with frequent excursions to diverse topics to stay fresh.

☛ Don't read the literature

Students are inevitably told to read the literature to get started. This advice is fine for students who are used to looking up the answers in the back of the book and repeating the examples they have seen. For the practicing professional, however, this first step can be inhibiting. First, it channels your thoughts too much into well-worn grooves. Second, a germ of an idea can easily seem insignificant in comparison to finished studies. Third, the sheer volume of material to read may intimidate one into abandoning any work in a new area. Medawar (1967) also advises against reading too much, arguing that study can be a substitute for productive work.

My recommendation for the first step (after getting the germ of an idea) is to put your feet up on the desk and stare out the window. Try to elaborate the idea as much as possible. Do some calculations or quick laboratory experiments. Write a few pages or sketch out a design. Only after the idea has incubated and developed will it be robust enough to compare it to existing literature. Given a certain level of knowledge in a subject, you know generally what is going on, so you are not likely to be reinventing the wheel. When you go to the literature, you may find that someone has preempted you or that your idea is invalid, but at the risk of only a few days or weeks of work. The cost of good ideas killed off too soon is much higher than the cost of some wasted effort.

Work habits

Work habits are a crucial component of strategic creativity. Many creative people are unable to follow through on an idea. Others are less productive than they could be or complain of distractions. This section provides tips on work habits in the context of enhancing creativity.

☞ Let's get bored

Boredom or inactivity is a seriously underrated part of the creative process. I do not, of course, mean that being creative is boring, or that boring people are creative, but that slack time – quiet time – is a valuable part of the total creative process. Consider an artist. If he or she walked into the studio and, instead of contemplating the canvas, immediately began to dab on paint and did so for eight straight hours, I would not anticipate seeing anything of real beauty. Novelists may go for months or years collecting facts, traveling, and searching for inspiration. Poets are notorious for working only when inspired.

Yet because a professional's time is valuable, we seem to expect an eight hour day of nonstop productive work. This is fine if you are doing routine work (e.g., screening 100 chemicals in mice for cancer risks using standard methods), but not good for work that requires deep thought. To quote Watson (1968), "much of our success was due to the long uneventful periods when we walked the colleges or read the new books," not exactly the factory style of working. As Cairns (1988) stated on reviewing Frances Crick's autobiography, "Many readers will be struck by the thought that Crick belongs to a bygone age, when biologists were given time to think. What granting agency today would give several years of support to a young scientist who just wanted to build models? What 30 year old would now dare to embark on such a perilous pursuit?"

In comparisons of student problem solving (Whimbey and Whimbey, 1976), it was thought that the better students would be found to read a difficult problem faster and solve it faster. In fact, the good students took much longer to read the problem, because they were thinking about it, but then took less time to answer the questions or do the mathematics. The poor students often were jumping ahead and solving the wrong problem. On simple problems, there was little difference in performance. This habit of jumping ahead leads too often in technical areas also to solving the wrong problem. The pace of professional life has become so frenetic that activity and motion have come to replace thought. The need for careful thought and planning is particularly acute for projects involving complex systems such as large-scale software projects, integrated manufacturing, large construction projects, and high tech product development. There is a simple test for freneticism; merely ask someone, "Why are you doing this task?" If they are too busy to answer or cannot explain it, the ratio of thought to activity is too low.

There are some techniques that have fallen out of favor in recent decades as

Unfortunately, deep thought looks very much like "goofing off."

being inefficient but which should be reintroduced. One of these is the highly sophisticated pipe-smoking technique. This instrument has its utility in the almost incessant and highly ritualized care it demands, which keeps the hands busy while the mind contemplates some problem, while at the same time leading a passerby into believing that the smoker is actually doing something (for detailed instructions, see McManus, 1979). In contrast, an unfocused gaze with hands behind the head is immediately interpreted as "goofing off." Of course, I do not recommend smoking, but some substitute for the pipe is sorely needed.

An equally effective technique, good for deeper contemplation, is the walk. This technique is looked down on today as being too low tech. Besides, someone

Figure 3.   Charles Darwin engaged in the arcane and almost lost art that today we would label "thinking." Illustration by Richard Loehle.

walking is obviously not working. Darwin used to take an hour's walk every day around a course he had laid out (Figure 3). He would become engrossed in his thoughts; therefore he put some small stones at the start, kicking one off at each round so that he did not have to keep track of how many circuits he had made or worry about time. It was during these walks that he wrestled with the deepest questions.

The practice of taking long walks as an active part of intellectual activity used to be a common part of academic life in Europe. Professors would take their graduate students on walks to debate, discuss, and question. These days graduate students are lucky to even see their professor in the halls. Our idea of a walk is going to the photocopy machine. Some psychologists have found that taking patients for a walk is very effective in getting them to open up and express themselves. With the short attention spans prevalent these days, it would no doubt require practice to be able to come to conclusions or formulate complex thoughts while walking and remember them back in the office, but it can be done and would lead to deeper thought.

☞ If you can't walk, try running

I have been a recreational jogger for 20 years. I sometimes find that a pain in my ankle that I feel when walking or jogging will go away if I switch to a sprint. This cure suggests a strategy to overcome writer's block (designer's block, etc.), which afflicts many professionals. The scenario I often observe is that someone finishes a project or gets a new idea and then sits down to "write up the results" but cannot get started. It reminds me of the *Peanuts* comic strip in which Snoopy the dog is trying to write a great novel and keeps getting stuck on "It was a dark and stormy night."

Starting at the first word to write up an entire document is rather intimidating. The walking writer, like Snoopy, is noticing the pain in his ankle at every sentence and is likely to stop and massage each sore spot, thus repeatedly getting stuck. Such jerky motion is also anathema to creative thought. Sprinting can sometimes cure both problems. One should sit down with a cup of coffee and define a short piece to be written in a defined interval, say the Methods section in one hour. The Introduction is not where one should start; rather it should be last, after the technical parts are all worked out. Then sprint without worrying about grammar or style, which can be corrected later. Leave blanks where the references and figures should go. Often this plan will get one off the mark and writing may continue for several hours. If it turns out not to be a good day, the sprinting technique at least allows for an hour or two of solid work. The utility of this approach depends on the style of the professional and is most useful for hyperactive individuals who do not like to sit still and for perfectionists like Snoopy who get stuck on the first sentence.

The cure for writer's block.

☞ The four hour work day

A frequent cause of inadequate creative and professional performance is mental fatigue caused by excessive pressure, hours, or effort. Many people wish to be perceived as hard working, so they do everything with intensity and put in long hours. Unfortunately, this can make the brain rather fuzzy, which is very detrimental to strategic thinking. Strategic thinking is not a brute force approach, but rather requires wise and efficient use of mental faculties to be more effective. The logic is that it is more important to be effective than to be busy, because in the realm of complex problems the most important thing is to not start off down the wrong path. An army of programmers can be busy as bees developing a new program, but if the basic design for the software is faulty, the result will be of no use to anyone. It is for this reason that I recommend the four hour work day.

Few of us can work at full capacity, thinking clearly and profoundly, for the duration of every work day any more than we can run at top speed for the same distance that we can jog. This is the myth of the modern work environment – that anything can be expected of workers and they must deliver. Most people fake it, and will not admit when they are at less than 100%. The result is that terrible decisions are made, product designs are compromised, and serious system errors are introduced by people who are fatigued. In contrast, it is much more likely that one can work at 100% mental clarity for about four hours. If one keeps this in mind, then a distinction can be made between critical issues that need full clarity and intense effort, which become part of the four hours of work per day, and those parts of a project that are routine and become part of the rest of the day. That is to say if you expect yourself to be brilliant for only four hours per day, then you may actually live up to this standard. During the rest of the day, there are plenty of routine tasks to accomplish such as returning calls, coding a clearly designed subroutine, ordering equipment, doing drafting (once the design is set), proof-reading reports, etc. We may again turn to Darwin as an example. He habitually spent about four hours writing, which he found exhausting because this was the creative part of his work day, and spent the rest of the day writing correspondence, doing experiments, reading articles, etc. Ralph Waldo Emerson also spent half a day writing, and then spent the rest of the day in his garden or doing other chores. In the case of Emerson, we may be confident that while gardening he was simultaneously engaged in rather profound thought, and was thus not really "goofing off."

To reiterate, the value of the four hour work day is that certain components of creative and technical projects are more crucial than others and thus require more intelligent thinking to do properly. In science, the choice of problem and approach for solving it are absolutely crucial to success, and require one's full attention. In architecture, the overall concept for a building is the crucial step, with much of the drafting requiring skill but not brilliance. In computer science, the functional specification for a piece of software and the basic layout, flowcharts, and algorithms are the crucial steps that require extra care. For these crucial steps, if one is not thinking 100% clearly, then one is likely to introduce errors that then require significant effort to put right. In all of these cases, if the difficult parts are not done well, subsequent work on the details is a waste of time. Therefore the recognition of which components of a project require extra care and attention is a critical component of ultimate effectiveness. Proper use of this approach can make one look much smarter and more efficient that one actually is, because so little time will be wasted and because difficult problems will be solved.

☞ Be unrealistic

It is a fatal mistake to have a realistic estimation of your mental capacities. Someone who is realistic will never attempt problems that seem hard, because few of us are Newtons. Nevertheless, creativity is only marginally related to IQ. That is to say, above a certain minimal level, IQ and college grades are not predictive of productivity, success, or innovation (Arieti, 1976; Gardner, 1983; Simonton, 1988).

As we look back on great scientific discoveries, many of them seem childishly simple to us now. The great innovation of Galileo was to avoid trying to explain *why* objects fall (as Aristotle had) in favor of quantifying *how* they fall. When Newton treated objects as point masses it was brilliant, but in retrospect it is a simple concept. The great innovation of Vesalius was to do dissections himself and base his anatomy book on what he actually saw rather than on the authority of Galen (Boorstin, 1983). His further innovation was to use medical diagrams in his book. All of these are elementary ideas.

Some may despair that all the easy ideas have been found, but this assessment is far from true. In the last two decades, fractals and chaos have transformed the foundations of science, yet the basic concepts and even some of the formal mathematics are intuitively obvious and simple once learned. Often the solution one seeks will turn out to be simple and well within the reach of our intelligence. It is puzzling why discovery is so hard when the final result can often be demonstrated to a class of 14-year-olds.

Let us be more clear on this point. At any given time it will seem that all the good ideas have been discovered. The head of the United States patent office in the mid-1800s suggested that it be closed down because all of the good ideas had already been discovered, but the flow of new inventions and scientific discoveries does not seem to be letting up even now. Even in the realm of business, innovation does not stand still. IBM was the obvious giant in the computer field and without serious competitors but nevertheless personal computers, work stations, distributed computing, and parallel computing originated elsewhere and have brought a reversal in IBM's fortunes. Sears was the dominant department store in the USA for decades but missed the boat on several retailing innovations and almost went bankrupt in the early 1990s. Impossible things like radial keratotomy for correcting nearsightedness, superconductors, worldwide e-mail, compact disks, giant shopping malls, movie special effects, buckyballs (60-carbon atom molecular cages), and fractals have all burst upon the scene in recent decades out of nowhere. The fact is that there are always surprises around every corner. Even in areas where it seems that everyone has come to agreement, there can be surprises. In astronomy, at the time of writing, the age of the universe seems to be less than the age of some nearby galaxies. This is certainly a surprise and shows that clearly we are missing something somewhere. The well-known "fact" that cholesterol causes heart attacks by clogging arteries has recently been challenged by a new theory that iron is the actual culprit. By this theory excess iron (which the body accumulates over years) catalyzes cholesterol into a form that causes the damage to arteries. This theory supports the fact that men with very high iron levels have higher heart attack rates and explains why women have an increased risk after menopause (they stop losing iron in blood during menstruation). This new theory is not proven, but shows how a well accepted theory (cholesterol is bad) may turn out to be completely mistaken. It also illustrates how simple a revolutionary theory can be and still be new. When we look at any domain, the same result holds: new results, ways of doing business, inventions, designs, and innovations are all around us. The realistic person "knows" he or she is not smart enough to discover or invent these things. The strategic thinker realizes that one does not need to be so smart, if one is clever.

☞ Inverse procrastination

The first priority of the innovator is procrastination. Only by putting off routine duties and avoiding committee assignments can one find time to daydream and browse in the literature. I do not believe it is fair to call this "procrastination" and avoidance *"irresponsible behavior."* Rather, it has to do with lead times being more important than deadlines. The gestation time for ideas, methods, and models is often quite long. The "Eureka!" phenomenon is usually the tail end of a long process of puzzling over a problem, reading about it, and discussing it with colleagues.

For example, ever since my teens I have been fascinated with the ability of some trees to live for thousands of years. I read accounts of tree life span and counted rings on stumps without any goal in mind for many years. But eventually this information led me to a new approach to the problem of the energetic costs of achieving great age (Loehle, 1988b).

I believe that most creative professionals have a long list, or zoo, if you will, of perhaps only partially articulated questions and puzzles that they mull over and that guide them. The need to feed the inmates of this zoo at regular intervals is strong, because these ideas will blossom into the next set of research problems. This drive leads to what I call The First Law of Inverse Procrastination: always put off some of what you should be doing today so you can do something that might be relevant later.

☞ Surfing

If I say that creative work is like surfing, you will think I am from California. By this analogy, however, I mean that good ideas come sporadically and unpredictably and should be pursued as they pass by, just as the surfer pursues the wave. Some waves are small, some large. Some days the surf is up, and some days it is not. For the big waves, it can take real effort to stay on the crest. The little waves can be caught by jotting down notes wherever you are. When the surf is up, it is crucial to recognize it and, like the California hot-dogger, "cut classes if necessary to hang ten." At such times, one should shut the door and disconnect the phone. In such creative waves, sometimes entire first drafts of papers can be written in a continuous burst or entire systems designed in one session. Authors have written entire books in a few weeks when inspired in this way. Edward de Bono wrote

When the surf is up, go for it!

Future Positive (Penguin, 1990) in eight days and Robert James Waller's recent best-seller *The Bridges of Madison County* (Mandarin, 1993) was written in three weeks. Such work is often of the highest quality even though hurriedly done.

Does such an approach mean one should be a prima donna, only working when the mood strikes? Certainly not. On days that are not good for surfing, there are articles to read, manuscripts to revise, equipment to order, papers to review, phone calls, meetings, and so on and on. The point is not to be moody but to be receptive to the creative muse. Designating a fixed time of day for technical work or following too rigid a pattern of work is detrimental to such receptivity.

Surfing applies to topics popping up, as well as to being inspired in general. To quote Skinner (1959), "a first principle not formally recognized by scientific methodologists: when you run onto something interesting, drop everything else and study it."

This principle points out a fundamental problem with the current peer review research and development (R&D) grant-giving process as well as with project scheduling for engineering. The current review (or planning) system requires one to lay out, in some detail, the steps and procedures one is going to follow through several years and what the expected outcome is going to be. The United States Department of Energy actually sent out a memo (which I saw) to its laboratories around 1990 requesting that it be notified at least six months in advance of any major discoveries! This demand is completely unrealistic, because research is a contingent process. Rigid scheduling also precludes following up interesting leads. Examining Michael Faraday's notebooks, one sees that he did several experiments per day in an iterative, tinkering type of research. How could he have planned this research in advance or presented it to a review panel? In the context of engineering, it is clear from the examination of the history of the development of any product or technology (see Petroski, 1992) that iterative tinkering is far more the rule than is following a plan set up at the beginning of the project.

Today's highly competitive climate has led to the misconception that the quality of proposed work and its outcome is predictable from a detailed proposal. Few if any really surprising discoveries are explicitly funded this way. As Koestler (1964) notes, "The history of discovery is full of arrivals at unexpected destinations, and arrivals at the right destination by the wrong boat." A much better practice is to fund investigators, as does the Howard Hughes Medical Foundation, for three to five year periods based on the individual's track record rather than to fund a detailed proposal. This practice frees up the truly productive from the huge overhead of chasing grants (as much as 50% of one's time) and from making overly rigid research plans. One cannot predict or control what the creative person will do, but he or she can be encouraged by adequate support.

Intensity

Certain types of creative task require exceptional powers of concentration, a certain intensity. This is most true of those types of task requiring strategic thinking. Tasks in which each short piece of work stands alone may be done in spite of interruptions. When I am opening my mail it is only a slight distraction if someone drops by my office or the phone rings, but in the middle of writing a complex computer algorithm I do not at all enjoy being interrupted. Such an interruption can in fact cause a bug to be introduced that requires hours to fix.

Let us clarify this point. An airline pilot must concentrate on the task in hand, but if he or she is interrupted or distracted for a moment the overall task is not at risk as long as the plane is not being landed at that moment. In contrast the unique aspect of creative endeavors is that complex mental constructs must be created and held in the mind for a task to be successful. An artist must generate a vision of the desired work and then hold this vision in mind while working. Sketches help to make the vision concrete. Because the artist must hold this vision in mind while working, most artists require privacy and long periods without interruption. Many also refuse to allow anyone to view a piece before it is finished. Since viewers do not "see" the painting the artist has in mind, they may react to incomplete design elements and thereby express emotions or opinions that are inappropriate or negative. This may cause the artist to react to these reactions instead of following the original vision.

In many creative and technical fields this same situation exists. An intense focus is needed to maintain a sufficient level of concentration to follow long trains of reasoning, to build up complex networks of relationships, to respond to subtle clues, and to envision complex structures. Without intense concentration, subtle thoughts and half-formed thoughts will slip away. We may in fact say that without intense concentration the benefits of taking long contemplative walks or of putting the feet up on the desk will not be realized.

Some years ago, I was debugging a very long piece of complex code written by other people. This bug was sort of a phantom that occurred only sometimes and was therefore really annoying us. I was tracing through the program code line by line and simultaneously following the machine instructions on the debugger. This meant that I had to trace through thousands of lines of code and keep in mind the entire flow of control and many values in the computer memory. During three attempts, each of which took three hours or more, I had gone a little too fast or missed something, and had failed to catch the phantom in action. On my fourth attempt I was very careful and did not move from my chair or think of anything else for three hours, at which point I trapped the bug: I caught it executing a simple FORTRAN statement such as $X = Y$, but the machine executed a WRITE op code. This meant that we had a hardware bug in our VAX computer, and it turned out to be in the disk drive controller software. This explained why the bug usually appeared after lunch: at this time we were working the machine rather hard, and the disk drive reader software became lost during high speed working. Only intense concentration enabled me to find this bug.

Examples abound where intense concentration is essential to success. Before computers were available, climatologist Milutin Milankovitch postulated that the tilt of the Earth's axis and the precession of its orbit could lead to sufficient changes in light interception by the northern latitudes that ice ages could result. He spent many long months doing the calculations by hand. Any mistake could jeopardize the entire calculation. Kepler before him performed a similar computational feat to demonstrate that the planets follow elliptical orbits. The writer Eric Hoffer, almost blind, would compose entire books while walking, and then dictate them later.

We may generally say that the types of problem of concern in this book require intense sustained work characterized by complete concentration. Any problem that is highly technical, involves synthesis of information, involves complex structures, or has multiple components falls into this class. It is simply not possible to jump from task to task when the problem is complex. A more formal analysis is presented in the following chapters, but at this point we can simply observe that interruptions of a complex task introduce errors whose seriousness increases with the complexity of the task.

These observations bear on several misconceptions about problem solving. A major focus of "creativity" workshops is to get people to relax and be spontaneous. Much effort is focused on brainstorming and allowing absurd or novel ideas to surface. While all of this is certainly useful for people who are overly rigid and afraid to entertain new ideas, this focus on spontaneity is seriously misplaced. It assumes that idea generation is the limiting step, and in fact is all that is needed to be creative. It creates the impression that leaping about and quickly generating clever ideas is sufficient for success; that is, it completely ignores the issue of follow through. In fact, given half a chance most people can generate many clever ideas, but lack the ability to follow through on complex problems that require sustained effort, long chains of reasoning, and concentration. It has actually been shown that there is no relation between scores on tests of divergent thinking and the ranking of scientists on a scale of creativity (Weisberg, 1986). Truly innovative work requires periods of generating new ideas as well as periods of sustained work to follow through on the initial good idea. Unless the problem is trivial, brain-storming is only the first step.

A second implication concerns work habits. I mentioned earlier that good work requires periods free from interruption. Such solitary work is difficult for many people. Those who are very gregarious feel the need to talk with others about their ideas or to call a meeting about it, but this mode of work does not lead to sufficient intensity or to the generation of sufficiently long trains of thought to solve very complex problems. In fact, complex problems have seldom if ever been solved in a meeting or by a committee. The focus on busy-ness and visibility in many companies means that everyone is almost always interrupted before a complex task can be completed. If someone went off to a remote site for six months to really solve a problem alone, they would come back to find they were no longer considered a player, and were no longer part of the power system. This is part of the reason many companies are so short-sighted in their planning.

Understanding the key role of intensity and concentration allows us to grasp the peculiar phenomenon of the overachiever. I remember in high school that following IQ testing, some students were identified as being "overachievers." With only an average IQ, they were doing exceptionally well in school. If we

It is doubtful whether a committee ever created a complex product.

believe that IQ tests measure anything at all, and they are said to be quite good at predicting success in school, then overachievement on this very measure of what IQ is supposed to predict would seem to be nonsensical. The simple explanation is that these individuals work with greater than average intensity. This extra focus and concentration lead to greater performance on complex tasks than is expected from performance on short-answer tests such as an IQ test (see Chapters 2–3 for more details). This same factor can also explain underachievement in many cases. To complete real work, even a genius must concentrate, but this is hard work and requires discipline. Without sufficient intensity, complex problems (involved in any type of high achievement) cannot be completed successfully.

How does one foster this critical intensity? It has been observed that when poor (in both senses) students join a good chess club after school, their grades go up. Attempts to find specific cognitive skills fostered by chess that might transfer to school work have failed. This increased performance could be attributed to a change in attitude, but I believe it is at least in part due to the students learning how to concentrate intensely. It is not possible to play chess without concentrating, and it thus fosters this particular skill. The same may be said of mathematics and computer programming, which also are not possible unless one concentrates. As noted above, performance on all complex tasks requires this kind of intense concentration, and thus the payoff from chess and similar activities can be substantial. In general, activities that promote intense concentration, particularly if this concentration is mental rather than attentional (one may be an intense fisherman, but this type of concentration is not useful for strategic thinking problems), will provide valuable training and the skill acquired will carry over into other domains of problem solving.

Conclusions

The path of creativity is strewn with the bones of those consumed by the vultures of mediocrity, accountability, and responsibility. One cannot schedule creative breakthroughs, budget for them, or prove them in advance to a review panel or manager. An entirely different, flexible approach to discovery is necessary to encourage creativity. To conceive of time as being too valuable for staring out the window or reading for pleasure is equivalent to riding a bicycle under water. Free and undirected thought and research are essential.

However, one must not live in the creative moment permanently. The imagination is very powerful and can easily mislead (Arieti, 1976). One whose ideas remain conceptual will never know whether they are valid, feasible, complete, or useful. They will remain in the realm of dreams and play. One's goal as a strategist is to produce finished products of some sort. This means that innovative ideas must somehow be converted into concrete form. Dreams must be converted into designs, inventions, systems, or some other product. Thus, creativity per se is only the first step. What is necessary to be an effective innovator is for the process of converting ideas into the realm of action to be facilitated and made efficient. To do this, one must understand the entire problem-solving process, not just the step of generating novelty. Chapters 2–4 discuss the steps for converting ideas into reality. First, one must take a vague initial concept or intuition and turn it into a substantive discovery. This process involves elaboration of an initially vague idea so that it becomes operational, measurable, and can be communicated. Next, one must convert a discovery into a product, such as a piece of software, or a theory, or an experiment, or a manufacturing system. Finally, one must check the new theory or product against reality to verify that it is useful, efficient, novel, or correct.

2 Discovery as a process

Introduction

At the heart of strategic thinking is the discovery of new ways of solving problems, new ways of organizing information, and new ways of designing products and systems. Therefore the discovery process needs exploration here. Chapter 1 on creativity set the stage for an examination of the discovery process by setting out the approaches and attitudes that make discovery possible. In this chapter the nature of discovery and innovation are explored and myths about them cleared up. The presentation of discovery will be in the context of scientific discovery, because this is the only field in which discoveries can be verified by others. In other contexts, a discovery (e.g., how best to organize a corporation, a new art form) is difficult to verify, and in the end can only be objectively tested by in fact applying scientific methods. The examination of discovery in the context of science, where one can examine the component steps out in the open and verify the analysis of the discovery process, enables one to learn how this process works and then apply this process reliably to other fields of endeavor.

Scientific discovery is one of the most dramatic and exciting products of the human mind and ultimately is the source of our advanced technology. There is tremendous pressure to increase the rate of discovery as more and more key societal issues are seen to contain a scientific component (e.g., AIDS, global climate change, tropical deforestation). Currently expectations of what science can deliver are very high because of science's past breakthroughs, but the general perception of how science works is not in harmony with its actual operation. This discrepancy leads to the attitudes reflected in protests in the USA that the government is not doing enough for sufferers of acquired immunodeficiency syndrome (AIDS), even though over $1 billion is being spent annually on research, which is more per mortality case than is spent for any other disease. The expectation that money alone is required to order a cure on demand results from a serious misunderstanding of the discovery process. This same misunderstanding is evident in corporations that expect to be able to order up new products from their R&D departments with the snap of two fingers, and become impatient with research when progress is slow.

A clearer understanding of how discoveries are actually made is necessary, so that barriers to discovery can be removed and discoveries can be rewarded and enhanced. As Bauer (1992) points out, science is not based on a fixed recipe or method (the "scientific method"). If it was, we would not be frustrated by problems such as cancer, and scientific progress would be predictable. Rather, science proceeds by a process similar to solving a puzzle. That is to say, discovery is a process, not an event, and in fact is rather complicated. The official version of how science is or should be done conflicts with this reality. Discovery is in fact best achieved by the application of strategic problem-solving techniques, as will be shown later.

Some persistent myths about scientific discovery cause a great deal of trouble and confusion in the practice and public perception of science today. Three great myths that contribute to problematic public attitudes and form a sort of triumvirate of misunderstanding are the Eureka! myth, the hypothesis myth, and the measurement myth. These myths are prevalent among scientists as well as among observers of science, and spill over into attitudes and approaches prevalent among those professionals who wish to appear logical and scientific. Following a detailed characterization of these myths, I present an alternative, developmental model of discovery.

☞ The Eureka! myth

It has long been assumed that the philosophy of science may be helpful in epistemology or in the logic of deduction, axiomatization, or justification, but that it has little to say concerning the process of discovery. Popper (1963), for instance, states that discovery (the generation of hypotheses) is not subject to formal rules, so that neither inductive nor deductive logic are reliable (though they are sometimes useful) paths to discovery. This idea has led to the view that scientific discovery is somehow a mysterious subconscious process, a conclusion that does not necessarily follow from Popper's argument. Many have written about flashes of insight, dreams, the psychology of discovery, etc. (e.g., Root-Bernstein, 1989). In this view, discoveries appear as a spontaneous act, in a flash. If one is not a "creative type," then one will not have creative flashes.

The view that discoveries, insights, or hypotheses are obtained in a flash is what I call the Eureka! myth. This is the myth that discoveries are made all of a piece, and consist of an event or moment or thing. It is reinforced by dramatic accounts such as Friedrich Kekulé's discovery of chemical ring structures in a dream and similar accounts (c.f., Hadamard, 1949). Conscious work → incubation → insight has in fact become the popular image of discovery, as documented by Langley and Jones (1988). Popular courses on creativity focus almost exclusively on such Eureka! moments. Such colorful, flash-of-insight accounts capture the imagination and are certainly interesting; however, they may be misleading, as shown by Weisberg (1986). They draw attention to only the dramatic cases and suggest that the process of discovery is not subject to study or dissection. They also draw attention away from valid insights or new ideas that require nurturing, development, and maturation. That is to say, if it isn't completed in ten minutes, then forget it. This is discovery as instant porridge.

The focus on insight is a holdover from the Freudian emphasis on the unconscious, which is supposedly more powerful than our conscious brain. The belief that our unconscious can solve problems during an "incubation" period and then deliver them to our conscious mind fully formed is simply a myth (Weisberg, 1986). What actually occurs is a mulling over of problems while one is engaged in other things, such as driving. The active worrying over a problem, however, tends to be forgotten later but if successful leads to a solution that *seems* dramatic as one may be in the bath!

In contrast to this Eureka! view, I would like to argue for the central role of pattern recognition in the discovery process. The human brain is wired for pattern recognition, as Margolis (1987) argues at length. This process is neither inductive nor deductive, nor is it rule based, though it can be mimicked by rules in some cases. For example, everyone can recognize, at a flash, hundreds if not thousands of faces, without using statistical hypothesis testing or deductive logic. Many people are equally good at musical patterns, being able to recognize thousands or even tens of thousands of songs. They generally would be unable to do so from the sheet music and absolutely unable to do so from a sonogram.

Besides visual and auditory patterns, some people have a facility for recognizing other, more abstract types of pattern. Einstein described his own thought processes as being of this type (Hadamard, 1949). Such a skill is particularly useful for finding relationships in phenomena that do not necessarily have a visual representation.

There is a crucial difference between detecting patterns in science and the popular concept of creativity. Creativity workshops focus on spontaneity, on being uninhibited, on play, on humor, and on dressing up in a gorilla costume. But scientific discovery is not a free, uninhibited, artistic-type process. It is far closer to puzzle solving or to mechanical work. That is to say, a pattern or mental structure or understanding does not necessarily come all as a piece and in a flash, but rather is built up slowly and piecemeal as one links facts together and builds and rearranges a mental framework for the problem. It involves tinkering, puttering, patience, and stubbornness. We may say that the scientist is involved in constructing patterns. These patterns consist of networks of relationships between facts, assumptions, mathematical relations and methods, measurement techniques, rules of thumb, and hunches. A "discovery" involves an expansion, rearrangement, or simplification of all or part of this network of relationships. A discovery is thus not a *thing* or *event* and rarely involves only a single step as argued at length by Weisberg (1986).

It is necessary to clarify here that there are exceptions that occur when a thing is actually discovered, as in being found. For example, Columbus is said to have discovered the Americas. We may discover a new species of plant, or a new moon around Jupiter. However, often we speak of a discovery such as the discovery of a

Discovery is akin to puzzle solving, not art.

new medicine or vaccine or of a fundamental atomic particle. These "discoveries" usually involve a long series of steps and are constructed piece by piece. It is not possible to look in the microscope and "discover" a vaccine; much work in DNA analysis, protein characterization, and cell biology goes into such a discovery, and in fact there is no single moment when the "discovery" can be said to have occurred. Similarly, physicists usually don't just find a bunch of Higgs bosons lying around on the laboratory floor and then run out and announce a discovery. The discovery of *things* such as moons or new species might therefore more properly be called findings or observations and should not be confused with other types of discovery.

☞ The hypothesis myth

It has become a truism that one cannot design a proper experiment without a clearly stated hypothesis. To an extent this is a reasonable approach as a response to the pure empiricist tradition, because the mere gathering and cataloging of "facts," leads only to a very large pile of facts and very little knowledge. The emphasis on hypotheses may be traced to Popper's (1963) "Principle of Demarcation", which gives testability as the demarcation between scientific and unscientific (e.g., astrology, Marxism) theories. This perfectly correct argument has been carried to too fine a level of detail, however, by the general scientific establishment.

The argument that a *theory* must be testable has been extended to the requirement that every aspect of science must involve a theory (hypothesis) and a test of that theory. This narrow interpretation of "testability" is blind to the fact that much of science is really technology. Scientists spend a great deal of their time developing instruments, software, and methods to measure and detect phenomena (Crease, 1992; Hall, 1992). This activity is science; however, it is not a theory nor a test of a theory. In addition, empirical, descriptive studies are a necessary part of science. It is from them that sufficient data may be obtained to allow a pattern (structure, relationship) to be detected, possibly forming the basis for further study. Such preliminary observed patterns are not hypotheses in the sense of Popper because they are empirical rather than explanatory.

We may trace this confusion over what is a hypothesis partly to the excessively simplified presentations of the scientific method taught in most schools and partly to the confounding of concepts between a scientific hypothesis and a statistical hypothesis. A statistical hypothesis is a probability statement in terms of outcomes. It concerns measurable events and magnitudes. In contrast, we may have a perfectly valid scientific hypothesis (theory) but be unable to specify its outcomes. A deductive step is required to go from the scientific hypothesis to the statistical hypothesis, and this step is not always easy or clear cut. After it was proposed that subnuclear particles, hadrons, are composed of quarks, it took much effort to determine how to test this idea. Superstring theory which is a unifying atomic theory, remains untestable at present. In contrast, if we conduct a purely empirical study of the efficacy of a pesticide (with no biochemical theory of how it works) by measuring dose versus kill rate, we have no scientific hypothesis about causation, but we do have a statistical hypothesis framed in terms of the experimental design. The way that statistics is taught contributes to these difficulties. The distinction between a scientific and a statistical hypothesis is rarely made. Statistical tests are presented with the assumption that the question is either obvious (difference in mean income between two groups) or already determined. No mention is made of how one derives a testable and useful hypothesis from a theory. In fact, statistical examples in texts are almost never in the context of testing or refining a theory; rather they are almost all purely empirical relations or questions (finding defective light bulbs, age versus income, comparing fertilizer effects). By making statistics a separate academic discipline, it has become cut off from science and the students exposed to it often learn it out of context and assume that *this* is what "experimental design" is. In practice, scientists learn the proper role of statistics as they see how statistics is used by more experienced scientists, and not from their statistics courses.

A final source of confusion arises from multiple definitions of "scientific hypothesis." If I say "I think X and Y may be related in some way," this is a hunch or intuitive guess. This is what we have when we *think* we have found a regularity (pattern) in nature. Comparing X and Y does not "test" this guess because being wrong on such a hunch or "working hypothesis" does not cause any change in a scientific paradigm. In contrast, a *scientific hypothesis* (theory) is based on cause–effect reasoning. A scientific hypothesis does not merely state that X and Y may be related, but it *explains* why they are related. Should we find that X and Y are *not* related when a theory predicts them to be, then something is wrong with the theory. If we have a hunch that they are related, but then find that they are not, we merely try something else. The correlation between body size and life span in mammals is not a hypothesis or a theory, but any potential explanations for this correlation are.

The essential point about hypotheses is that there are different types and levels of hypothesis. At the first stage of discovery we have a hunch or intuition that we have detected a pattern or relationship in nature. This *working hypothesis* is a perfectly valid subject of study. A *working hypothesis* may lead to the discovery of an *empirical relationship*, which may be quite precise but is not a theory. A *working hypothesis* becomes a *scientific hypothesis* or theory when one offers an explanation for a pattern or relationship in terms of cause–effect or structural properties. A *statistical hypothesis* may be purely empirical (dog food brand A is better), or descriptive (a quadratic line fits these data), or it may be used to test a *scientific hypothesis* after suitable deduction and definition of variables.

☞ The measurement myth

The measurement myth is the assumption that the fundamental objects or variables (primitives) that are our objects of study have real existence or are unambiguous. That is to say, once we define objects or variables and use them in discourse we come to assume that they are real and that we can measure or study them: this is reification. We then base our statistical (experimental) analysis on the measures of these objects and assume that our analysis bears on the real world. For example, the concepts food web and ecosystem seem concrete and are used as if they are concrete, but in fact they are fraught with observational, boundary, resolution, and other difficulties and ambiguities. Similarly "gene" as commonly used refers to the one gene one trait assumption, which is often not valid (there is no "gene" for producing an arm or the eye). We may also recall Gross National Product, Consumer Price Index, and consumer confidence as variables that are often treated as if they were concrete and objective properties of the real world, which they are not. In reality neither do we make discoveries on the basis of clearly defined variables, nor are the meanings of any such variables as we use fixed and unambiguous. Pattern recognition violates the assumption that the objects to be measured are initially well defined or even identifiable. This fact becomes clear when we examine pattern recognition in some everyday contexts. It is not at all obvious what features we use for recognizing a familiar face. We never measure facial features to identify people and would not even be able to say what variables are informative nor how to measure them. Furthermore, we have no clue about how we are processing this information. The same ambiguous use of information is a fundamental aspect of scientific discovery.

Initially, a discovery is like the recognition of a face; the discoverer feels sure that he or she has found a pattern, but at first this pattern is intuitive. The elaboration process must make this intuitive pattern explicit, which means putting it in terms of measurements and data. As a discovery unfolds and is elaborated, the meanings of previously unobjectionable data (facts, metrics, variables, objects) may be called into question. The solid atom may turn out to be composed of parts. Fixed continents may turn out to move. Rulers may shrink and grow and clocks move at different speeds. Therefore, the basic assumption of hypothesis testing, that the variables to be measured are *a priori* well defined and quantifiable, does not hold up in the early stages of scientific discovery. The path from pattern to theory to experiment is not necessarily straightforward.

It is stated by some philosophers of science that there are no "facts" separate from theory. From the above we can see the sense in which this is true. As a theory develops, it impacts and changes our concepts and our interpretation of facts. Quantum physics alters our concept of "empty space." The modern concept of wealth in economics includes informational and quality of life types of wealth that were not considered wealth in the 1800s. It is also unfortunately the case, however, that the implication is drawn from this that it is impossible to truly test a theory because it is all-of-a-piece. In reality, a theory does not alter all of our definitions or perceptions of facts, only certain ones. There are generally many facts, metrics, or observables we may use to test a theory that are not influenced by it.

A new model

I would like to propose an alternative to the standard model of the scientific method. My model emphasizes pattern and its elaboration as being prior to formal statistics and hypothesis testing. The four steps are the following:

1 A pattern is found, a defect in an existing pattern is found, or no pattern is found where one was expected. The pattern may be in data, or it may be a meta-pattern, relating abstract concepts.
2 Elaboration takes place. A vocabulary must often be developed to describe the pattern. Methods of measurement (of shape or form, statistical properties, instruments, laboratory protocol) may need to be developed. Characteristics of the pattern are refined.
3 A theory or explanation for the observed pattern is proposed. The theory may need elaboration, rearrangement, or analysis before it yields testable predictions.
4 Experimental, statistical testing of hypotheses begins.

The usual concept of discovery compresses stages 1–3 into a product (a hypothesis or theory) with the process being hidden. During the conduct of routine science, one can often move rapidly from stage 1 to stage 4, and the processes of stages 1 through 3 tend to be glossed over or lost in the final scientific report of a study. In many cases, however, the real work of discovery takes place iteratively at stages 1, 2, and 3, but differs in nature and is often done by different people at different stages. That is to say, "discovery" really involves this entire process of iterative refinement, elaboration, and explanation of patterns perceived in nature. The same argument may be made about invention, which is typically viewed as an insight or "aha!" experience, but actually usually involves a prolonged elaboration and refinement process. The original idea for the invention is not the invention itself, which may in fact take years of fiddling and refinement before it is worthy of a patent.

In the initial stages of pattern detection, it may be clear that a pattern has been found but not at all clear how one is to proceed next. In chaos theory, strange attractors were not well received at first when expressed mathematically (Gleick, 1987a), but when they were presented visually it was recognized instantly that real patterns were involved. For example, the sequence in time of water dripping from a faucet appears random, but when the dripping is plotted as an attractor (Gleick, 1987b), the pattern becomes apparent. Once attractors were recognized from graphic plots, it became clear that a descriptive vocabulary was needed. For example, the patterns of chaotic attractors are clearly not random, but are very difficult to describe. Statistically demonstrating the difference between random and chaotic time series is quite difficult and new methods have been needed (e.g., that of Tsonis and Elsner, 1992). The initial intuitive recognition of attractors has thus been augmented by the development of tools such as the concepts of scaling and universality and the use of Poincaré sections, though the descriptive vocabulary for attractors is still deficient.

We might recognize patterns via the Gestalt process of figure–ground reversal. For example, we might fail to see a consistent pattern in locations where a species is found but see a pattern in locations where the species is *not* found. As another example, one might study not only the attractor of a dynamic system but its repellor, which may provide new insights (Sidorowich, 1992). We might make a discovery by observing the lack of a pattern or response where one was expected. Such was the case in the discovery of symmetry breaking in physics (for example, in the generation of the asymmetry that produces a magnet). Finally, we may make a discovery by observing a defect in a pattern, an anomaly (Lightman and Gingerich, 1992). Such was the origin of relativity, a defect (largely ignored) in Newtonian mechanics.

The process of pattern elaboration is central to the study of patterns for which cause and effect cannot be discerned immediately by experimentation. During the elaboration stage, the problem of how and what to measure is crucial. For example, in the early X-ray diffraction studies of DNA (Watson, 1968) what was being measured and how to interpret the data were not at all clear. What is foreground and what background, what is data and what noise, all need to be worked out. In addition, a vocabulary for description is essential. The trained taxonomist need only glance at most trees to identify them, but in doubtful cases he or she must refer to a key that uses a specialized descriptive vocabulary for leaf shape, flower parts, etc. Much of mathematics serves to provide a descriptive vocabulary. The process of developing a vocabulary in itself may change the perceived pattern. For example, in describing body form in the context of taxonomy, it was found that axis of symmetry was a useful descriptor. Radial symmetry is characteristic of simpler, more primitive forms (such as sea urchins) as compared to the bilateral symmetry exhibited by all vertebrates. The recognition of bilateral symmetry led to the examination of symmetry breaking, such as the handedness of the large claw in crabs or right-hand dominance in humans. Thus, the process of elaboration for both description and measurement may change our perception of the original pattern or uncover further patterns, all without necessarily involving hypotheses, explanations, or statistical tests. Further aspects of pattern elaboration are discussed by Loehle (1988a).

Discussion

The human brain not only recognizes patterns but it seeks them out and will generate them even where they do not exist, as in clouds or ink blots. We may characterize much of science as: the identification of complex natural patterns; their elaboration, quantification, and explanation; and, finally and definitely last, their statistical testing. The admonition that real science requires that one begin with a hypothesis and then test it is the death knell of discovery, largely limiting the practitioner to questions such as "the effect of levels of X on Y." Clinical trials, drug safety testing, agricultural research, and other fields are held in a death grip by this formalism. For example, simple-minded linear extrapolation of dose–response experiments currently governs our food, drug, and contamination regulations but totally ignores the complex machinery within cells that combats low levels of oxidative damage and that repairs DNA. This is not to say that experimentation is bad, far from it, but simple dose–response experimentation, whether for fertilizer, dog food, or carcinogens, is totally incapable of refining a vague theory, or of truly testing how things work. No single experiment or test will clarify the functioning of the immune system, the processes governing ice age cycles, or the factors regulating evolution. Such topics require complex and abstract theories which, because they are complex, require a concern over their internal structure and their development.

Another implication of the present argument concerns the lack of progress evident in certain fields of science. Bauer (1992) notes, for example, that in the social sciences conflicting theories and schools of thought exist without any resolution in favor of one or the other for indefinite periods of time. He attributes this problem to the ineffectiveness of the "reality therapy" that other sciences must endure. I would in contrast argue that lack of progress in such fields is due to failure of the elaboration step. As Hall (1992) and Crease (1992) point out, technique is a crucial aspect of scientific progress because it allows us to measure things so that hypotheses become testable. In the social sciences there is no shortage of "scientific method" or hypotheses or advanced statistics (Bauer, 1992), or even of data, rather what is missing is the capacity to reliably measure things or to define entities that are measurable. The type of elaboration of technique described by Hall (1992) and Crease (1992), such as development of X-ray diffraction technology or radioisotope tracers, often stops at the preliminary stage in the social sciences. Concepts are proposed that might be important or causative, but the further steps of elaboration are often not successful. How do we reliably measure alienation, social unrest, happiness, or culture? Such terms illustrate the fallacy of reification that, just because one can use a word therefore the word refers to a thing that exists. Instruments such as questionnaires and tests have been developed, but it is not clear what they actually measure. For example, an IQ test measures something that predicts success in school, but it is not clear that this something is "intelligence." Theories in the social sciences tend to be built of such concepts that we seem to understand but cannot precisely quantify, and as such are subject to multiple interpretations. In spite of the use of good scientific method, vague concepts interfere with rigorous testing against reality. This is not to say that true insights are not obtained in these fields, but rather that it is impossible to eliminate beliefs that do not accord with reality because tests that are acceptable to all parties as a proof cannot be obtained when the basic concepts are vague. In ecology one can point to similar problems that result from the use of concepts such as ecosystem, fitness, and biodiversity that are also ambiguous. As an antidote, I suggest that more effort be expended to develop theories that are based on the mechanisms of operation in the system. For example, cognitive psychology focuses on how people process information and make decisions, with a good linkage between theory and experiment. Certain phobias can be shown to result from faulty reasoning and have been successfully treated by providing information and experience with the phobic activity, such as taking the bus or giving a speech. In economics one can point to studies that ask what behaviors will result from a system consisting of imperfect decision makers operating on the basis of incomplete and even erroneous information. This approach is much closer to reality than the standard analytical models of omniscient utility maximizers.

We should not underestimate the danger posed by the myths of the scientific method. For example, Robert Gallo, co-discoverer of the AIDS virus, was accused of scientific misconduct for, among other things, supposedly taking an AIDS culture from a French scientist and claiming it was his own. In fact, cross-contamination turned out to be the likely culprit. Immunologist David Baltimore's team was accused of fraud and misconduct for what, in the end, turned out to be sloppy record keeping. Both men were cleared of misconduct but only after immense cost to their careers. The treatments of the Gallo and Baltimore fraud cases suggest that the auditors expected the type of rigor and formality in these studies that might be found in a bank ledger, on the assumption that the scientists were (or should have been) following a set procedure. In reality, scientists on the cutting edge are struggling to measure things that no one understands, using methods that no one can prove are right. No one can see the dust in the air that results in cross-contamination; there is no bad guy. Similarly, inventors struggle to create something they cannot define by methods they cannot defend. Aside from outright fabrication, the types of error being criticized in the Gallo and Baltimore cases can be found in any laboratory where really innovative work is being done. Legitimate arguments about laboratory technique, artifacts, and interpretation of data can occur in any field and for any experiment. Similarly, the expectation that any drug or vaccine can ever be declared totally safe results from this same misconception. Clarity, certainty, and well-defined laboratory protocols become available only long after the discovery phase. In fact, when we reach this stage the work is commonly turned over to technicians, as are AIDS blood testing or soil fertility testing today. During the early days of the AIDS epidemic, for example, there was a complete muddle concerning symptoms and causation. Similar confusion exists now about chronic fatigue syndrome. In the case of AIDS, measuring the level of the human immunodeficiency virus (HIV) and correlating that to the degree of symptom expression gives a negative result because of the long latency of the virus and its odd behavior.

Much confusion and misdirection results from the mistaken idea that first and foremost the scientific method is about doing controlled experiments with statistical rigor. In fact, it is largely about the struggle to convert an intuitively perceived pattern into something sharp and definite. By the time experiments are feasible and standard statistics apply, the battle is mostly won.

Once we see, as above, how discovery operates in science, we may apply this approach in other domains as well. From this we can see that several aspects of discovery in other domains could be substantially improved. For example, the techniques of brainstorming commonly promoted for business problem solving are clearly inadequate in the context of strategic thinking. Brainstorming may be adequate for naming a new product or discovering features people would like to see added to a car, but it is too superficial to address complex problems because it fails completely to address the pattern elaboration stage, in which one uncovers the complexities and subtleties inherent in the original insight (Weisberg, 1986). For example, brainstorming would not have helped Beethoven develop his unique and sophisticated musical styles, nor would it be of much help in developing a complex software system. The same may be said for the standard model of discovery in psychology: analysis–incubation–insight. This model assumes that one pass at the target is sufficient to achieve a final result. In fact, any really original design or problem solution requires elaboration, iteration, and evolution (Weisberg, 1986). Again, both brainstorming and the standard model of discovery neglect any mention of testing whether the insight or solution one has achieved has any relation to reality. That is, hypothesis testing is not incorporated into these techniques. Thus, we cannot say that these techniques are reliable in general or even useful for complex problems in particular. Strategic thinking, in contrast, considers all of the above-mentioned solution steps specifically in the context of complex problems.

3 Strategic problem solving

Introduction

In this chapter I discuss the problem-solving process itself, not in terms of the mental operations of thinking about a problem but in terms of the actual actions one takes to obtain a finished product, whether that product be a design, a plan, an experiment, an invention, or a piece of software. In particular, I build here on the discussion of discovery in Chapter 2 and put discovery in the context of the practice of solving real problems and producing technical products. The discussion here is where the material in the first two chapters is put into practice as components of an overall model of practical problem solving.

The structure of a problem has a great deal to do with the best way to organize one's work. For cleaning up the house, almost any order of doing the work will be equally efficient, but for complex tasks the way work is done has a significant bearing on success and productivity. In particular, a strategic problem-solving approach becomes crucial in this context to avoid a high risk of failure or a low level of productivity. The risk of failure in complex projects is not trivial. Gibbs (1994), for example, documents very large project delays (up to twice as long as planned) and large probabilities (up to 50%) of project cancellation for large software projects (over 10 000 function points). Many of these failures result from a lack of knowledge about the inherent differences between simple and complex problems and how they must be approached and managed. An analysis of multistep problems shows how such failures as noted for software projects are a natural feature of their size, how failure risk can be assessed, and how complex projects can be approached to minimize failure and increase productivity. This same type of analysis provides a guide to the organization of work on any technical or professional project, from writing software to construction project management to inventing. This analysis is presented next. While the following few pages entail a little more heavy reading than the rest of this book, they provide key tools for understanding both the structure of complex problems and large-scale failures and fiascoes. The reader should therefore stick with it. Nothing more advanced than a little multiplication is required to get through it.

Problem solving as a multistep process

In considering the problem-solving process, I wish to distinguish three basic types of problem: parallel, sequential, and iterative. In parallel problems, steps are independent of one another. For example, for a set of simple addition problems, each problem is independent. One's score thus represents the number of successes divided by the total number of tries. If one is skilled enough to get 90% of the problems right, then on a long enough test one's score should be a 90. Most tests in school are parallel in nature.

In a sequential problem, the success of the whole depends on each part or step. The classic example is electronic components in series. If any single component fails, the whole device stops operating. If each component has a 0.1% chance of failure during some time interval and 20 components in series make up a critical device, then the probability of failure of that device is $1.0 - 0.999^{20} \approx 0.02$, which is unacceptable for a critical device such as those aboard a space shuttle. Even with a component failure rate of 0.0001, there is a 0.2% failure rate for the device, which is still unacceptable, especially considering the thousands of devices and systems of devices involved. The only solution is redundancy, the course taken for rocket systems. The probability that n redundant components will fail simultaneously is the nth power of their single failure rates. For the example above with a 0.1% chance of failure per component, if even two redundant units are used for each of 20 components in series, the risk of failure goes down to $1.0 - (1.0 - (0.001)^2)^{20} = 0.00002$. Alternately, if there are two entire redundant systems of 20 components each, but with no redundant parts internally, we have $(1.0 - 0.999^{20})^2 = 0.0004$, which is still a very low failure rate.

Iterative problems have quite different properties. Examples include writing and editing a document such as this one, computer programming, and painting. Iterative problems have the property that work previously completed can be fixed, reworked, and improved. No one has ever written more than a few hundred lines of computer code without errors, but the errors can be fixed iteratively without starting over each time.

Technical and planning tasks consist of problems of all three types. Proof-reading a report for mistakes is largely parallel; the errors found are mostly independent of one another. Complex calculations are highly sequential, but they are typically repeated to check the answer. Laboratory work is also often highly sequential. Writing a paper, theorizing, and data analysis tend to be highly iterative.

The basic premise of my model is that much research, invention, and design work is a multistage, multistep process, where stages are qualitatively different sets of related tasks (e.g. theorizing versus experimentation) that themselves consist of discrete tasks (steps). A discovery or end product such as a patent, device, software system, or publication is not a single "thing." It is rarely complete with the initial "Eureka!," but rather it represents a cumulative series of steps or solved problems all (most) of which must be correct. Newton had to invent calculus before solving mechanics, a stage that itself consisted of many steps. In a typical experiment one must: have an idea; design, set up, and execute the experiment; perform statistical analyses; interpret the results; properly compare these results to the literature; and then communicate the results to an audience. An inventor must generate and elaborate a concept, create a prototype, test it, refine it, and document the result. Individual steps, such as performing transplant surgery on laboratory animals or observing the behavior of lions in the field, have a significant risk of failure. Failure at any step certainly leads to lost time and effort, thereby reducing productivity, and it may destroy the entire experiment. (I deal with creative use of failures below.) A certain level of failure (or even reworking) may use up all the available time and money on a particular project, leading to total failure or the waste of a large block of time. Even when the specific component tasks in a technical project are parallel or iterative, the overall success of the project depends on most of them being done correctly. For example, a finished manuscript can be rejected because of poor writing, improper statistics, inadequate experimental technique, or other causes. Only a single serious flaw is needed to make publication unlikely. In addition, even a delay can be equivalent to failure if someone else makes a discovery or brings a product to market first.

These effects can be quantified by using standard critical path analysis models applied to problem solving. The simplest critical path (failure analysis) model where all steps are in series, is simply $P_{success} = p^n$, where p is the probability of success (assumed constant) for a single step, and n is the number of steps. For a problem that consists of 10 steps, the probability of success is p^{10}, where p is the probability of doing each step correctly. Two individuals could have an "A" average in college with respectively 90% and 97% correct answers on tests. However, for a 10 step sequential problem, $0.90^{10} \approx 0.349$, whereas $0.97^{10} \approx 0.737$, more than a two-fold difference in the chance of success for any given project (and thus in productivity). For a 20 step problem, $p = 0.9$ gives only a 12% chance of overall success, while $p = 0.97$ gives a 54% chance of success. This simple calculation does not tell the full story, of course, and I develop a more complete model next, but this calculation does point out something that has been overlooked in the past: small differences in problem-solving skill lead to widely divergent results for multistep problems.

A critical path model of productivity

At this point, I would like to introduce a more complete simulation of multistep problem solving. Consider the office of a professional as a factory whose products are inventions, designs, computer systems, plans, proposals, patents, discoveries, or publications. I wish to model first the small "factory" with perhaps a few assistants, but in which most of the ideas, analyses, and writing and much of the laboratory work is done by the professional per se. We can see that the "raw materials" of this factory are not really mice or chemicals but concepts, hypotheses, experimental skill, base knowledge, computing skills, etc. There are many ways to model this factory. In a study of a furniture craftsman's shop, one might distinguish design, wood working, assembly, and finishing stages to partition labor costs and find bottlenecks. In my model of the professional as factory, I have defined three basic stages: ideation (I), execution (E), and communication (C). Each stage consists of multiple steps. Success in a step of any of these stages is given by p, which represents problem-solving skill. We are interested in the number of successful projects (productions) completed in a period of time. The products of completed projects are publications, patents, software, machines designed, etc. The model is a mix of sequential and iterative components. In operations research terms, the model is a queuing model. Jobs (productions) queue up for the attention of the single operator. Each job is processed through three work stations (I, E, and C). Multiple jobs can be in process, but the operator can work on only one at a time. Errors are randomly introduced but are not detected until the specific checkpoint (defined below). Errors lead to reworking, thereby tying up the operator (the professional). Therefore, no simple equation defines the level of productivity. Rather, a simulation of the process is necessary. The simulation model is defined as follows:

1 The probability of success at each step is p, a measure of technical skill. In the simulation, uniform random (0, 1) numbers (R) are drawn and compared to determine success at each step. For $R > p$, the step is a failure. Each step counts as 1 time increment.

2 Stage 1 (ideation) has I steps; all must be completed successfully. Failure leads to the loss of all time required for both stage 1 and stage 2. That is to say, a failure means that a useless experiment or design project was performed because of a nonfruitful idea.

3 Stage 2 (execution) has E steps. If a step is unsuccessful, the model is reset to the beginning of stage 2, representing a mistake in an experiment, product development, or design project that is based on a basically sound idea. The mistake leads to repeating the execution of the project (an iterative action). The entire time required for stage 2 is lost by failure, on the assumption that errors in the execution stage are not detected until the end of that stage.

4 Stage 3 (communication) has C steps. Unsuccessful steps are repeated (as in rewriting a paper). Complete failure of communication is not allowed because of the iterative nature of writing. (One can always rewrite a document.) Allowing failure at stage 3 would accentuate the nonlinearities and differences between short and long productions discussed below.

Although projects are assumed to vary in length, the average project is modeled. Few-step versus multistep projects are modeled explicitly below. Since the scientific method allows for some experimental error, "failure" in this context refers, for example, to ruined or uninterpretable experiments, not just to occasional measurement error, or to a useless software system, not just one with a few bugs. A lifetime of professional output was simulated by setting $T = 8750$ time steps. For a 35 year long, full-time career, this equates to one real workday per simulated step. One day is a reasonable estimate for a discrete piece of an overall project, such as writing a section of a paper or analyzing data. The overall number of projects completed over a career as a function of p is given in Figure 4. The upper line is for simpler problems with few steps ($I = 5, E = 7, C = 6$). The lower line is for more difficult problems ($I = 11, E = 13, C = 6$). These parameter values were chosen on the basis of my experience, but they could instead be empirically determined. The maximum possible total productivity (at $p = 1.0$) is of course lower for the problems with more steps.

The output of the model, shown in Figure 4, corresponds fairly well with reality. The maximum possible lifetime productivities (for $p = 1.0$) shown are in the range of that observed in real life (486 for short problems, 291 for long problems). For skilled scientists who must teach full time with only summers free, this would give lifetime productivities of 121 and 73 for short and long productions, respectively. Again, these numbers are in accord with reality. Employment

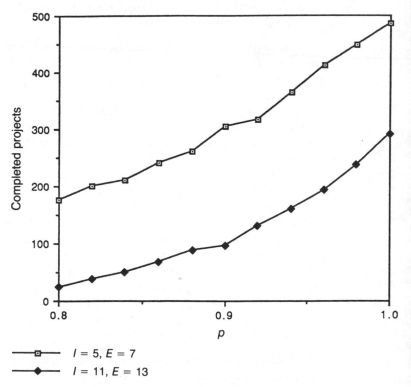

Figure 4. Productivity for short versus long problems. $T = 8750$ time steps.

Table 1. *Lifetime productivities predicted by the model for long problems*
(I = 11, E = 13, C = 6)

	Full-time researcher	Full-time with assistants	¼ time (full teaching load)
Brilliant scientist ($p = 1.0$)	291	582–1000	73
Average scientist ($p = 0.8$)	24	48	6

I, number of ideation steps; E, number of execution steps; C, number of cummunication steps in a problem.

of technicians and students and coauthorship practices can effectively double or triple these figures, giving maximum lifetime productivities that closely match all but the most prolific (Table 1). The most prolific scientists overall are usually heads of large teams (Anderson, 1992), in which the average number of papers per worker may be only one to three per year (total papers divided by total laboratory staff). For example, Boxenbaum *et al.* (1987) showed a strong negative correlation between percentage of sole-authored papers and total number of publications. Publication records for some of the most famous, working largely alone and on difficult problems, include Einstein (248), Galton (227), Binet (277), James (307), Freud (330), and Maslow (165) (Albert, 1975). However, much of these authors' productivity was in the form of books, so their true productivity was higher than these figures indicate. An example of what can be accomplished by a single person working largely on smaller (though still difficult) problems is the case of I. J. Good of the Statistics Department at Virginia Tech, with a lifetime total of over 1600 publications (personal communication), many of them notes or commentaries. Other examples include John Cairns, Jr (Biology Department, Virginia Tech), with over 800 (personal communication), Carl Djerassi (chemistry) with over 1000, and Linus Pauling (chemistry) with over 700 lifetime publications, respectively. Similar results obtain from examination of famous inventors, engineers, and software designers, such as the inventor David Rabinow with over 225 patents and Marvin Camras with over 500 (Petroski, 1992). Qualitative correspondence between this model and actual experience can also be observed in the nonlinear increase in failure probability for software projects of increasing length (Gibbs, 1994).

The range of productivities predicted by this model for more typical full-time research scientists with average skill levels ($p = 0.80$) ranges from 24 for very difficult problems to 175 for very simple problems. Numbers between these extremes are quite reasonable for actual full-time research scientists at the lower range of productivity. Teaching responsibilities of course diminish these numbers considerably. Thus, the p values, the structure of the model, and the number of

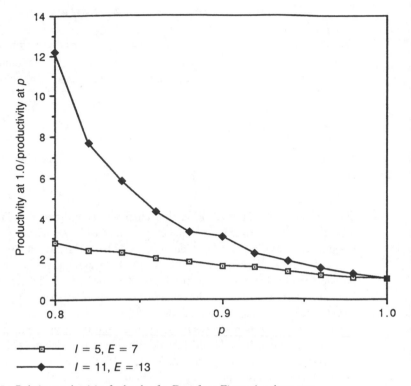

Figure 5.   Relative productivity for levels of p. Data from Figure 4 and see text.

steps simulated lead to quite reasonable results in comparison to real scientists, and may safely be extended to other professionals on the basis of data from engineers, inventors, designers, and software producers.

In Figure 5, relative productivity is shown for short and long productions. That is to say, the value plotted at a given value of p, $\text{Prod}_{1.0}/\text{Prod}_p$, allows comparison between each level of p and the most productive. Relative productivities are relevant here because professional advancement opportunities are based on relative performance measures. The difference between these two curves indicates that the relative advantage of choosing simple, few-step problems (or those that are more parallel or iterative) increases as p decreases. For few-step problems (the lower curve) the most skilled professional ($p = 1.0$) is 2.8-fold as productive as one at $p = 0.8$. The relationship is rather linear with shallow slope, suggesting that to a major extent it is possible to substitute perspiration for inspiration on this type of problem.

Thomas Edison, famous for his "science is 99% perspiration and 1% inspiration," actually followed this strategy. Much of his work was trial and error or incremental (e.g., he tested hundreds of items for his light bulb filament), and he put in record-breaking hours in his laboratory. He also had an army of assistants. On projects that involve few steps, therefore, sufficient variation in the number of hours individuals work or the number of assistants they have can account for the large variation in individual productivities. The upper curve in Figure 5 represents the opposite case. For long, multistep problems such as difficult proofs in mathematics, the effect of p is very nonlinear. In the upper curve, the person with $p = 1.0$ would be 12-fold as productive as one with $p = 0.8$. Perspiration cannot be substituted for inspiration on such problems because there are insufficient hours in a day to make a difference. In fact, if long hours lead to even a slight decrease in p due to fatigue, then Edison's approach will be counterproductive. In addition, an army of assistants may not necessarily be helpful but work habits and various personality factors such as persistence might alter p slightly and have a major effect on long multistep problems because of the strong nonlinearity of the relationship.

Discussion

This model suggests a reexamination of our focus on idea generation as the alpha and omega of creativity. The typical picture of the highly creative person is the individual bursting with breakthrough concepts and ideas; the "Eureka!" experience is common for such a person. Most books on creativity focus almost entirely on this step of the creative process. Whether this flood of ideas is translated into a flood of finished products, however, depends on the length and difficulty of the elaboration, execution, and communication stages. Thus, starting with the basic model presented above, it is useful to consider how various factors affect p, the nature of the problem (iterative versus sequential), and the number of steps at each stage.

Consider the physicist Michael Faraday. Because of the nature of his problems and his skill as an experimenter, he could perform dozens of experiments per week. Thus, even though he had many hunches that came to nothing, he could still achieve a high productivity (measured as successes). In contrast, in some fields progress becomes rate limited at the execution stage. For example, in field ecology single experiments are very time consuming, and the logistics of running them dictate that a single researcher can handle only a few such projects at a time. Observing the behavior of lions in the field may require thousands of hours. One needs only a few good ideas per year in this context, and 50 might not help at all. Rather, meticulous attention to detail and a long attention span are essential. Clinical trials can also be very time consuming and are a major rate-limiting step in medical research. The communication stage can also be rate limiting. Richard Feynman hated to write. Much of his work saw the light of day only because of his coauthors (Feynman, 1984).

Creativity can also have an effect on productivity. Creativity leads some individuals to recognize problems that others do not see, but which may be very difficult. Charles Darwin's approach to the speciation problem (Darwin, 1958) is a good example of this; he chose a very difficult and tangled problem, speciation, which led him into a long period of data collection and rumination. This choice of problem did not allow for a quick attack or a simple experiment. In such cases creativity may actually decrease productivity (as measured by publication counts) because effort is focused on difficult problems. For others, whose creativity is more focused on methods and technique, creativity may lead to solutions that drastically reduce the work necessary to solve a problem. We can see an example in the development of the polymerase chain reaction (PCR), which amplifies small pieces of DNA. This new technology greatly reduces the number of steps in a scientific procedure, and thereby increases reliability.

The above factors, I believe, explain why little relationship has been found between creativity and productivity. Creativity can have a large positive effect, a negative effect, or no effect on output rate, depending on the stage of the problem-solving process to which it is applied and the nature of the bottlenecks inherent in the specific field. Further, the role of work habits versus skill level will differ on few-step compared to multistep productions. Taking creativity into account in the context of the whole process of creating technical products should allow a more complete understanding of its role.

This model also explains how those who are not brilliant can still do good work. If p is lower, it is still possible to finish difficult projects if the nature of the problem allows indefinite repetition of any step until it succeeds (i.e., the problem allows an iterative approach). This iterative strategy leads to lower productivity, because each stage takes longer, but increases quality. Some writers, for example, must edit a document through many drafts but achieve good quality in the end. Peer review also raises p and is most effective if it occurs not just at the final stage (when it may be too late) but at the early stages as well. Repeated review during a project decreases the nonlinearity inherent in the process by reducing the number of steps that must be repeated when a failure is detected. Such reviews can be particularly valuable for software projects. Peer review is also analogous to redundancy in circuit design: independent reviewers are very unlikely to make the same mistakes as the author. Thus, peer review (of the constructive variety) has an extremely strong positive effect on quality. Unfortunately, pressures on the individual professional today make it difficult for peers to find sufficient time to review the work of others.

From the perspective of this analysis, it can be seen that standard views of the "genius" are seriously mistaken. When there is too much focus on the flash-of-insight type of discovery, and simultaneously the genius is held up as the exemplar of creativity, then the ordinary person feels he or she will never do any quality work. Who can expect to produce a great theory at a single stroke? The reality is far different. Most historical figures of exceptional renown in fact applied an iterative problem-solving approach. They did not just burst forth with finished products in an unpremeditated way, but sketched, revised, reworked, and polished. Darwin spent 20 years working on his theory of evolution. Throughout this period he struggled with the parts that did not seem to fit or that were weak. Picasso tried out huge numbers of ideas in rough sketches before settling on a finished product. The same can be said of most such figures. What perhaps distinguishes such people is not the brilliance of their initial insight, but the fact that they keep working on a problem until the result is exceptional. They can recognize when a solution (or work of art) is incomplete or inadequate in some way, and keep trying to improve it. Many people conceived of the light bulb, but only Edison and a few others kept at it until they had one that worked. Interestingly, Edison also realized that he would never sell many light bulbs unless an electrical power network existed, and he therefore established one. He thus followed through on the implications of his invention more thoroughly than others did.

This multistep view of productivity has implications for improving the productivity of the individual professional. Writing skills are highly amenable to training and practice. Particular attention should be paid to bottlenecks in the project that are time consuming or have a high risk of failure. Such bottlenecks can be overcome, for example, by using meta-analysis to combine information from a series of clinical trails or studies (Mann, 1990). This approach is very useful because conducting the "perfect" single experiment is highly unlikely in fields such as medicine. A bottleneck at the ideation stage may be overcome by certain work habits (Loehle, 1990, and Chapters 1 and 2). Development of new experimental techniques or instruments may also eliminate error-prone bottleneck points or make them less time consuming (Crease, 1992; Hall, 1992). Molecular techniques such as PCR, gene sequencing, and hybridization have removed bottlenecks in the study of biology and genetics.

We may also apply this model to the problem of professionals whose productivity is deficient in spite of their skill and industry. Some professionals are very busy and do very good work, but much of their work is never completed in a finished form. A close examination of the files of many scientists will show dozens of manuscripts that have been started or are even almost finished but that will never see the light of day, as well as drawers full of data that will never be analyzed. Inventors end up with file drawers full of partial designs, almost finished prototypes, and partially written patent applications. Writers have partial stories and half-finished novels filling their office. All of these people know that greater productivity would lead to greater rewards, to promotions or raises or an enhanced reputation, so why do they leave so much unfinished? Are they lazy? Observing them in action clearly rules out laziness as a factor. I believe the answer lies in the fact that for any such complex product, there is a high chance that at least one step will prove problematic (will be a failure). One key piece of data will prove elusive; one design criterion will be left unfulfilled; one analysis will prove too difficult; and the project will be put aside for a while. Since there are always many things to be done that are not so difficult, that are even enjoyable, projects in which a step has failed may be put on the back shelf and left and eventually they become forgotten or outdated. In most such cases, the failed step can be repeated or fixed, but the level of effort for that step may be greater than the average required for other projects. The single equation holding up a manuscript might require days of sustained effort of a rather unpleasant sort, or a key experiment might require equipment that is not available in one's own laboratory. Therefore, because these single steps appear to be too formidable, the entire time spent on that project may go to waste. All of this results from the inevitable probabilities of multistep problem solving. The productive professional, the strategic thinker, recognizes that key tasks may require more effort than average, and also recognizes that such extra effort on certain tasks is warranted to avoid losing the time invested on a project prior to the encounter with the difficulty. These difficult or problematic steps may also require teaming with experts in other domains.

This view of productivity has implications for the management of professionals and of technical projects. In hiring, subsequent productivity apparently cannot be predicted from test scores or college grades (Simonton, 1988). However, an established record of productivity is probably stable over a lifetime (e.g., Simonton, 1988; Parker, 1989). The model presented here suggests that more task-relevant tests are needed for predicting professional performance. For example, measures of attention span and task persistence might be more relevant to predicting technical productivity than measures of either creativity or subject knowledge. Creativity tests that focus on analogy, novelty generation etc. are unlikely to be relevant unless the task of the professional is specifically to generate novelty (as in advertising). The model presented here also suggests that inter-ruptions and distractions can be detrimental to total productivity. This conclusion is supported by historical examples. Many famous scientists have isolated them-selves for long periods. Skunk works* in industry have led to extraordinary accomplishments because the design group was protected from interruptions and because they allowed rapid feedback at each step, so that single steps could be repeated immediately (Peters and Austin, 1985). In contrast, when control is exerted from the top (e.g., in the name of administration), two things happen in addition to interruptions. First, the number of steps increases greatly. Military procurement is a classic case in which hundreds of people (and steps) are involved in writing specifications for a product. The probability of a mistake rises nonlinearly with the number of steps. Second, the long planning and specification process may cause a prototype not to be built until "the end," when mistakes may require massive reworking. Thus, excessive control and accountability can lead paradoxically to nonlinear increases in time or money expended and chances for

---

* A separate building for a design team, freed from usual rules and procedures.

failure. The recent high tech systems fiascoes such as the Sargent York military vehicle in the USA and the Hubble telescope may therefore not reflect stupidity but merely a specification-and-design process with too many steps and players and not enough iterative problem solving (see also McDonald, 1990). Specifically, when a task becomes extremely sequential (as are many large software projects), it may become nearly impossible to prevent major failures, however careful the participants. This was recognized as one of the reasons why the United States Star Wars (Strategic Defense Initiative) program was unlikely to succeed and why it was finally killed. In this context, we can see clearly one of the benefits of virtual reality. When applied to buildings, a virtual reality system allows a trial of the building as designed. The ability of a person in a wheelchair to navigate the building, for example, can be tested. The safety hazard of projecting pipes and equipment in a factory can be assessed by a simulated "walkthrough." In this way the building can be assessed before it is built so that changes can be made cheaply, at the design stage. This, in essence, converts a sequential process into an iterative one, with consequent increased end product quality and reduced costs.

Productivity has become a principal measure of success and a key to promotion. The nonlinear model presented here suggests, however, that problems can arise from simple publication counts as measures of professional output. Choosing small, simple problems (or "salami slicing") can radically increase output, and therefore rewards, out of all proportion to the significance of the work performed. Tackling the really difficult problems may give the greatest payoff for science or the corporation but not for the individual professional if he or she is judged on patents or number of publications. Promotion practices may thus be inherently unfair when comparisons are made between, say, biochemists (inherently high output rate) versus evolutionary biologists (inherently low output rate). In addition, it is possible to achieve higher productivity by avoiding difficult problems, for example by applying standard methods to well-defined problems. Innovative ideas are both more difficult (more steps, at least at the ideation stage) and riskier (p may be lower if new methods or tools are used). The discoveries that receive the most attention may require several really innovative steps and thus be very unlikely. In the extreme, high productivity can be achieved by using mass production approaches or by doing many descriptive studies (e.g., species lists), as noted with examples by Simonton (1988), in which case the number of steps at stage 1 is greatly reduced (new ideas are not really needed), and p for stage 2 is increased (because well-tested methods are being used). These considerations point out the pitfalls of measuring success purely by publication counts.

These results also have implications for educational systems. Most educational systems are geared toward adequate performance, but most real world jobs require far higher levels of performance. If a car mechanic knows where only 85% of your carburetor parts go, this is not a "B" performance but rather rates an "F." This is particularly so for highly sequential tasks. Unfortunately, most school systems almost completely lack emphasis on the skills or work habits that lead to successful multistep problem solving (Thelan, 1972; Hunter, 1978). Term papers, long-term observation, diaries, science projects, building machinery etc. are all largely skipped because they are too demanding of the teacher, in favor of multiple-choice tests based on short-term memorization. Thus, parallel rather than sequential or iterative problem-solving skills are emphasized. Subject mastery rather than minimal competence should also be emphasized. For example, if a term paper is inadequate, the student should be required to redo it. Problems in science and business require not multiple choice, but instead multiple-step solutions. Our educational system needs to reflect that reality. It is notable that the United States graduate education system, praised as among the best in the world, is strongly hands-on and apprentice based. The graduate student generally becomes a junior partner on a team and is given tasks to do that require original thought, but within the structure of the overall project and with the guidance of the advisor if problems arise. The sink-or-swim approach to graduate education (almost no advice provided) used by some professors is not optimal and only works effectively with particularly mature and independent students. However, the graduate-student-as-laboratory-technician approach denies the student the chance to develop critical thinking skills and does not produce an independent scientist. In fact, such graduate students may remain as laboratory technicians and never mature into scientists. An optimal apprentice program thefore allows independence but provides some guidance and feedback on performance.

Conclusion

The new operational model presented here can tie together cognitive models of problem solving and sociological models of the scientific process. Such factors as available technology, reward structure, and marginality (Simonton, 1988) affect the type of problems chosen (short or long) and the base level of the probability of success of a single step, p, for the professional culture as a whole (we now routinely solve problems that would have been too difficult for the average professional 100 years ago). For example, members in an elite department or group can increase p by having access to feedback, advice, techniques, equipment, and appropriate collaborators. The model presented provides a quantitative framework for converting test scores (e.g., college grades, standardized test scores) into predictions about productivity that specifically account for the nonlinearities involved. The model also makes specific predictions about how test performance should change on simple versus multistep problems as a function of skill level. The importance of bottlenecks to productivity is pointed out. Differences between fields are also explained. Some fields focus largely on short problems (e.g., Faraday's simple experiments on electricity), whereas others (e.g., economics, ecology, sociology) face difficult-to-control, complex systems that cause studies to be often long and tedious. The model developed is applicable to industrial or technological problem solving and large-scale software projects as well as to individual productivity. Overall, critical path analysis of technical problem solving can provide a new perspective that links cognitive and sociological aspects in a single framework based on observables such as problem type, operator skill, and problem size.

This analysis clearly shows why novelty or creativity alone are inadequate. Creativity only becomes innovation when a novel finished product is produced. Producing finished products requires attention to the entire sequential problem-solving process. The final critical step in innovation and problem solving is the testing of the value or validity of the finished product, discussed next.

4 Reality check

In previous chapters, the process of discovery and the harnessing of our mental machinery in the service of discovery, problem solving and invention were discussed. By definition, when creating something new or solving a novel problem, we are stepping somewhat into the unknown. Clearly, in such cases we cannot look up the proper answer in the back of the book. It is not always clear and evident, however, that the discovery or problem solution is correct, useful, or the best. For an artist or composer it is only necessary that the product be pleasing to the author and/or the public. No further test is necessary, in spite of the presumed central role critics give themselves. In other realms of endeavor, however, it is essential that some type of test be used, some reality check, to verify the solution arrived at. This is particularly critical for complex systems, as is discussed in Chapters 5–7. There are two types of test that we may apply. First, we may be somewhat confident of the product of our work if we can be sure that the problem-solving process itself did not lead us astray. In this case we cannot be sure that our result is correct, but we can assert that we did not make any obvious blunders. This is an internal reality check. Second, it is useful to check, if possible, our results against some objective standard. This is an external reality check. These checks are discussed next.

Internal reality check

There are several types of pitfall that lie in wait for the strategic thinker. Our mental machinery is very unreliable in certain domains, and has some distinct blind spots. As Margolis (1987) discusses, our minds work primarily by recognizing patterns. We are very quick and proficient at recognizing faces, musical tunes, and places. This same capability aids us in making discoveries by finding new patterns, new structures, and new connections between data and in discerning data from noise. However, just because the brain detects a pattern does not automatically mean that the pattern is real. As children, we find the darkness is full of monsters and the clouds are full of Disney characters. As adults, we misread the pattern of stock prices, of economic indicators, and of spousal moods. The pitfall here lies in our tendency to accept these patterns that we observe as real because the process by which we discover them is hidden. Just as we are unaware of how we identify a face or a song but are nevertheless confident about our identification, we are also unaware of how we identify other patterns and thus have no opportunity to question our judgement. Because of this it is crucial that we examine the structure of the patterns we observe, construct, or "discover" out in the open as much as possible. The use of logic and examination of pattern or structure coherence are particularly helpful in this regard. It is also very useful to become aware of how we assess probability (risk, chance) in decision making and in weighting evidence that goes into our judgements.

☞ Faulty generalization

As mentioned elsewhere in this chapter, our reasoning processes are far from foolproof and rigorous. One universal flaw is the Law of Faulty Generalization (A. A. Furutan, personal communication). This law states that we tend to overgeneralize from single incidents to entire classes. If we are in a distant city and someone helps us when we are lost, we believe the entire city is full of kind people. If we visit another city and get mugged, we will never go there again. We can understand the basis for this response in ingrained survival mechanisms. For example, it is extremely important in an evolutionary sense that you never forget that a certain food is poisonous and that it made you sick when you ate it. The second time you try it you might not survive. Thus, people can develop extremely strong food preferences based on experiences that made them gag as a child (even when a hair in the food, and not the food itself, caused the problem) or caused them to become sick. The same is true of almost drowning, almost being caught by a lion, or almost falling off a cliff. We are therefore not wired to accurately find the long-term odds of falling off a cliff or to accurately sample the people of a city for friendliness, but rather to entrain into memory any particularly good or adverse situation and to generalize it. We may note that this is the origin of superstitions – a close coincidence in time between some unusual event such as seeing a black cat, and a subsequent serious adverse occurrence. While certain people are far more likely to overgeneralize than others, and thus to become fearful or superstitious or compulsive, we all do it to some extent. Whereas generalization from single encounters with dangerous animals or foods is adaptive, we also generalize about abstract categories such as ethnic groups or places or social situations.

While it may not matter much that you do not like eggplant because the first time you tried it it made you gag so you won't try it again, in other situations this propensity to overgeneralize has serious consequences. When we see a television report of an airplane crash, we overgeneralize ("That could be me") and are so horrified that we become afraid of flying even though it is far safer than driving. In puritanical societies, the proscription against adultery (sex outside marriage is bad) has become overgeneralized (sex is bad). We have now overgeneralized in the other direction: if sex is good, then sex with anyone any time must be good, so that all standards become lost. We conclude that, if salt in the diet raises the blood pressure in the short term, then salt must cause permanent high blood pressure in the long term, a conclusion totally without merit.

Let us look at a more extended generalization problem: recycling. The concept that recycling could be a good thing for conserving resources is not without merit. During World War II extensive recycling, especially of metals, was practiced. Recycling practiced by industry can clearly be shown to be a money maker while at the same time helping the environment. From this the generalization is made: recycling is good, therefore residential recycling will also be good. Experience has shown, however, that residential curbside pickup of recyclables has been a money loser almost everywhere in the USA where it has been tried (Bailey, 1995) because the cost of curbside pickup is just too high and the items are too mixed and low value. Even when it is not an overt money loser, it can be sustained only because the labor cost of sorting the rubbish is not counted, since the residential consumers do it for free before collection. In contrast, in the factory tonnes of an item to be recycled are generated at one discrete point, which makes it cheap to collect. A related example of faulty reasoning is the perception that landfill space is running out in the USA. A few local examples of landfills that are full have been generalized to a presumption of a national crisis (Bailey, 1995) but closer examination usually reveals that these local cases result from NIMBY (not in my back yard) lawsuits, not from actual lack of suitable locations. Further, modern landfills are filled not just to 15 m but to 30–90 m in depth, which makes them last much longer than old ones. This phantom crisis results from using superficial impressions rather than actual data to make decisions. The Long Island refuse barge *Mobro* that wandered the seas for two months in 1987 was perceived to be wandering looking for a dump that wasn't full, like Diogenes with his lamp looking for an honest man, but that was not the real story. The barge owner was a novice at garbage disposal, and sent the barge down to North Carolina without ever making an arrangement for acceptance. This caused the dump owners to ask questions (Was there toxic waste in the refuse? What was the rush?) and stall, which meant that the barge was not allowed into the harbor (since it would block traffic and occupy dock space) and was therefore sent back to sea (Bailey, 1995). Once this happened, the barge became famous and no other dump would touch it. A false conclusion about why the barge was not accepted (no dump space) was over-generalized to the conclusion that all of our dumps must be full, especially as the barge continued to wander, causing a feeling of widespread panic. Never mind that no other barges were wandering the seas nor were trucks full of refuse wandering the highways. One could not even show that dumping refuse was particularly expensive as it would be if space were short.

We can demonstrate excessive generalization even in cases where experience is extensive. For example, at annual review time for employee performance, the most recent few weeks have a disproportionate influence on the supervisor's performance appraisal. This is not the time to take a holiday, decide to grow a beard, or fumble a project. Similarly, at any point in a relationship, the emotional response of one's partner is strongly biased by recent events which are heavily overgeneralized – What have you done for me lately?

The general solution to this tendency to falsely generalize is to learn to depend more heavily on numbers (rates, odds, rankings, etc.). We should automatically dismiss the single encounter with the person in a new city, because it cannot possibly be representative. We do this when a beefburger makes us sick; our long experience with them makes us realize that this single burger was not representative. In the case of the performance appraisal, the employee should keep a log of concrete accomplishments during the year and provide this as a basis for review.

This approach actually provides a method used to treat phobias. Phobias, while sometimes having a biological basis, also have a strongly learned (or perhaps we should say mis-learned) component. The common and successful treatment of phobias such as fear of heights or of crowds or of public transportation is to gradually expose the person to the stimulus in a safe environment using very small doses. For example, for a person afraid of heights, they will first be asked to step up on a very low platform and back down to see that nothing happens. They can then work up to going up in an office building. The emphasis is to overcome the false generalization with lots of valid data, delivered in small, safe doses. Direct confrontation does not generally work because when a panic reaction becomes habitual it becomes self-fulfilling: the person panics at the shopping mall even though there is no reason to, so their experience is disastrous even though objectively nothing went wrong. The fear of panic itself sets off a panic. Small safe doses must therefore be used to allow the person to experience the situation and not have a panic attack. This technique applies learning to extinguish an inappropriate overgeneralization, that all situations like the one that triggered the original panic are just as threatening.

As is the case with the other deficits in our reasoning, only knowledge of how we fail to think clearly can allow us to compensate and therefore to think more clearly.

☞ Logic

People are notoriously bad in their use of logic. While most can handle simple declarative logic, more complex logical trains of thought, particularly if they include negations or exclusions, prove daunting. For example, the commonly used negative argument "No pain reliever proven more effective" is very convincing to many people, but does not in fact mean that the brand in question is superior. It may only mean that no comparative study has been done, or that you cannot tell this brand from the others statistically. The computer as a model for intelligence is therefore completely misleading. We reason neither like an expert system (by using sets of rules), nor like a hierarchical classifier, nor like a FORTRAN computational loop. In fact, our formal reasoning abilities are rather limited. For this reason, we can often observe illogical arguments in spousal "discussions" and in political debates. Margolis (1987) argues that we do not think by a process of sequences of logical deductions, but rather in terms of patterns. If certain items seem related or connected (form a pattern), we will believe that they are related in a causal way. We will consequently reason in an illogical way about them (e.g., explaining why they are related) and never notice that our reasoning is fallacious. In particular, the mental operations we use to explain or communicate the patterns we have observed are equally facile at explaining a real pattern and a fictitious one, according to Margolis. For a conspiracy theorist, all types of data fit together seamlessly, even data that later turn out to be erroneous or merely rumor. This means that one must take special care when attempting to reason logically, and should apply particular techniques that are less subject to this type of pitfall.

Another faulty type of logic concerns reasoning by opposition. We often enough experience exclusive relations (one cannot be in two places at once, one can buy either item 1 or item 2 with a certain amount of cash, the person is either alive or dead, it is either true or false that a certain event happened) sufficiently often that this approach to reasoning comes to seem reliable. When applied to complex issues, however, such reasoning is inadequate. If one argues that pure communism is bad, it does not follow that its opposite, pure capitalism, is perfect. If one spouse is wrong, this does not mean that the other spouse is right. Black-and-white reasoning is prone to reducing a complex issue to an either–or question, when in reality neither alternative may be the best or a compromise may be the best and not either extreme. Extra care must therefore be taken to avoid this type of logic because it seems much more conclusive than it is.

Because we can operate fairly reliably on simple "if . . . then" type logical statements (if I buy this item, then I will run out of cash), since such statements correspond to our usual sense and experience of cause and effect, such declarative logic provides a useful tool for examining our reasoning about patterns. We can use it in two principal ways: to examine the premises underlying our idea, and to examine the consequences of our idea.

Underlying any discovery, pattern, invention, or structure, is a set of premises or assumptions. Such premises are often much more easily examined than is the overall pattern or theory or concept. The successful introduction of the minivan was based on the correct premise that for families a station wagon (or estate car) was just too cramped but a full size van was too big, too hard to drive, and too expensive. In other cases, the premises may be suspect. For example, if one assumes that there are few homeless and that most of them are mentally disturbed or substance abusers, then one will support a very different social policy than if one assumes that all homeless are down on their luck and eager to take advantage of an opportunity to better themselves. In many cases the assumptions people make about the homeless are based on no data at all and no personal experience but rather on social theories (world views). Reliable data are desperately needed to characterize the population of concern in this case because otherwise incompatible solutions are offered by groups starting with these very different (usually unspoken) assumptions.

If we examine Darwin's development of the theory of evolution as presented in the *Origin of Species*, we see a very successful use of the testing of premises. Darwin believed that the patterns he saw in nature could be explained by natural selection acting on heritable variation. At the time, the genetic code had not been discovered, so he could not examine the mechanisms of inheritance directly; but evolution occurs so slowly that he could not directly observe it in operation either. However, after considerable reflection he realized that he could collect data to evaluate the premises of his theory. One premise was that variation in traits is heritable. He showed this to be true, indirectly, by exhaustive collection of data from plant and animal breeders. A second premise was that organisms are all descended from common ancestors. A challenge to this assumption seemed to be posed by life on distant oceanic islands. If these remote plants and animals could not have traveled there, then they must have been specially created, which would invalidate descent from common ancestors. He tested this premise by showing that seeds of many species can float in salt water for long periods and still germinate, and by noting that the animals found on these islands can all either fly or survive long periods without water and thus can travel on mats of floating plants for long distances (e.g., reptiles).

Historically, the examination of premises has been critical to finding flaws in ideas. For example, Freudian analysis seems to be a coherent system, and it is good at "explaining" many aspects of human behavior. However, as psychology has matured, investigations have failed to find any evidence for the assumptions underlying the Freudian paradigm, such as penis envy, the Oedipal urge, etc. As a result, Freudianism is more popular among the public than among psychologists (Stanovich, 1992).

In contrast, it is typical of those holding irrational beliefs (in folklore, crackpot theories, superstition, perpetual motion machines, etc.) that they resist efforts to examine the premises of their belief system. People holding such beliefs recognize the utility of testing assumptions and premises only in as much as such efforts make them nervous. Freudian psychotherapists and Marxists have never been particularly interested in examining their premises and both groups are notable for their lack of enthusiasm for experimentation, which is why neither philosophy has progressed and why both are rapidly fading from view.

We may also use "if . . . then" logical reasoning to examine our ideas, concepts, or inventions by making causal predictions or extrapolations. Because this type of reasoning matches one of the natural abilities of pattern reasoning and involves only simple conditional logic, people have a natural talent in this area (though it is far from foolproof). We habitually try to imagine the scenario at a picnic so that we will remember to take everything we need. We try to imagine our old age when planning for retirement. This type of reasoning can be used to derive tests of our ideas or to draw out the implications of them. We can imagine how a consumer might use a new product or try to predict the reactions that might follow a foreign policy action. We can try to see what follows if a particular scientific theory is true. Scale models, mathematical models, and virtual reality simulations are particularly useful for projecting the consequences of our ideas or actions.

It is particularly useful to extrapolate our action or idea to see what it entails. For example, I was considering painting my kitchen because of a large stain above the stove. When I followed through this action in my mind, I got to the edge of the kitchen and realized that the wall is continuous with the living room, dining room, and family room. There is no place to stop. Therefore, I matched the paint and just painted above the stove (for now). We may similarly extrapolate the effect of a policy decision. In the United States education community, it has been decided that bilingual education is a good thing. We can debate the logic behind this policy (in particular, the prescription does not follow from the premises, as discussed below), but here I just want to extrapolate this policy. If bilingual education is a good thing, then we should apply it everywhere. However, some schools have immigrants from dozens of different countries. Do we provide bilingual education for them all? Doing so will totally bankrupt the school district (or the nation) by leading to class sizes of one in some cases. If we provide bilingual education for only Hispanics, then we are either being condescending (the others don't need help, only Hispanics find it too difficult to learn English), or we are practicing favoritism. Extrapolating the situation from the area on the Mexican border (large numbers of Hispanics) to the entire USA (multiple nationalities of immigrants) shows the policy to be impractical.

Let us take another example. It has been argued that extenuating circumstances should be considered in criminal cases. For example, if a woman murders her husband (in cold blood, not in self-defense) because he was constantly beating her, there will be a tendency to view her situation with some sympathy and she might get a reduced sentence in the USA and in France. It has similarly been argued, however, that other individuals have been traumatized by parents or by society, and that this likewise excuses their criminal actions. The danger here clearly is that when we extrapolate the reasonable argument for abused wives to other cases, we enter a domain where almost anything can be argued. Husbands have argued that their wives abused them verbally or had affairs and that this justified murder. Gang members have argued that they are hopeless and oppressed and therefore their lifestyle is excusable. There is virtually no end to the excuses that can be made in this fashion, and we end up weighing imponderables about who has been victimized or abused sufficiently that they will be excused from a crime. Again, extrapolation shows this policy to be unworkable. We must insist that there are always alternatives to violence or crime, and that while we offer sympathy to the abused or oppressed, we cannot excuse criminal actions.

A difficulty with examining premises in practice is that the reasoning processes many people use are not consistent, such that their conclusions often do not follow from their premises. That is to say, the truth or falseness of their premises (assumptions) may not bear on the truth or falseness of their conclusions. There are several reasons for this.

The first type of reasoning failure is that we are often working with incomplete information, though the incompleteness of our set of premises is not always obvious (except with hindsight, of course). It is a fundamental error to attempt to draw conclusions logically from a set of incomplete premises. Such a situation is indeterminate and many different conclusions can be shown to be compatible with the given premises. Consider a designer creating a consumer product for outdoor use. He or she considers sun, rain, heat, and dirt as factors affecting product durability, and designs accordingly. However, because the designer lives in Iowa, he or she does not envision the widespread use of the product by the ocean, where it corrodes overnight. I have in mind here two brands of folding chairs I bought in South Carolina. One was all aluminum and performed well by the beach, but the other was steel and rusted in no time. There are only two types of protection against this difficulty: first, actively seek out all possible impinging factors; second, test any decision, invention, or theory against reality (see below). We observe the consequences of failure to guard against this incompleteness pitfall in the lives of grand theorists (social, political, or other) who are so confident of their reasoning ability that they never stop to think that they might be missing something (Johnson, 1988). Thus are born an endless series of popular psychology prescriptions for improving your love life, self-esteem, weight, addiction, etc.: each is based on a set of only partially correct (to be generous) premises.

A related problem is caused by faulty reasoning per se, such that the conclusions do not follow from the stated premises. We observe this frequently in politics. One cause of this is the tendency to jump from premises to prescription. For example, from the premise that crime is high, we are immediately given the prescription that prison terms must be longer. The analysis is presented as though the prescription follows inevitably from the premises, which it does not. The prescription is only one of many possible solutions. An alternative prescription might be to intensify police presence and to make jail time more certain (rather than longer) for an arrested criminal. This would make capture and punishment seem more likely to the criminal. A second cause of conclusions that do not follow is the single causal factor fallacy (Stanovich, 1992). For example, from the fact that childhood sexual abuse is traumatic and can cause adult adjustment problems, certain therapists have drawn the conclusion that every adult who has problems (or even every adult) is the victim of sexual abuse. This conclusion does not follow, however, because there are many reasons why an adult can have problems besides sexual abuse.

A further difficulty is that in many cases the reasons given to explain a decision actually have nothing to do with the decision. Often the articulated "reasons" are nothing more than rationalizations or justifications. People are quite good at offering "explanations" for chance or even nonsensical events (Margolis, 1987) and are even better at it when trying to justify their actions. The "reasons" offered for the choice of a particular job candidate often obscure irrational decisions or outright biases. The steel company president who goes wild and buys an oil company while ignoring the modernization of the steel mills may offer elaborate logic for this decision based on business cycles and return on investment, but the real reasons may not be rational at all (maybe the oil business seems more glamorous than the steel business). One should likewise be suspicious of the reasons offered by people for their choices of cars, careers, and houses.

A final difficulty arises from the decision criteria people use when reasoning from their assumptions. There are usually several conflicting goals in any decision-making context. If the wrong one is chosen, the resulting decision or product will be deficient. For example, let us say that a company sells a cheap automobile. Some complaints come in about various missing features. The goal of fixing these "problems" conflicts with the goal of keeping the price down. If fancy features are added to a slow, small, boxy car, it will no longer be the cheapest car, but it will not attract higher end buyers. Better fuel mileage on a luxury car may not expand the market for that car; this is not a major criterion for such buyers. Individuals often choose a horrible spouse because the criteria they use for picking someone to date (wild, fun, a heavy drinker, a flirt, unpredictable) leads them to become acquainted with, and therefore to marry, a real no hoper. A common response to conflicting goals is to look for a compromise, but often an exclusive choice is necessary, as in the car example above, because a compromise actually satisfies no one. One can become either a doctor or an artist, but very few can do both. In the dating context, conflicting goals lead to a cycle of dating and breaking up, because the fun person chosen for dating becomes annoying or impossible to tolerate in a long-term relationship. The problem may therefore lie in the decision criteria and not just in the premises or methods of reasoning.

Thus, we can see that it is necessary and useful to examine the premises behind a decision, design, or theory, and the reasoning used to get there. Everyone believes they reason things out like detectives Sherlock Holmes, Philip Marlowe, Colombo, and Hercule Poirot, but few of us can or do.

☞ Coherence

As mentioned previously, the tendency to detect pattern is strong enough that even disconnected events or forces can seem to be part of a pattern. We see this tendency run amok in the paranoid schizophrenic's tendency to weave random, unconnected events into a vast government conspiracy. We can counter this tendency by checking for coherence. In a coherent series of events there is some type of logical or causal dependence. A check for coherence is also a search for pattern, in a sense, but is a search for items that make a pattern by being causally related. Following a hurricane, for example, we may observe high prices, emotional distress, and looting. All of these are caused by the effects of the hurricane and are thus coherent (though independent) effects. A corporate

The detective we all think we are, but aren't. Illustration by Richard Loehle.

reorganization can affect productivity, morale, and stock prices, again in a causal and coherent way. In an incoherent "pattern" there is no such connection. I recently came across a hollow Earth enthusiast's letter to a major government research laboratory, seeking their support for his theory. He attributed auroras to light escaping from a sun inside the earth via a hole at the north pole, unidentified flying objects (UFOs) to flights by the people living inside the earth, etc. Not only were the "facts" he put forth completely incoherent with respect to each other (there was no necessary relation between them), but they were completely out of synch with dozens of other facts (a hollow Earth would collapse and the oceans would run into a hole at the north pole, for instance).

As another incoherent system we can look to New Age philosophy, which incorporates astral projection, past lives, healing crystals, vegetarianism, UFOs, and New Age music. There is no necessary relation between these separate beliefs. They do not derive from a set of premises, and are not logically or causally related. In fact it is possible to substitute alternative beliefs for any one of the ones listed in an arbitrary way. It is thus a collection, not a system.

As an example of an incoherent scientific theory we can again turn to Freudian psychoanalysis. As Stanovich (1992) notes, the component parts of this theory contradict one another. Consequently one can come to almost any conclusion that seems convenient. This is a telltale sign of an incoherent system: it is too loose and permits too much, so that anything goes. Stanovich cites as another example folk wisdom: there is an aphorism for every situation, but they can be contradictory ("look before you leap" but "he who hesitates is lost").

Incoherent beliefs or systems are held by people with magical thinking, by children, and sometimes by the mentally ill. Most people are guilty of incoherence in at least some part of their lives, for instance in their views on love or politics. We may believe that government meddles too much, but at the same time expect it to fix every problem and right every wrong. In love, a woman's stated views on what makes a good husband may conflict sharply with the type of men she dates. A man may be promiscuous but still expect to marry a virgin. In contrast, in science and engineering there are multiple logical and causal connections between different components of the enterprise, each contributing to and supporting the other, and giving high coherence. Thus, coherence is a very useful tool for examining our beliefs.

☛ Figuring the odds

In strategic problem solving, one is often faced with risks or with chance events. In planning a factory expansion, one must factor in the odds that interest rates will rise. One must balance the extent of insurance coverage with the risk that it will be needed. Unfortunately, people are *extremely* bad at estimating odds and risks. In cards and games of chance, people seem to be almost without a clue as to their odds of winning, which makes casino owners very rich. One notes that slot machines are designed to make a great noise as the coins fall into the tray, thereby

The strategic thinker doesn't count on luck, and keeps chance in mind.

creating the appearance of many winners and big winnings. In estimating risk, people are equally incompetent. People feel perfectly safe on a bicycle, but bicycles are far from safe. Many parents are terrified that their child will be kidnapped and murdered, though they are actually much more likely to die in a car crash (Stanovich, 1992). Dramatic events, such as airplane crashes, seem much more prevalent than they are. Similarly, people misjudge the risk of stroke because death by stroke is much less dramatic than is death from cancer or heart disease. People's behaviors are often influenced by these incorrect perceptions.

Strategic problems often involve a probabilistic or risk component, and failure to recognize that people are quite bad at assessing risk or probability often results in adverse outcomes. A mother in a quiet suburban neighborhood may refuse to let her children ever play outside for fear of them being kidnapped. A manager may fear making a mistake so much that he or she refuses to make a decision, not realizing that failure to act also carries risks. In certain hurricane-prone areas such as Florida, insurance companies have long had actuarial tables showing the risk from storms, but during recent decades they ignored their own perfectly sound analyses in favor of the perception that risk was low because there had been no major storms for a while. Thus, during Hurricane Andrew in 1993, insurers were exposed to excessive liability, especially from oceanside homes and cheaply made homes. In fact, the course that insurance companies take, figuring out the odds of various risks explicitly, is the proper course and it usually serves them well. Their failure in Florida was because they ignored their own calculations.

This actuarial type approach is the only protection against the failure of our mental machinery to deal properly with probabilities and risks. In the context of any strategic problem, whether product design, urban planning, invention, etc., one must specifically and quantitatively account for chance events. In engineering design, for example, failure analysis is a standard, quantitative design criterion. In military campaigns it is standard to hold troops in reserve in case of unexpected reversals. In science one is expected to account for the odds that one's experimental results were actually the result of chance.

We can see, therefore, that there are a number of tools we can apply to examine our ideas, models, designs, and theories to see whether they pass muster in terms of not being the result of obvious mistakes caused by the imperfections in our reasoning abilities. Unfortunately, it is far easier to apply these techniques to the examination of the work of others than to ourselves, and thus more objective, external reality checking is also necessary.

External reality check

Given that one has taken precautions against the pitfalls noted above by checking for coherence, examining premises, and making any assessments of risk or probability explicit, it is still not guaranteed that one's result is correct or useful. A logical and coherent theory can be wrong and a clever invention can be too expensive to sell or never work properly. For this reason, an external reality check is necessary. Two basic types of external reality check are available: peer review and experiment (testing).

☛ Break it

Once you have created something, it is very important to break it. Of course, the very last thing that the creator of something novel has the heart to do is break it, but it must be done, for if the creator won't break it the public will. If the creation is a building design, it will be found by someone to have some type of flaw and many will think it is ugly. If it is a piece of software, you can be certain that a certain number of users will make it fail. The perfect assembly line is subject to a change in the products that it will be expected to produce. Even the best scientific theory has some kind of flaw. If the developer of a product can summon the courage to break it, he or she is in the best position to envision the possible ways to do so, and perhaps to thereby fix it. There are several specific topics in this respect that can help us to focus our thinking about the breakage/failure question.

☞ Physical breakage

For most physically realized creative products (i.e., not a theory or abstraction), it is useful to search out the possible modes of physical breakage. Every parent with small children has had to (or tried to) prevent them from inserting various objects into the video recorder, but one must wonder about whether the video recorder designers envisioned this problem. In the same vein, cassette tapes don't melt if left in a hot automobile, but video tapes do. If you wish to return a tape on the way home from work, you cannot leave the tape in the car but you risk embarrassment if you take the children's cartoons or your favorite horror movie to work in your briefcase. Thus, modes of breakage may turn out to be common even with widely used products.

Let us consider "breakage" for a building. An obvious type of breakage is earthquake damage. Careful consideration of how an earthquake operates (e.g., maximum lateral velocities and displacements, vibration frequencies) is necessary to design protection against this type of damage. An unusual type of "breakage" occurred in 1992 in Chicago when the Chicago River broke into a system of old freight tunnels that connected to the basements of major office buildings. The water shorted out most of the electrical power to the entire downtown Loop area and proved to be very difficult to remove. Many large buildings had their heating and electrical stations on these lower levels, and their owners had never really considered flooding as a risk.

In general, it is safe to assume that if some mode of physical breakage exists, then it will happen eventually. If that mode involves human misuse, then it will probably happen on a regular basis. Any household item should be able to survive being dropped, for example. If it shouldn't become wet, it probably will. Such abuse should be allowed for in the design.

☞ Side-effects

It is well known that almost every medicine has some sort of side-effect. We usually watch for them. We are not so alert to side-effects in other contexts, but they are just as inevitable. That is to say, we should actively and explicitly search out side-effects.

Let us consider a high rise building again. What could we mean by "side-effects" for a building? As many pedestrians chasing their hats down the streets of the "windy city" Chicago can attest, high rises can funnel and amplify the wind, creating almost gale force gusts during storms. Under such conditions I have seen an entire rubbish bin full of inside-out umbrellas. A second side-effect, noted particularly in waterfront locations, is that a large building can block the view for other buildings, thereby lowering their value. A skyscraper also typically displaces small shops, thereby making a neighborhood less easy to live in. Thus, we can see that side-effects are not so hard to find, even for a building.

In ecology, side-effects are pervasive. A major impetus to the environmental movement was in fact the documentation by Rachel Carson in *Silent Spring* (1962) of the side-effects of the insecticide DDT, manifested in very much increased fragility of birds' eggs. Many human activities create environmental side-effects that may even occur a long way away (as with acid rain). Tracing and managing these side-effects remains one of the major tasks of ecology as a science and as a management art.

Identifying side-effects is an effective technique for guarding against problems that otherwise seem to come out of the blue.

☞ Difficulty in use

No product will be universally easy to use. This is obviously true for consumer products such as kitchen appliances, tools, and bottle caps, but applies elsewhere as well. A revolving door seems like a simple thing, easy to use, until you try to go through it with a baby carriage. Computers have been notorious for the difficulties many people experience with their use. The increased ease of use personal computers afford has contributed to their growth at the expense of mainframes.

We may equally apply this question to abstractions. When a new scientific theory is introduced, we should anticipate that someone will have trouble grasping (using) it. In the case of evolution, this "someone" was largely the public and the religious community. For other theories it may be other scientists who have trouble adjusting to a new world view.

It is the frequent experience of inventors that the public doesn't grasp how wonderful their invention is, of companies that ordinary products lead to many complaints about them being hard to use, and of scientists that their work is not understood. These all result from the fact that consumers will not find a product or theory as easy to use or grasp as the inventor does. This should be borne in mind.

☞ *Your worst nightmare*

A good way to scare up some of the flaws in a product, idea, or design is to think about what would be your (the inventor's) worst nightmare about it. For a toy, this might be for a child to get hurt. A scientist might have a nagging fear at the back of his or her consciousness that something might be wrong with the new theory or that an experiment might be flawed. For an inventor, the worst nightmare might be that the idea has already been patented, and that he or she is therefore wasting time.

The reason a "worst nightmare" is so useful is that in thinking about and working on a product or theory, the possible flaws have usually occurred at least in passing. Often, really serious flaws may occur to the inventor, but there is a strong tendency to suppress these thoughts "until later," since it is in truth unreasonable to expect an early stage design or a prototype to meet all possible objections. Once these difficulties are pushed aside, it is too easy to keep them out of the picture, but if really serious they may continue to resurface as nagging doubts or fears. It is best to face them directly once a project has achieved sufficient proof of principle. At this stage, bringing the feared flaws out in the open can provide a critical reality check and either improve the product or allow a timely retreat from it if the flaw is real.

☞ *Change of environment*

Another way to "break" a product is to change the environment in which it is being used. For the developer, this means thinking about the consequences of a change in environment. The fuel-guzzling cars of the 1960s, for example, were damaged by the change of the fuel-price environment in the mid-70s. The typewriter has declined due to the introduction of the word processor. In fashion, it is well known that a change in public taste can lead to the "death" of a product line. In fact, clothing manufacturers actually plan for such changes in environment. Many products have also failed when subjected to a new physical environment, from standard motor oils that freeze up in the Arctic to house designs that are inappropriate for the tropics.

We may also consider a change of environment in the case of abstract products. Computer software is always subject to a change of environment. As operating system architecture changes to provide new capabilities and to keep up with hardware advances, the software running on it must also change lest it fall behind and eventually fail to operate in the new environment. Conceiving of a change in environment can also help to point out where a scientific theory may fail. For example, Einstein noted that at speeds near the speed of light the laws of Newtonian physics fail. In the micro-world of atoms, it is also observed that the laws of our macroscopic world fail. The lawful economic relations we observe in a developed economy fail in an environment without a monetary system, such as in a jungle village.

Overall, searching out how we can break our product or theory is a good way to make it stronger. When this effort is not made, the inevitable side-effects, customer complaints, lawsuits, and critical reviews come as a surprise. Facing the ways in which a product can be broken requires a nontrivial amount of detachment, discussed in Chapter 5.

☞ Peer review

Every time you ask your friends what they think of the car you are thinking of buying, you are practicing peer review. Reviewers can be extremely valuable because they bring different perspectives to bear on the problem at hand, and they may be less emotionally involved and thus more objective. In medicine it is useful to get a second opinion before surgery. In science, every grant proposal and every publication must pass muster with at least two to three reviewers. Movies and plays must endure critics (though often after they are in final form). Some movies are tested in limited release, and modified if reaction is negative. A test audience is used only to predict whether a movie will be popular, not whether it is historically accurate or even of artistic merit, so in this case we only worry about whether the audience is representative of what the movie will encounter after release. For other types of review, it is also possible that the reviewer can be wrong.

The ideal reviewer knows enough about the topic to be useful, is objective, helpful, thorough, and polite. If anyone knows the whereabouts of this mythical creature, please send me their address because I could certainly use some help. In the real world, each reviewer has various shortcomings and these must be taken into account by the reviewee.

The most serious problem with reviewers is that they tend to be too negative. It is easy to criticize anything, especially if the person views their role as being that of a gatekeeper. After all, what kind of a critic are you if you can't find anything wrong? New inventions are particularly easy to criticize because they are usually not in final, "bug-free" form and do not necessarily have a ready market. The original photocopy machine was rejected by many companies because they viewed carbon paper as sufficient and because the initial copy quality was poor and they could not imagine that quality could be improved. The initial zipper design had many failings (Petroski, 1992) such as a tendency to jam open. It took 20 years to perfect the design, create machines that could reliably make them with minimal waste, persuade manufacturers to incorporate them into their products, and persuade consumers to buy them. Throughout this process, it would have been correct to state that the product was deficient, but such a judgement would have been premature. In fact, any new idea or invention must go through a period of maturation and development before it can withstand rigorous scrutiny (as noted earlier in this book). A movie concept is not a finished movie. A tentative scientific hypothesis is not yet ready for experimental testing and it might not even be clear how it *can* be tested. No one would expect the outline for a novel to be a best seller. Yet very often a new management scheme in business or an idea for a new product is subject to intense scrutiny and review by management at an early stage of development, and often only an abbreviated, itemized form of the idea is presented. Under these conditions, it is not surprising that most new ideas are killed off prematurely and without an adequate hearing. The number of inventions that were difficult to market but are now major products is truly amazing. Review of an idea, plan, or product therefore is not without a significant risk. It is wise to shield it from review by those in a position to kill it off until the idea is sufficiently developed that it can withstand scrutiny. During this phase, reviews should be sought from those outside the lines of authority. A new idea should not be presented in an abbreviated format because the audience will be almost certain not to understand it. Sufficient detail should be presented so that the concept is conveyed clearly. If further development is needed, the path forward should be clearly stated.

As a reviewee, one must develop a thick skin. Try to glean the useful suggestions out of the negative comments while letting the disparaging remarks about your mental stability and IQ slide. It is often the case that a reviewer has a pet theory, invention, or point of view that colors his or her opinion of what is being reviewed. This also must be taken into account.

A second difficulty is that reviewers rarely put the time into their review that is required. The inventor spends a year on a new product but gets only 30 minutes in front of management to promote it. A scientist spends four months on a project but a reviewer may spend only an hour or so reading the manuscript. Something really novel is difficult to digest, especially upon quick examination. A reviewer with only a partial grasp of the concept is likely to dismiss the idea or focus on trivial or irrelevant aspects of the product. It is difficult to overcome this tendency. Because most people are busy and since one is usually asking a favor in obtaining a review, one cannot control how much time a reviewer spends looking over one's work. One can partially overcome this problem by obtaining several reviews and taking into account that each is going to be incomplete. A more satisfactory solution is to pay a consultant or some other party to perform a review. If one is in a position to control budgets sufficient to do this, it is well worth it, because consultants or paid reviewers will take the time to be thorough, will be more objective, and are not in a position to steal the idea (by contract) or kill the project. One must be aware of the danger that paid reviewers may try too hard to please and may be reluctant to be too critical lest they lose any future work.

The nit picker is a particularly useless type of reviewer, and can be deadly if in a position of power. Nit pickers are often observed in bureaucracies, where the proper filling out of forms and the formatting of reports can come to assume greater importance than the work itself. The nit picker does not merely find grammatical and formatting errors, but focuses on them exclusively, sending a report back to the author with a sneer because of the errors. To such a person the trivial errors invalidate the whole project or report. One can easily identify the nit picker because they are unable to make any useful comments on the overall product, just on the format. Nit pickers are useful if they are performing merely an editorial task, as long as they know what they are talking about. Otherwise, they can interfere with real work and can be a deadly bottleneck in an organization by refusing to ever approve anything.

☞ Testing and experiment

Generally, when people think of tests and experiments they think of the procedures of scientists as a model. This is a partially useful viewpoint, but it tends to magnify the difficulty of the process so that people think testing involves expensive laboratories and a doctorate degree. This is not the case. Many types of testing are a part of regular business practice and may even be quite simple, for example opinion polls, market surveys, engineering failure analyses, prototypes, dry runs, scale models, project flow charts, and statistical quality control. What all of these types of test have in common is that they provide objective information about the workability or quality of our wonderful new idea or product. These are now explored in turn.

☞ Surveys

Surveys and opinion polls are a common component of marketing and political decision making. Many new products are test marketed and surveys look for the public pulse on political issues. For test marketing, the issue is largely whether the test audience is representative. Those individuals who are easy to persuade to participate in a market test, however, may not be representative. For example, those willing to see a sneak preview of a new film, which is in reality a test screening, are not likely to be representative of the many people who depend on newspaper reviews and word of mouth before choosing which film to see. Market niche groups such as urban singles or business travelers may be very difficult to locate and persuade to participate in market surveys. Market surveys do not enable one to evaluate such factors as long-term satisfaction with a product, word of mouth, and repeat buying.

Opinion polls are a whole different kettle of fish. Polls are routinely presented in the media on every issue imaginable, from political issues to how people feel about dogs and spouses. A standard part of these presentations is the measure of error (e.g., $\pm x$ percentage points). This is commonly taken as a measure of accuracy, but is in fact only a measure of reproducibility. That is to say, it measures how likely a repeat of the same survey is to yield the same results. For example, a survey of the readership of a particular women's magazine will have what appears to be high accuracy because of the large number of people responding, but when the results are extrapolated to all women, or even all the magazine's readers, including those who tend not to fill out surveys, they may not be representative at all. A second problem is that the phrasing of questions can have a significant impact on how people answer. Although this is well known in sociology, it is often ignored in political polls. For example, to the question "Is health care too expensive?" a large majority will answer yes, but to the question "Do you approve of a government bureaucrat deciding whether you can have bypass surgery?" a large majority would answer no. Such questionnaires are often phrased in such a way that the sponsoring organization tends to obtain answers that help it. A great deal of cleverness is necessary to obtain answers that are not biased, and private opinion poll organizations do not necessarily take the time to do so. Academic surveys are more likely to be objective in this sense.

A second issue is that people often lie in surveys, even when they know their identity will be kept secret. This is a common problem on surveys of sexual behavior, but also occurs in other contexts. For example, in surveys, whites sometimes express fewer negative stereotypes about various minorities than do members of various minorities about each other or even about themselves. It may be that this is accurate, but it could also be that whites are acutely aware that they should not admit their negative feelings, and thus lie in the surveys.

A final problem with surveys as a reality check is that what people say they want and what they do often do not coincide. For example, it is frequently observed that people will say they are in favor of the environment and schools, but will not necessarily approve a recycling center or a school bond issue. This is because, at the point where attitude hits the pocketbook, various goals come into explicit conflict. Overall it is necessary to take survey results with a very large pinch of salt.

☞ *Prototypes*

A very useful type of reality check is the use of prototypes. Prototypes have the advantage that they can be touched and examined, and may reveal many deficiencies that are not evident in a verbal description of a proposed object. This is particularly so because each person tends to interpret or visualize a verbal description in a personal way. Even a drawing of a proposed product may be more glamorous or attractive than any physical realization could ever be. Artistic sketches of new or proposed cars are glamorous but have visual properties that no real automobile can have. A prototype removes this subjectivity. Prototypes have long been used in engineering, where models of a new aircraft, for example, are tested in a wind tunnel. In architecture, scale models are useful prototypes because a drawing of a new building can easily be made attractive with good artistry, whereas a scale model looks more like the real building. The construction of a three-dimensional prototype in the computer allows explicit calculation of turbulence in the wake of an airplane and how the wings will generate lift. Light penetration into a proposed building can be explicitly viewed. Such prototypes are extremely useful. Scale models of harbors, of road systems, etc., are likewise valuable. Prototypes of new consumer products are often produced and tested before full-scale production begins. With prototypes one should always be aware of the scale-up problem: a 200 m tall building made of steel and glass will look inherently different from a plastic model; the mass-produced version of a radio will look different from the prototype; and the mass-produced cookie will taste different from the sample cookie.

In social engineering, one of the problems is that prototypes are difficult to construct. Almost any social system (welfare, rapid transit, socialized medicine) can be made to sound good (or disastrous) on paper, but without a prototype it is difficult to tell what will really happen. Depending on public opinion for making decisions in this context is a serious problem, not only because of the difficulties with opinion polls described above, but because without a prototype the public is responding not to the actual consequences of the policies they are being asked about, but to the promises about those policies. For example, one can make any promise one wants about a health care system, but it is more useful to look at particular countries or states with different systems to see what has actually happened, how much it actually costs, etc. Thus, for social systems prototypes are a valuable source of information, but in this context the prototypes are provided by different social bodies that have implemented different policies.

☞ *Quality testing*
Quality testing has become an essential process in manufacturing. For example, a key element in the invasion of Japanese cars into the USA in the 1980s was quality deficiencies in American cars. Clearly, automobile quality had to be designed in, but it also had to be tested for. Tests of product quality are now common and are an essential reality check for manufacturers. Quality testing, if done correctly, is a vast improvement over waiting for consumers to complain. Care must be taken that one knows what to measure, however, and how to interpret the results.

A type of testing that often seems to be overlooked is consumer operability. It seems to be increasingly common for a product that requires assembly to come with an instruction manual consisting almost entirely of drawings with helpful instructions such as "attach handle." In many cases one cannot believe that the ability of anyone to follow these instructions was ever tested, and in some cases it is not even possible to do what is depicted in the diagram. Whereas I have purchased a broom that had instructions for how to sweep (!), it is more likely that instructions on consumer products will be inadequate. Testing of these products on naive consumers could help to eliminate such problems.

Consumer product testing is a particular type of testing that is done by third parties for various purposes such as safety and product evaluation reporting. In these tests it is common for a standardized treatment to be applied to a product to see how it holds up or performs. The standardization is a key element that removes the subjectivity inherent in merely asking people how they like a product (which is a measure of consumer satisfaction). Consumer satisfaction can be influenced by clever advertising campaigns, for example, and may not be related to actual product performance. Just as with opinion polls, however, standardization increases repeatability but not necessarily accuracy. For example, a measure of durability of a dish-washing sponge obtained from a mechanical dish-washing device may be irrelevant if sponges are commonly disposed of because they begin to smell long before they ever fall apart.

☞ *Analysis*
Various types of analysis are used in different settings to provide a reality check based on calculations of various sorts. In construction planning, one lays out a schedule to make sure that materials are on hand when needed and that different crews do not obstruct each other. In financial planning, explicit calculations of costs over time are used to test the feasibility of a given project. A dry run of a medical operation, film scene, or military exercise is a test of the verbal description of the operation to make sure it works. Dry runs are particularly important for testing emergency plans (e.g., a hospital evacuation) because when the plans are used for real it will be an emergency with serious consequences if a plan is faulty.

☞ *Experiments*
For certain types of test, true experiments in the scientific sense are necessary. It is easy to believe, from initial results, that a new drug is wonderful and will have a major impact on disease. To have it approved, however, hard data on efficacy and side-effects are needed. This necessitates controlled experiments. Conducting and interpreting such experiments are discussed in more detail in Chapter 2, but it is useful to point out here that even controlled experiments can be subject to error, bias, and misinterpretation. For example, in the world of medical research, it is rare that a single study has been sufficient to demonstrate the risk of a toxic agent, the benefits of a medical procedure, or the effect of diet or exercise. Some of the studies that have been effective in defining the roles of diet and exercise (etc.) on health have had tens of thousands of participants. Such large numbers are necessary to detect small effects reliably. Thus, while one can view the controlled experiment as the ultimate type of test, in practice caution is necessary even here.

Discussion

Anyone who enters a fun house at a carnival is aware that much of what they see will be illusory. As disconcerting as it may be, it is also the case that in the realm of decision making much of what we think is also illusory. If this were not so, we would not find ourselves embroiled in foolish wars, monsters such as Hitler would not obtain power, people would not believe in magic, and those running get-rich-quick schemes would not be so prolific. While the human brain is excellent at many tasks, it is not very logical or consistent. It is far too easy to believe what we wish to believe. This is why reality checks are so important. By recognizing where we are likely to be weak, we can compensate with reality checks of various sorts. For decisions, we must be aware of wishful thinking and self-justification. We must be alert to long chains of reasoning and not put too much trust in them. We need to be aware of jumbled collections of unrelated ideas and not give them undue credit by calling them a philosophy. Any time there is risk or chance, we should try to base our decisions on an explicit calculation of probability, as in an actuarial table. We can obtain useful information from reviews by colleagues, while at the same time keeping in mind that a reviewer has all the same limitations of reasoning that we do. Other types of reality check such as prototypes, tests, surveys, and experiments are also invaluable. Overall, it is very dangerous to proceed without some type of reality check.

5 A matter of style

Personality significantly affects problem-solving style, the subject of this chapter. Problem-solving style is the overall pattern of how people tackle problems, the types of problem they choose, and their emotional relationship to problems. Rather than probing for the deep psychological reasons (motivations) behind different styles, I merely present them here and comment on their utility and limitations for different types of problem. Problem-solving style is particularly relevant for complex problems, because certain problem types are only solvable (or even identifiable) using certain styles. Some of the styles we will explore include the fault-finder, the visionary, the obsessive, the counter-puncher, the efficiency expert, the synthesizer, and the artiste. I conclude with a discussion of cognitive style, as it contrasts with emotional style.

The fault-finder

We normally think of fault-finding as a negative trait, and when dealing with people it generally is. When dealing with problems, however, fault-finding can be a very productive approach. Petroski (1992) points out that most inventors and industrial designers begin with a perception of some fault or deficiency in an existing object, and then devise an improvement to that device, tool, or product. One cannot readily improve upon an existing object if one cannot see the deficiencies in it. Inventors are typically driven to improve upon existing devices and to create new devices that do jobs that currently no device does well or at all. In this sense they are continuously dissatisfied. Catastrophic failures, such as airplanes that lose their wings and bridges that collapse, have always been a tremendous spur to invention, but even subtle failures are an indication of something that can be done better. The distinguishing characteristic of a successful inventor is that he or she has a good understanding of what is possible, and what are the constraints and tradeoffs (those are discussed further in Part 2): that to make a hand tool smaller but maintain strength may require a stronger, and perhaps more expensive, material; that to make a tool better for a particular job may make it worse for some other job, which is why combined hammer–screwdriver–paintbrushes have never sold very well. This firm grasp of the tradeoffs, the limits of materials, and the deficiencies of existing objects provides guidance to the inventor so that changes lead to an improved product, and work as intended. Politicians are similarly always dissatisfied with existing systems, since expressing a desire to improve things generates political support and may even have provided their motivation for entering politics. However, they do not have a firm grasp of the tradeoffs and limitations of their materials, and are constantly trying to control things that cannot be controlled and invent perpetual motion machines, which is why the USA (among others) has such a large budget deficit.

The engineer's drive to improve a product does not necessarily lead to progress. For example, there is a tendency for any new car model to become fancier with each model year as improvements are added, but this tends to increase the cost. It is very difficult for a car maker to resist this tendency. As personal computers have become fancier and more powerful, everyone wants the latest model even if they are only going to send e-mail and write letters. One must wonder, for example, what in the world the typical user plans to do with a gigabyte hard drive.

The evil twin of the fault-finding inventor is the nit picker. The nit picker finds fault with everything, but is not able to distinguish the significant fault from the trivial. The typical destructive nit picker is a boss who is never satisfied with a subordinate's work, but typically focuses on the formatting of reports, minor grammatical mistakes, and similar trivia, and may completely ignore the serious flaws in a piece of work. Conversely, he or she will not praise a good or even excellent idea or result because there is always something about it that can be picked apart. Such bosses become enamored of word processors and know all the details of formatting, fonts, type styles, and report organization. The consequence completely escapes them that endless picking at and revising a document can make it a year late, and therefore useless.

The tinkerer

The classic picture of the inventor is the tinkerer, who is constantly hunched over a workbench, fiddling with inventions. The tinkerer takes a very hands-on approach, and is not given to grand schemes but rather is fascinated with the details. Many tinkerers are fault-finders to some degree, being driven by the imperfections they see in existing products, but not all fault-finders are tinkerers. The dominant mode of the tinkerer is to try it, to work with it, to take it apart and put it back together. Their orientation is practical, not theoretical, and they like to use their hands. Some scientists fall into this category, with Faraday being a notable example. Hobbyists are often of this type with respect of their hobby, as are computer hackers. The advantage the tinkerer has is that he or she has experience manipulating materials and understands how they work in a mechanical sense. If a project calls for a grand vision or for an understanding of some consumer quirk, tinkerers may not be so successful. The biggest pitfall they face is not knowing when to quit working on a project, because the process of manipulation is in and of itself so rewarding.

The visionary

The visionary is a different breed from the tinkering inventor. Once the visionary perceives a problem, he or she does not seek to improve it incrementally, but to start from scratch to design an entirely new product or system that will be perfect or ideal. The visionary wants to design a car from the tires up, all new and revolutionary. CAD (computer-aided design) systems have made it much easier for the visionary to do this. The inventors of the personal computer, John MacReady with his Gossamer Albatross human powered plane, Alexander Bain (the inventor of the fax machine), Henry Ford with his pioneering assembly line, and Ray Kroc (founder of McDonalds), who pioneered fast food, were visionaries. The visionary is driven by images of perfection and by pictures of entire products, processes or systems, not by ideas of tinkering with the hifi's tweeters or woofers or making a doorknob easier to grip. A visionary may be very unhappy if not in a position to carry out his or her vision. Many visionaries are frustrated engineers or designers who never get to do a grand project but are instead given pieces of larger projects to do. They can become distressed and disillusioned because their job conflicts with their style. Those visionaries who lack the technical skill to carry out a grand design are what we typically call dreamers: the salesperson who designs and sketches "cool" looking sports cars at home that will never be built, the fringe political types who are sure they know how Utopia should be engineered, etc.

Designing from scratch can be an expensive approach in industrial contexts. For example, if every car is designed from the bottom up, then many potentially standard parts such as nuts and bolts not only must be designed, but become nonstandard between models. Further, there is a tremendous overhead cost to keeping track of 100 different types of fastener and keeping them in stock. In addition, components that work perfectly well (e.g., windshield wiper motors) when redesigned will typically have design faults at first, thus leading to a defective product and reworking. Thus, care must be taken when an employee is a visionary, because the tendency will be to redo everything, including things that do not need redoing. This is even more the case when a visionary type takes over an organization. He or she wants to shake it all up, reengineer it, restructure it in a completely new way. In a large organization such restructuring is not without costs, both direct and in lost productivity, and may not necessarily lead to improvements. Restructuring for its own sake can therefore be seen to be a consequence of the visionary's inner drives and desires, and is not necessarily justified by the bottom line or by any rational plan.

The jurist

The jurist focuses on legalistic problems: rules, regulations, permits, procedures, forms, and formalities. This type of person is concerned with structure and feels uncomfortable in an unstructured environment. The successful jurist can devise a working procurement system, approval forms, permitting procedures, etc. In this sense jurists can be successful problem solvers. They are also useful when enlisted to help an organization run smoothly. For instance, a good budget person for a department should make sure everyone hands their financial reports and proposals in on time, head off procurement rules problems, and generally provide preemptive strikes against delays and mistakes. There is an unfortunate tendency, however, for jurists to be so focused on rules and procedures that they lose sight of the need to get anything done. The result, common in government agencies, is approval processes for documents or actions that are arcane and labyrinthine, or actually impossible. For example, at one United States government site one could not send a soil sample out to a laboratory for analysis to find out what contamination was in it unless you knew what contamination was in it. Similarly, department A might require that department B sign off first, but B requires that A sign off first. A common problem in government procurement is requiring that one spends a month of effort (at more than $12 000 per month total cost) to document and justify a sole source procurement of $6000. Bidding requirements may be such that the cost to the bidder of preparing a bid package exceeds the value of the contract, leading to offers with no bidders. All of this results from the narrow legalistic approach of the jurist, who believes that one can pass detailed rules to prevent all possible problems (such as in procurement). This is analogous to stopping and searching every single shopper to prevent shoplifting, or stopping every car and conducting a sobriety test to prevent drunk driving. This view has taken over many government agencies in their passage of rules to govern very specific behaviors. This view totally overlooks the cost of regulation and rules. In procurement, the cost of ensuring that every bidder has the ultimate health, safety, and quality assurance plans, complies with all federal labor laws, etc. etc. is that one must pay twice as much (via hidden costs) for products and services. The cost within a bureaucracy of overly arcane procedures and protocols is gridlock. Rules and procedures can help things to run smoothly, but when procedural perfection is demanded and procedures are enforced to try to ensure that no mistakes are ever made, then actually making sure something is done can become like swimming in molasses.

The obsessive

A very successful type of problem solver is the obsessive, not because he or she has any particular technique advantage, but because the problem solver has single-minded thinking. The phrase "get a life" applies to most obsessives. A hacker is an obsessive, and thinks about almost nothing but computers. I know a zoologist who is obsessed with turtles and snakes and another who thinks about nothing but ducks (his house has duck paintings, duck decoys, duck pillows, duck sculptures, etc.). Such individuals somehow have become intensely interested in a particular topic, to the exclusion of almost everything else. This provides them with several advantages. First, they are fascinated by every detail, every dimension of their chosen obsession. Because of this, they know all the trivia and raw facts that on some problems make all the difference, because many times the devil really is in the details. For example, when a computer virus strikes, a hacker is a useful person to have around because he or she has experience of all the obscure hardware and operating system features that are key to tracking down the virus. Second, obsessives develop an intuitive feel for the object or problem. My zoologist friend thinks like a duck (no, he doesn't look like a duck) and has a real feel for their behavior. Another person might have a real feel for motors or model airplanes. This intuitive feel is deeper than factual knowledge or book learning about a topic and is very useful for solving problems. Third, because they are obsessed, they think about for example ducks or computers when they are driving, when they are in the shower, when they are cutting the grass, and thus spend much more time thinking about the topic than other people do.

The obsessive approach to problem solving, however, is not without its pitfalls. An obsessive may spend most of his or her time on unproductive fiddling around, as has been noted for hackers. Obsessives may also be too narrowly focused if the problem involves other domains (interaction between hawks and ducks, computer user ergonomics, etc.). In such cases, the obsessives' overly narrow focus can be overcome by teaming them with someone with other skills, but an obsessive working alone may not realize that such collaboration is needed.

The counter-puncher

The boxer Muhammed Ali was a classic counter-puncher. When his opponent would swing, he would jab, and gradually he would pound the opposition senseless with his many hits. In problem solving, a counter-puncher is one who reacts to a solution, product, or idea posed by others. Just as in boxing, the action of the opponent opens up an opportunity. The counter-puncher is typically angered by arguments or ideas that seem erroneous or fallacious or is annoyed by products that are ugly or inelegant. The anger that is provoked is an indication that the person somehow recognizes that the argument of the opponent is in error, though he or she may be unable at first to say what the error is. This anger simultaneously provides a motivation to prove the other person to be wrong. The philosopher Kant was angered by the (to him) fallacious arguments of Hume, and set out to build an entire new system of rational philosophy to counter Hume's "false" doctrines. The counter-punch style can be seen in the development of the Apple Macintosh computer, which was a reaction to the mainframe way of thinking.

The efficacy of this style depends on several factors. First, counter-punchers must have a good instinct for what is worth getting angry about. If they get angry about silly ideas like astral projection or healing crystals, then they will not be productive. Second, they must have the technical skill to convert the anger into a productive alternative. Finally, they must not become so angry that their judgement becomes clouded. Karl Marx, for example, was so angered by an unjust system (nineteenth century capitalism), as well as being angered by being an academic outsider, that he went to extreme lengths to prove his thesis, thereby losing all regard for facts and logic (Johnson, 1988).

The efficiency expert

Some people have a fascination with problems of efficiency. They love the challenge of finding a faster, easier, or cheaper way of doing something. Since real world problems often involve efficiency considerations, the contributions of the efficiency-minded problem solver can be valuable. We may wish to reduce electrical consumption in a refrigerator or speed mail delivery, reduce waste in a factory or shorten the checkout lines at a grocery store. The efficiency-minded person is inherently irritated by material waste, inefficiency, and wasted time. Thus, he or she notices waste more than others and is motivated to find ways to reduce it. Efficiency improvements are most valuable in the context of existing products or services. The delivery service Federal Express is an example of a company built around a concept of efficiency, but it required a visionary to create the company, not an efficiency expert alone.

Efficiency experts can cause difficulties in certain contexts. New product development, for example, is risky and therefore wasteful. Such messy, inefficient operations drive efficiency experts up the wall, and are likely to be stifled if such experts are in charge because the latter will tend to request proof that any given action or expenditure will produce results, such proof of course not being available. Efficiency experts also become impatient with the slow and tedious R&D process and may cut projects off prematurely. Finally, an efficiency focus can lead to short-sighted behaviors. During the rapid growth phase of a successful new company one should not try to optimize every process because all processes are likely to change rapidly. Further, "bean counting" can take effort away from high profit activities in favor of marginal returns resulting from cost-saving efforts or efficiency considerations.

The tendency to push a system toward more and more efficiency may make it brittle. For example, the perfectly efficient assembly line does not allow for workers to use the bathroom or take into account equipment failures. The perfectly efficient business does not have any slack for rush jobs, and will therefore lose some business and maybe lose customer loyalty. This is the fallacy of the downsizing fad: on an economic downswing it always appears that there are excess personnel but as soon as the economy picks up a little, those excess personnel become essential. Companies end up in a cycle of hiring and firing that is destructive of morale and not even optimal for profitability because hiring is expensive and newly hired employees are not that productive at first. Thus, the tendency to view efficiency as virtuous and essential must be resisted, because efficiency is only one of the goals to be achieved in any problem context and because efficiency and growth are not necessarily compatible.

The synthesizer

A very particular skill is possessed by the synthesizer who relishes drawing all the threads of a problem together and weaving a comprehensive, integrated solution. A synthesizer pulls it all together to write the definitive textbook on a subject. The best biographers and historians are synthesizers (the worst being mere catalogers and list makers). If one wishes to trace the consequences of a foreign policy action, a synthesizer is needed. The synthesizer wants to arrange all the pieces of the puzzle on the table and manipulate them until they all fit together. If they cannot be made to fit, then the synthesizer may be working on a problem prematurely, and is at risk of achieving a false synthesis. Karl Marx was a synthesizer as well as a visionary, but pursued his vision by forcing facts into place with distortion and fabrication (Johnson, 1988). When the facts do not all fit together, what may be needed is a tinkerer or visionary who can redefine the problem. Synthesis requires time to contemplate, to gather facts and sift them, to formulate overall structures and explanations, and is thus difficult to do in our fast paced modern world. Even when a synthesis is achieved, it may be difficult to communicate to those who only have time for one-paragraph summaries because a true synthesis does not fit into an itemized format.

The tool master

The tool master has mastered one or a few tricks or techniques. Being a person with a hammer, everything looks like a nail. He or she can do anything with a spreadsheet, but not much else. This is the person who wants to computerize everything, all data, all communications, everything, because that is the preferred tool. Tool masters become most visible when there is a clash of technologies: those of this type wedded to old tools and techniques will be in tooth and nail conflict with those of the same type (usually younger) who have adopted new tools. The difference between the tool master and the obsessive is that the obsessive is in love with a subject (turtles, cars, the Civil War) whereas the tool master has hitched his or her professional wagon to being a competent user of some tool or technique that has commercial value. Such people can command high wages if the tool they have mastered produces value and is in demand. One can observe many such people in academia who have mastered some technique (optimization, gene splicing, literary deconstruction) and apply this technique to one problem after another. That is to say, such people are not subject matter experts but are experts in technique. The problem with this strategy is that real problems may have many dimensions and may require many tools for their solution. Thus, the tool master may be restricted in what he or she can accomplish to those problems that fall within the scope of his or her bag of tricks.

The artiste

Those whose problem-solving style is governed by aesthetic sensibilities are not all artists in the traditional sense. Rather, they are driven in their search for problems and solutions by aesthetic criteria such as symmetry, harmony, elegance, beauty, and simplicity. A mathematician, for example, may be most attracted to an elegant proof, and an inventor annoyed by a clumsy piece of machinery. A good aesthetic sense is very difficult to describe, and even more difficult to inculcate in a student. In ancient Egypt, artisans were trained from a rigid manual that prescribed exactly how human figures should be drawn. Little aesthetic sense was developed from such training and all artists' work was nearly identical. In modern art, it almost seems that anti-aesthetics governs because the motivation is often to shock, to be different, to irritate, or to make some social or political statement.

Nevertheless, when designers and inventors are guided by a search for beautiful or elegant solutions, they are often on the right track. This is because beauty is often consistent with such useful design principles as efficiency, balance, and utility. For example, if an electronics board has wires running all over the place, creating an ugly appearance, then it is probably badly designed and will be both slower and generate more heat than would a better design. An elegant mathematical proof is often more powerful and general. An awkward computer operating system will be hard to learn and the user will make many mistakes.

The recognition of beautiful patterns is often the first step toward the discovery of simple or interesting organizing principles. The shapes that soap bubbles make on wire frames are directly due to least-energy principles, as are the shapes that crystals take. The haunting beauty of the Mandelbrot set galvanized interest in fractals. Symmetry of animal body form has been found to be upset by deleterious mutations. Our perception of lush greenery somehow relates fairly well to the absence of soil mineral deficiencies. An intuitive sense of harmony, symmetry, and elegance can be a very useful guide to discovering or creating.

Aesthetic considerations are not a foolproof guide to one's work, however, because they can be influenced by fads. Automobiles have been influenced by various views of what is aerodynamic, with a common "low-drag" car (e.g., many sports cars) being tapered in front and squared off at the back. However, since the most drag is created not by the nose but by the creation of turbulence at the rear, such cars would actually have less drag if driven backwards. Our aesthetic concepts of what is modern or space age often conflict with what is efficient or useful, which can be seen most clearly when looking at old magazines purporting to show what the future would look like (as far ahead as the 1980s or 1990s!).

The craftsperson

The craftsperson, a dying breed, is concerned with the total product and wants every aspect to be perfect. The product is not necessarily an invention, and may be something that is made the same by others. Traditional craftspeople made things by hand and took pride in their work. As used here, the craftsperson is concerned with the aesthetics of the product, its functionality, and with the details. If a person with this style is a scientist, he or she does the experiments rather than delegating the work to students or a technician. If the person with this style is a store owner, the store is not just a source of income, but is a source of pride. This store owner will be found tidying up and making the store look good, helping customers, and answering the phone himself. Certain consumer products have the feeling of having been overseen or designed by a craftsperson, because there was great attention to overall functioning and the integration of every detail. Other products, in contrast, look like a different person designed every part and then they were all bolted together.

The craftsperson will have trouble doing a rush job or creating a rough prototype of a product, will tend to tinker too long, polish too much, and worry about style and format on projects that do not warrant such care. It is important to know when detail and polish are warranted and when they are not.

The eccentric (the genius)

It is commonly believed that really groundbreaking work requires that one be an extreme personality, like Vincent Van Gogh, and cut off one's ear, or drink too much like Ernest Hemingway, or have long hair and wear wild clothing. That is to say, one must be an eccentric; genius is inextricably linked with manic depression, with melancholy, with flamboyance, and with deviance. The facts, however, do not support this view (Arieti, 1976) This is a romantic notion that results from an extreme bias in historical and popular reporting such that those individuals who are both innovative *and* deviant receive undue attention because they are the most interesting. Einstein was not the only prominent physicist of his day, but he created great photo opportunities, spouted popular philosophy, wrote letters to presidents, and had endearing eccentric traits such as getting lost on his way home from work and never combing his hair. In my opinion, Richard Feynman was another such wild and crazy guy. Such people make good copy, and in particular fit the stereotype of many writers that the genius must be eccentric. This is extremely misleading. First, some of the most prolific people, and the greatest minds, have not been written about at all. Frederick Sanger, one of only three people to ever win two Nobel Prizes, is absolutely normal, modest, and humble (Jones and Douglas, 1994), and consequently is virtually unknown outside his scientific field. There are inventors who have changed our technological world almost single handedly (Petroski, 1992) but about whom no one has heard because, frankly, they are boring. The high percentage of major literary prize winners who appear depressed, disturbed, or suicidal similarly results, in my opinion, from the bias in awarding literary prizes toward those who write disturbing, moody, or depressing works. Those who write best sellers, detective novels, or science fiction novels rarely win such prizes. Second, I believe there are far more eccentric people who never achieve anything than there are high achievers who are eccentric. There are thousands of UFO enthusiasts, flat Earth aficionados, collectors of 10 000 hubcaps, and obsessive Civil War buffs who squander their enthusiasms on trivia or the fantastic. The eccentricity of these individuals does not help them solve real world problems. Further, a focus on personality, particularly a focus on the roots of extreme behaviors, the neuroses of the great creators and their obsessions, does not help us to uncover the problem-solving techniques they used (Arieti, 1976), techniques that may in fact be useful to more well-adjusted individuals as well as to the eccentric.

What we can say is that in some circumstances the eccentricity of an individual may help them if it allows them to come to a unique perspective or to be oblivious to the fact that they are out of step with the standard way of thinking. In particular, those in the creative arts tend to be much more likely to be afflicted with mood disorders, particularly manic depression, which may help them to be more expressive than they would otherwise be since they tend to be flooded with unbidden images, word associations, and moods, particularly during their manic phase when their level of creative output may be enhanced (Jamison, 1995). What seems most likely to me is that when high intelligence is combined with a mood disorder, the individual in question feels compelled to turn their energies toward artistic creative expression. Since such expression need not be functional, they may be successful in such efforts. We may note, however, that those with mood disorders, and particularly manic depressives during their manic phase, exhibit extremely poor judgement with respect to real world affairs, tending toward extravagant schemes, unrealistic plans and impulsive behaviors (Jamison, 1995). This is why no such correlation of mood disorders with success in science or in business can be found: in these domains steadiness and clear thinking are essential.

It is quite possible to be normal and also brilliant. In particular, this book is based on the proposition that whatever level of ability one has can be used more effectively. In fact, it is likely that almost anyone can be from twice as effective up to an order of magnitude more effective (see Gilbert, 1978, for documentation) if they can learn (1) to use their mind and creative abilities, (2) to not work against their style (discussed in this chapter), (3) to use their time effectively, and (4) the techniques of strategic problem solving. We should resist the temptation to undervalue our ability because we do not appear to be an extreme personality such as Freud or Picasso.

Discussion

The suite of problem-solving styles discussed above is not exhaustive. The noted problem-solving styles are also not personality types, and an individual may use different styles at different times or in different domains. A flexibility in this respect is a good safeguard against the potential flaws inherent in each style. This examination of style explains a long-standing puzzle in studies of creativity. There exists an extreme disparity between the personality traits assumed by different psychologists to be conducive to creativity (Arieti, 1976; Sternberg, 1988). Some assert that the innovative person is flamboyant but others that he or she is withdrawn or introverted – some say aggressive and others say detached. By examining style, we can see that much of this disparity results from a failure to characterize the type of problem the persons studied were successful in attacking. It is not the case that creative persons are creative in all domains, nor that their approach to problem solving will be universally applicable. What we can say is that those noted for their accomplishments have been successful in solving some type of problem or creating some type of product, but if we characterize their work it may often turn out to be dominated by a particular type of problem or to have been created in a certain way. That is, the effect of personality is to influence problem-solving style, which affects problem choice, method of attack, emotive content, problem scope (tinkering versus reengineering), and other factors, and thus the domain within which the person will be successful (or not). There is no single creative personality, as also argued by Weisberg (1986).

A further consideration is that problem-solving style may interact with intellectual talent or special strengths. Gardner (1983), for example, believes that there are seven distinct types of intelligence, including linguistic, mathematical, musical, spatial, interpersonal, and others. In this book it is argued that strategic intelligence is a further basic skill or ability. An IQ test may be a highly inadequate tool for assessing mental abilities. Individuals are likely to have ability in these different domains to differing degrees. Degree of talent in an area, of course, is relative to how much training one has obtained, so that individuals with a mathematics phobia may actually have considerable native mathematical ability but had negative experiences when young. Nevertheless, to the extent that these particular dimensions of intelligence (native and/or polished by training) coincide with the style of the individual, then that individual will be more successful (or not if not). For example, someone with a strong spatial ability and a visionary style could be successful as an artistic designer, but not necessarily as an industrial designer. Some individuals have strong aesthetic motivation, but do not necessarily have much talent in this area (e.g., no ability to visualize, no spatial intelligence). Such people may become collectors of music or art or become critics. Some people are fortunate enough to be able to overcome mismatches between their problem-solving style and their intellectual strengths by forming partnerships with others. Such teaming is common in the arts, where singer/ songwriter pairs often become inseparable. Teaming is also common in the sciences.

Overall, problem-solving style has a significant effect on the work individuals choose to do, how they go about it, and how successful they are. Differing styles between managers and subordinates or between project team members are typical causes of workplace conflict. Style is a very significant factor in problem solving, a factor that is often overlooked.

6 Attitude: The inner strategist

The purpose of this chapter is to explore the role of attitude in enhancing strategic problem solving and innovation. Attitude is well known to be important in sports, sales, and the arts, but is not as appreciated in the context of problem solving. However, because our thinking processes are nearly as subject to derailment, delusion, and mistake as are our aesthetic and athletic performances, the role of attitude (the inner strategist) is even more important. As a model for assessing the role of attitude in problem solving, I take not the arts, but science. The arts are primarily a vehicle for emotional and intellectual expression rather than practical problem solving. Furthermore, in the arts no objective criteria exist for judging success or truth. Therefore, if an artist attributes his or her creativity to having taken drugs, it is very difficult to evaluate this claim. I have focused on science because the creative act in science must result in a practical, workable solution to some problem. There is an objective criterion for judging success in science by which we can evaluate whether some attitude or behavior helps or hinders creativity. It would also be possible to use engineering as a model here, but there are too few accounts on which to base an analysis.

The creative act

Not everything done in science may be considered creative. A major part of the edifice of science consists of a toolbox of techniques and instrumentation. We are interested here in the subset of scientific problem solving that we may label truly creative. Such work is easily recognized in retrospect; virtually every scientist who makes it into the history books has done creative work (though not all scientists' work would qualify). The historical perspective selects those who were both creative and correct, though we must note the historical bias toward colorful individuals that taints this source of data. It is much more difficult to evaluate creative work as it is being produced. There are many characteristics shared between the truly creative and the misguided. Bold hypotheses, eloquent presentation, and beautiful analogies characterize both groups. What separates the crank (such as those who continually invent perpetual motion machines) from the true innovator, in my opinion, is a fatal flaw in a key behavioral dimension of the creative process in the crank. Such flaws include a lack of humility, self-aggrandizement, lack of introspection, and dishonesty. Please note that I am not suggesting that great scientists are saints. They tend to avoid church-going and have little interest in participating in charitable organizations (Simonton, 1988). However, the focus caused by work that is reality oriented and provides constant feedback leads to certain positive attitudinal consequences. It is impossible, for example, to conduct research while one is hung over or in a rage. Most creative scientists are particularly conscious of the factors that interfere with their work. Likewise, because the creative act is subtle and easily disrupted, the connection between inner realities and concrete results is perhaps more easily demonstrated in the context of science where objective testing of results is possible.

Hubris and humility

Making creative contributions in science requires a delicate balance between hubris and humility. Hubris is defined as insolence or arrogance resulting from excessive pride. It is generally a pejorative term, but in fact insolence and arrogance (of a special kind) are essential qualities for making truly innovative discoveries. The creative innovator is insolent, having little respect for authority, because his or her experience is that authority is often wrong. In fact, the innovator's career depends upon being able to show that the current wisdom is wrong or at least that it has overlooked something important. He or she is arrogant because of an expectation of uncovering the secrets of nature, and in fact makes a career of pursuing it. This is hubris in the sense exhibited by Prometheus who

The creative person needs the arrogance of Prometheus. Illustration by Richard Loehle.

stole fire from the gods, though it is often viewed by outsiders in purely the pejorative sense. The original thinker must endure periods of solitude and must expect to be misunderstood and perhaps bitterly opposed by peers. The ego must be strong to withstand these hardships. While ordinarily we would consider hubris to be a negative trait, in the case of the explorer or innovator in any field the above argument indicates that it may be an essential quality for success.

The key to the successful use of "hubris" is that it be tempered by humility. Such tempering leads to a balanced type of confidence that we may label strength of character, for want of a better phrase. The difficulty here is that even if someone is truly humble, the mere fact that they are doing or attempting something great or difficult leads others out of jealousy to view them as arrogant or proud. Many people resented the great American sprinter Carl Lewis, who was able to state factually for over ten years that he was the fastest man on earth, as demonstrated by his several Olympic gold medals, and yet I have never seen him boast or act proud. Jealousy among academics is rife and can be bitter. Those who dare to achieve greatness and challenge authority by discovering new things risk the label of arrogance and pride due to the jealousy of others, even when the charge is unjustified.

Several considerations can help one achieve humility. First, one can, of course, make mistakes and therefore must be careful not to state too strongly that one is right and others are wrong. Further, the fact that one's work supersedes previous work does not make one's predecessors stupid. Second, most discoveries, systems, inventions, and theories are eventually superseded by better, more precise, more comprehensive ones. In rapidly moving fields (e.g., that of computers) this can happen within a few years or less. One must dare to have a grand hypothesis but remember that it may well be soon forgotten. If one has as a primary goal of one's work service to all humanity, then the product of one's labors becomes a gift to be given rather than a status symbol or a bid for immortality. When individuals desire success not merely for the sake of achievement but to show that they are really better than, or superior to, others, then this is the death of humility. That is to say, one must ask whether the climb to the mountain peak is for the challenge and the joy of achievement or to make one feel taller.

Failure to balance these factors properly is at the root of both underachievement and barriers to strategic thinking. Lack of confidence leads to underachievement because the professional refuses to speculate. Without bold hypotheses, models, and experiments one is reduced to plodding routine. Such attitudes lead to a desire for absolute certainty and a tendency to dismiss anything new as "mere speculation." Failure to understand that the intellect is far more powerful than we assume also leads to confusion between one's self-esteem and one's actual abilities. Those whose self-image is damaged by events in their lives or who feel themselves to be young and inexperienced will fail to take seriously their true level of talent. They will then not attempt the "difficult" or important problems. But many problems in retrospect are seen to have simple solutions or to have yielded in the end to pure persistence. Many of today's key problems are as open to solution as more mundane problems with far less payoff. The lack of hubris, therefore, causes a great deal of underachievement.

Hubris not balanced by humility leads to several types of sins of excess. The most visible problem is what might be called the "crackpot syndrome." When a brilliant and successful strategist becomes convinced of his or her own freedom from error or the certainty of a particular hypothesis, he or she can become immune to criticism or to contrary evidence. This leads to many endless rounds of debate in academic fields because no amount of evidence is sufficient to change the mind of the fanatic (Loehle, 1987). In political fields it leads to great disasters (the invasions of Russia by Napoleon and by Hitler). In business it leads to overly rapid expansion of a new enterprise or the entry by a business into a new venture about which it knows nothing. A tricky aspect of evaluating particular cases is that many who seem to be crackpots at the time turn out later to be right. When Alfred Wegener proposed the idea of continental drift 80 years ago this must have seemed exceedingly crazy to his contemporaries (he was in fact vilified for his views) and yet he was essentially correct. There is a key difference, however, between his behavior and that of a crackpot; Wegener was not immune to criticism and fully acknowledged that a weakness of his theory was the lack of a mechanism by which continents might move. Thus, we can see that he was ahead of his time, but not suffering from irrational adherence to his hypotheses. Darwin likewise was tenacious in his views but was also acutely aware of the mechanisms and facts that were lacking to establish his theory of evolution. He spent many years attempting to fill in the gaps in his theory. The extrapolation of these examples to other realms of endeavor is obvious; however, the farther one moves away from the pure sciences the harder it may be to tell who is really a crackpot and who is a visionary.

Far more common than the crackpot is the "expert." The expert has also forgotten all about humility and is very proud of the fact that he or she knows all about his or her chosen specialty. The expert criticizes new ideas because they contradict what we "know" to be true. The expert is frequently also intolerant of those who intrude on his or her intellectual territory. Even worse, becoming an expert actively interferes with creativity and discovery, as discussed in Chapter 1. Failures perpetrated by "experts" include the complete inability of mainframe computer makers to see the future strength of the personal computer market and the frequent rejection of new products and inventions within a corporation by the senior brass. Humility constantly reminds us that the certainty of yesterday will be completely toppled tomorrow; we should therefore be ready at any moment to discard any piece of knowledge and start afresh.

Detachment

A key to maintaining the proper balance between "hubris" (or confidence) and humility and avoiding the pitfalls inherent in any type of creative or innovative work is a spirit of detachment. Detachment is a rather alien concept in current Western culture, which vaunts the self and personality above all else and holds self-esteem as the highest good.

Detachment is an attitude that arises from the realization of several key truths. The first of these is that our true worth is unrelated to our material attainments. When one realizes that the most valuable things in life are the quality of one's life, the strength of one's character, and one's family, then one is on the way to true detachment, because these most valuable things do not accrue from material success nor can they be taken away. They are entirely internal and are not subject to success or failure or the opinions of others. In any problem-solving domain one's accomplishments and discoveries are quickly obliterated by new discoveries and better products, so the ephemeral nature of material accomplishments is more obvious than in certain other fields of endeavor.

A spirit of detachment is a great gift in the pursuit of the creative solution of problems. One of the most important characteristics of creative individuals is independence of thought (Root-Bernstein, 1989). To be truly creative or innovative one needs first to have a mastery of the tools of the trade, but then one must go beyond what is known and create something new. Detachment enables one to recognize that the current state of knowledge is ephemeral and not fixed in stone. Furthermore, by removing excessive concern over the opinions of others, one's mind becomes free to consider new ideas clearly and on their own merits. New ideas are fragile and easily destroyed by premature criticism. Detachment leads to the kind of objectivity that can nurture truly original ideas.

Detachment is also a mighty shield against the slings and arrows that face the would-be innovator. Detachment shields one from fear of failure and fear of criticism, the two big fears that cause many to shy away from the new or unusual. True innovators are bound to seem odd or to receive unwarranted criticism, and detachment can help to deflect negative responses without the individual needing to isolate himself or herself or develop a bitter, defensive persona in response.

Conversely, detachment helps to combat the rigidity, conservatism, and know-it-all-ism that tempt the expert but kill innovation. Since the knowledge of even the most brilliant person is but a drop from the ocean of all knowledge, and since all around us the unknown far outweighs the known, the idea that one could ever truly "know it all" or be an expert can be seen clearly as an exercise in self-delusion. The extreme forms of hubris that result from the identification of one's self as the owner of an idea (and thus the crackpot's refusal to change his or her mind) are likewise tempered by detachment. Not only does one see then that one's discoveries are not really due to one's own efforts (because one's very skill is a gift), but one sees that these products of creativity do not belong to oneself at all but are truly gifts of service to humankind.

Tranquillity

In our increasingly frenetic world, tranquillity is a scarce commodity. It is not, however, merely our nerves that suffer. Lack of place and time for reflection have an adverse impact on our inner lives. The need for outer tranquillity in the search for inner tranquillity has a long tradition and is institutionalized in various forms of retreats. What is not so well known is that inner tranquillity is also conducive to success in creative endeavors, including the type of strategic thinking discussed here. Consider the sport of orienteering in which one attempts to navigate across country using a map and compass. The winner of an orienteering race is rarely the swiftest runner, but the one who has the correct bearings. In complex problem solving also it is crucial to have one's bearings. The ability to still the mind, to achieve a calm, reflective attitude can contribute significantly to innovation and creativity. This is because the most important and yet most difficult step in solving a complex problem is the formulation of truly original ideas. Yet good ideas typically start as urgings, hints, wisps, vapors, images, or vague analogies. Only the rare individual has them pop up in a concrete form, ready to be acted on. More likely is that the phantasm will need encouragement and its owner the patience to watch it drift by at its own pace. A hurried, impatient, "busy" person will not give these ideas sufficient play or attention and will tend to rush on to more "productive" work. Whereas the painter typically works alone and is almost forced into some sort of meditative or introspective state, in which verbal modes of thought are suppressed, it is all too easy for the professional to rush from meeting to airport to computer, and the phone is an all too frequent interruption. A frenetic pace is very detrimental to the formulation of complex thoughts and to receptivity to nascent breakthroughs.

The achievement of tranquillity, however, is more than just a technique such as walking or the safety of a remote office, free from phone calls. One can take a quiet walk in a remote wood yet still find one's mind racing with thoughts and anxieties. True tranquillity is brought about by the cultivation of certain key attitudes. First among these is detachment. Constant dwelling on getting the Nobel Prize or that next promotion poisons the intuition and receptivity to new and subtle ideas. The realization of the smallness of even the greatest of our accomplishments allows one to maintain a degree of emotional distance from the work at hand so that the needs of the work itself provide the guidance for how to proceed rather than our hopes and wishes. Detachment also allows ideas to enter our consciousness that may contradict our previous results (and perhaps contradict our cherished hopes); a busy and emotional mind may suppress or ignore these but they are crucial to correcting one's course. Tranquillity may also be enhanced by practice of various disciplines such as meditation.

Honesty

One might not think of honesty as relevant to strategic problem solving, but in my experience prominent strategists are quite honest, both with themselves and with others. Note that this is not necessarily true universally, because some reach prominence due to the labors of subordinates or by being prolific at the expense of being innovative. Why might this quality of honesty be important? After all, problem solving has never been considered a domain for ethical difficulties as are law or politics. The reason is that if one is to successfully confront complexity and create innovative products, designs, or solutions, absolute lack of self-deception is required. One can deceive the customer, bluff in sports, and bully in business, but nature cannot be tricked. When one builds a space shuttle or designs a computer system, the outcome is not influenced at all by one's bluffing or charm or good looks. On the contrary, self-deception is devastating in such a context. There is a natural psychological tendency to seek evidence that confirms what we already believe and to ignore evidence that contradicts our beliefs (Loehle, 1987). Collecting data that can only confirm what we already believe is useful as a check on knowledge acquired by others, but it does not lead to progress. One must constantly ask oneself "Am I interpreting this data according to my preferences or am I really seeing what is there?" Failure to be honest can lead to tragic consequences. For example, a prominent turn-of-the-century geologist became convinced in his later years that all rocks were fossil deposits of aquatic micro-organisms. His self-deception was so complete that no matter what type of rock he looked at under the poor-quality microscopes of that day, he saw microfossils. During the last years of his life no one would publish his work because it was so obviously biased and immune from criticism.

It is well to remember that slightly crazy ideas are crucial for successful strategic problem solving. The wild analogy or model is often useful or even correct. Those who become passionate advocates of such ideas are therefore not necessarily deceiving themselves. It is instructive to examine how such people deal with facts contrary to their beliefs. When the first experiments to test Einstein's theories seemed not to support his hypothesis, Einstein insisted the experiments were wrong. He had reason, however, to be skeptical because of the power of his theory and the difficulty of the experiments. Consider the case of Louis Pasteur (Root-Bernstein, 1989). He had a set of grand hypotheses or goals that in retrospect we can see to be not only wrong but a little crazy. For example, he dreamed of creating left-handed organisms (constituted from chirally left-handed organic chemicals) and thus becoming famous for creating a new form of life. In attempting to prove his theories he came upon many experimental results that were not what he expected or what he was looking for. He had the scientific honesty (or perhaps objectivity) to confront these results for what they were and publish them. Other scientists of his day had previously observed many of the same phenomena but failed to believe them because they contradicted what they already "knew" to be the case. Thus, in the case of Pasteur, his honesty saved him from becoming a crackpot (though of course, he was not a saint nor even always honest (Root-Bernstein, 1989)). It is clearly important to be honest with the facts and not let one's biases lead to self-deception. No one is ever free from bias, but honesty about its existence can prevent its negative effects.

Conclusion

I hope I have demonstrated that how one works is not unrelated to one's attitudes and behaviors. Not only do attitudes enhance problem solving, creativity, and productivity, but it is doubtful whether one's full capacity can be achieved when negative attitudes intervene. Furthermore, serious dangers await those brilliant minds who attempt to scale great intellectual heights without the protection of humility, detachment, and honesty. By harnessing positive emotional states one can risk less and achieve more than one would otherwise dare to imagine.

7 Strategic thinking exercises

One might ask what exercises can increase an individual's strategic thinking ability – besides reading this book, of course. There are in fact a number of concrete skills, practices, and techniques that can substantially enhance one's abilities in this area. It was mentioned earlier (p. 29) that intense concentration is essential for success on strategic problems. Games such as chess and problems in mathematics both help to foster this ability to concentrate. So experience with chess and mathematics carry over into other domains, even though the specific skills involved may not.

A key difference between the thinking of an untutored individual and a practiced strategist is that the strategist has mental structures at hand for organizing information and connecting events, whereas the untutored individual has disordered thought processes. The simplest example is the ability to order things in time. An impulsive person takes actions without following out the sequence of what will happen next, and is thus always being surprised by consequences. Such people do not schedule their errands so that their driving time is minimized and so that they finish in time, but are likely to go to the store and then find that the ice cream is melting in the car while they stop to shop for clothes. An impulsive person starts a major outdoor yard project 30 minutes before it gets dark, and ends up trying to cut the grass in the twilight, thereby running over the hose with the mower. A simple strategic structure in this case is merely the ordering of a sequence of events such that the time each takes is accounted for and the tasks fit in the time available. This is a linear structure. The many courses offered on time management suggest that sequential scheduling is not an inherent skill for most people but must be learned.

As we will see in the chapters that follow, skill in scheduling is an essential requisite to successful strategic problem solving. For example, the generation of scenarios is dependent on sequential scheduling ability. This ability is most easily learned by example. Graduate students who work for a professor who is skilled in this area can pick up the feel for ordering tasks in time so that time is not wasted. Working on a construction project also provides experience in this area as well as providing many examples of problems caused by scheduling failures (supplies that have not arrived, crews getting in each other's way, etc.).

A second type of structure is hierarchical. The organization of a textbook is hierarchical, because there are headings within sections within chapters. The practice of writing term papers in school helps to teach this type of organizational skill. Another very useful discipline for learning hierarchical structures is computer programming. By this I do not mean the use of a spreadsheet or a word processor, but procedural languages such as FORTRAN, Pascal, or C. In these languages, certain tasks are compartmentalized in subroutines, and subroutines arranged into a structure according to the computations required. Training in computer programming can be an extremely good experience for learning to organize complex tasks into a structure. Programming also has the advantage that one can incrementally improve the program until it works, thus learning how to track down problems and improve a structure.

More complex structures are not necessarily hierarchical, but are often represented by various types of flow chart. Learning to read maps, blueprints, and diagrams is good training for these other types of charts. Those who routinely use such charts may be surprised to discover that many people have great difficulty with maps and diagrams. Some people, for example, have trouble reading road maps. This trait is somewhat gender specific (Gardner, 1983). When giving directions or finding their way, for example, men tend to use ordinal directions and distances as a guide, as if they were looking at a map. Women, in contrast, tend to focus on landmarks. Similarly, there are differences between individuals in their ability to visualize a map or chart. Those with a visual-type memory have an advantage here, although they must still learn to relate the map abstractions to

Familiarity with blueprints and other diagram forms provides training in organizing complexity.

LOGIC FLOW CHART FOR QUALITY CONTROL

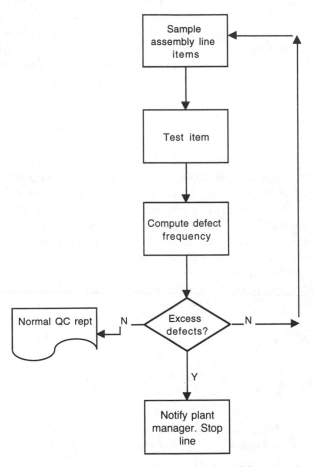

Logic diagrams can depict complex sets of actions. QC rept, quality control report.

physical landmarks and directions. Those without the ability to memorize visual information may be able to learn to read a map but cannot necessarily pull it up for reference mentally while driving.

Charts that capture more complex structures include topographic maps, project flow charts, organizational charts, decision trees, simulation model structure diagrams, and software flow charts. All of these types of chart capture a great deal of complexity in a single diagram and are thus extremely useful. Becoming familiar with these diagrams also provides tools for the internal organization of information and for planning.

Military campaigns provide invaluable examples of strategic reasoning. There is a goal to accomplish, risk and uncertainty, tactics for reaching the goal, constraints, and obstacles. It is very useful to read about such campaigns because we can follow through the consequences of the strategic decisions that were made, particularly in campaigns that are well documented such as much of the Allied effort in World War II. The small-scale model for war, of course, is team sports. It is often held that team sports provide good training in strategy. One must size up one's opponents and assess what they are likely to do, assign tasks to members of the team, who in turn must keep in mind not only the overall strategy and their part in it, but also the likely actions of their own team members so that they can interact properly. Board games also provide training in this type of strategy, though in a more restricted domain. Chess is held up as the ultimate strategy game. Experts in chess learn to recognize strategic patterns in play.

It is true that team sports are good training for some aspects of military-type strategy. In real life, however, the "game" is often much more similar to "Calvin ball" than to a traditional game. This is the game played by Calvin and his toy tiger in the comic strip *Calvin and Hobbs* in which the rules change constantly. In business settings the rules also can constantly change as one's opponents invent new technologies that make one's products obsolete. A new advertising strategy can cleverly cause consumers to focus on elements of the product that were never considered relevant before. This element of rules that change constantly also occurs in warfare (the winners usually have changed the rules, as when Hitler's troops introduced the *blitzkrieg* tactic), but does not occur in sports or games, which is one reason why the latter are really rather unrealistic forms of warfare. That is to say, a good game player does not necessarily make a good life strategist.

It is well to remember that not all strategic problems involve an opponent, as do board games, sports, and military campaigns. Inventing a device or product, planning a trip, moving to a new house, and investing are all strategic problems but do not involve an opponent (unless of course you believe that life is your opponent and is out to defeat you). In personal strategic action, one's opponents are fuzzy thinking, inertia, self-deception, disorganization, lack of information, and lack of requisite skills. One must obtain and organize information, come up with good ideas, organize components of a task, and be properly motivated. None of these components of strategic problem solving are enhanced by most board games, or particularly by video games.

In many strategic problems, there is an element of risk or uncertainty. A business we invest in may fail; the stock market may go down; the weather may spoil our camping trip. As mentioned earlier, people are extremely bad at assessing risks or chance events. Unfortunately, the only solution to this problem is to specifically become proficient at calculating odds. One type of odds is given by games of chance such as a card game where there is a known domain. In this arena, one can figure out exactly how likely is any given hand of cards. The same holds for coin tosses or dice. Familiarity with such problems is useful in other contexts also. For example, the odds on having a boy or girl, or a given number of each out of x children is exactly analogous to a coin toss, and can be figured in the same way. For other types of risk, it is useful to become familiar with historical odds, such as those for the actual risk of death from car accidents or airplane crashes. For such data, it is useful to look beyond the initial figures and examine a breakdown of the numbers. For example, one's risk from automobiles may seem high, but a large percentage of total deaths involving automobiles happen very late at night and result from driver fatigue or solitary drivers who have been drinking and hit a stationary object. If one neither drinks nor drives late at night, then one's risk is much reduced. To take another example, the risk of small business failure is often given as 50% in the first two years or something similar. What is not stated is that "failure" is defined as the number of businesses that are no longer in business after a given period. However, many of these businesses may no longer exist because they were sold to a larger company (death by assimilation), because the owner died or retired (the eventual fate of many sole proprietorships), or because the owner made a change in careers. In none of these cases is it necessarily true that the owners lost money. To properly deal with these kinds of odds-based issues, it is crucial that one have experience with calculations of risk and probability.

Logistics is a useful domain for learning about organizing complexity. In a typical logistics problem, one must get the right materials to the right place at the right time, under various constraints and risks. Not surprisingly, battles have been lost because of bad logistical operations (at the Battle of the Bulge in World War II, the Germans ran out of fuel). Conducting a logistical operation provides good training in various aspects of strategic thinking. Of course, few of us will be in charge of a military supply operation, but there are other situations that can provide similar training. A simple and accessible one is preparing for a backpacking trip. One must bring not merely food containers (cans, plastic pouches) but a means to open them and often a way to carry the waste home. One must balance the risk of rain against the extra weight that rain gear entails. One wants to bring just enough food (because it is heavy) but never go hungry. Items must be packed so that snacks and sweaters are accessible while hiking but without the need to unpack the whole backpack. This type of problem is analogous to other strategic problems where the limiting factor may not be the weight one can carry but the amount of time available or the amount of money one has to invest.

A surprising type of useful exercise comes about from being a critic. When one volunteers to be a critic of someone's project or is on an official review body, this provides an opportunity to check another person's work for flaws and errors. It can in some instances provide real insights into how someone else thinks if you can find the flaw in their reasoning. This experience is invaluable because once a habit of being an effective critic is established, this habit can be turned to examination of one's own work. Self-criticism is the best type of all because it can be applied in private and before effort has been wasted.

Finally, I must mention that building and making things is a particularly good type of training in strategic thinking, particularly if the thing built or made has some complexity. When children build model kits or make things out of LEGO bricks or using a construction set, they learn how to integrate many separate objects, how to convert a design into a finished object, and how to overcome obstacles. Home remodeling or building an extension has all the elements of a typical logistics problem, as well as being a puzzle-solving exercise. Such experiences are invaluable, but are becoming increasingly rare for children due to movement of populations to towns and cities and the elimination of technical courses in many urban and suburban schools.

Overall, there are many types of model, structure, and experience that serve to exercise the component skills of strategic thinking or develop one's overall facility with this approach.

PART 2 Strategic thinking in practice

The first part of this book presented the techniques of strategic thinking in terms of the nature of problem solving, how discoveries are made and tested, how creativity can be harnessed and enhanced, and how attitude and style affect strategic problem-solving effectiveness. This provides the foundation for actual strategic problem solving in terms of the mastery of one's cognitive tools and abilities. Such an understanding is essential to success, but there is more to it than this. There are characteristics of the problems themselves that one must also get a feel for before even the best strategist can be successful. To make an analogy, it is not sufficient for the sculptor to have an aesthetic vision, to know the symbolism he or she wishes to convey, and to have harnessed mental faculties to the task; it is also essential to understand the nature of the materials – the way that different woods respond to carving and polishing, the receptivity of these woods to stain, the susceptibility of different types of stone to cracking, and so on. That is to say, one must know something per se about the subject to be tackled. This is usually considered domain-specific knowledge (of cars or of diseases, of pizza or of electronics, for example), which of course is beyond the scope of this book because there are hundreds of domains and their intersections where people are faced with problems. However, there are common elements across these different domains, common factors that may be incorporated into an understanding of the system such that one can effectively apply the strategic problem-solving skills presented above. For example, we can note that any object or device or system behaves differently when scaled up to a larger size. This provides an angle for looking at problems. As another example, in any process there are potential bottlenecks and constraints. Using the search for these properties as a guideline can increase one's problem-solving ability.

To the strategist, then, a pile of sand, the stock market and earthquakes may share certain similarities (all may exhibit cascades on all scales, following a similar power law relationship, and perhaps for similar reasons). A ship capsizing and a coup may share certain stability properties, again for similar reasons. These analogies are not just clever but rather are structural: cases where similar results obtain for similar causal reasons. That is to say, in these cases there are general rules of behavior that extend across domains. We may use these rules and general properties in strategic problem solving. The reason it is so useful to do so is that in real problem solving we are always faced with problems that have an element of novelty (for problems where this novelty is missing, we merely have business as usual and need not be clever at all). For novel problems we need to seek efficient ways of coming to an understanding of the problem or system because otherwise we can waste incredible amounts of time learning all about it (and this often represents conventional wisdom about it in any case). This section explores these general principles and ways of approaching and dissecting problems, using concrete examples and analyses.

Few of us can lift the front end of a car, but with a jack even a child can do it. This is leverage. The essence of strategic problem solving in practice is the use of leverage. With leverage, we can identify problems more effectively, expend less time and effort analyzing a problem, and exert more control over a system.

Leverage is a theme song or advertisement jingle so catchy that people whistle it. Leverage is a cruise missile that can fly to a designated building and go down the ventilation shaft. We may contrast this to a brute force approach that uses dozens of high altitude bombers to hit the same target. Leverage is the polymerase chain reaction, which can amplify trace amounts of DNA. The strategic thinker shuns brute force approaches because time and energy are valuable and need to be used to obtain the highest return on invested effort. He or she seeks not to be busy but to be effective.

As mentioned in Chapter 1, the most important single task for the strategic problem solver is finding a problem, since in real life problems do not arrive as numbered homework assignments. Problems can be business opportunities, ideas for an essay, an idea for an invention, or "problems" in the negative sense of perhaps recognizing that one's company is beginning to slip in the market. In contrast to accepting the conventional wisdom about what problems exist or need solution, the strategic thinker looks for leverage points: a problem no one has noticed; a place where a new technique can be applied; a controversy that can be resolved elegantly. Problems identified in this way are more likely to be solvable with less effort and therefore to have a higher payoff.

Once a problem has been identified, there are certain effective tools of analysis that can be applied. In contrast to brainstorming and lateral thinking, which mainly just help to generate alternatives for simple (one-step) problems, the strategic thinker needs tools that allow him or her to reason through multistep problems. A number of such tools are presented in Part 2.

The objective of the strategic thinker is to generate solutions or products. To do so, leverage must be applied effectively so as to promote understanding the system (in a research setting) or otherwise to control or manipulate it. For example, in science one of the key problem elements is determining what in the system may be reliably measured and which of these measures tells us something useful. For systems one wishes to control (the profits of a business, the economy, a fish population) one must clearly identify what are the control points and how these determine system behavior. In Part 2 all of these issues are dealt with.

8 Problem finding

How does one find a problem worth working on? This is the most serious issue facing graduate students trying to start their research. Among practicing scientists, success in problem finding can make or break a career. In business, one may ask how one can recognize a new business opportunity or trend. Conversely, how can one recognize an organizational dysfunction?

The simple answer is that problems (including opportunities), just like diseases, have symptoms. An inconsistent theory will generate contradictions. An incomplete or inadequate theory will be confronted by anomalous data. Unexploited economic opportunities will generate unusual behaviors, dislocations, and unexpected rapid growth by certain companies. Undiscovered phenomena or processes will generate behaviors that cannot be explained. In all of these cases one observes something that does not fit. In particular, one is looking for something that doesn't fit that is important or that has implications for other issues. This chapter explores these topics.

8.1 PARADOX AND CONTRADICTION

In searching for critical aspects of a complex problem, it is useful to develop an eye for paradox and contradiction. By focusing on a point of paradox, contradiction or contention, one can avoid the need to learn everything about a topic. In any domain of knowledge, many things are well known to the experts, but to learn everything that the expert knows about a topic means that one must become an expert as well. This is clearly not efficient (or even possible) if many problems from diverse areas must be dealt with on a regular basis. In contrast, by focusing on a paradox or contradiction, one can locate those aspects of a complex problem that are not understood by others and that represent potentially key dimensions of the problem. In this sense, paradox indicates an opportunity, because it is a point of leverage. By focusing on a paradox, one can identify the key elements of knowledge and focus in on these, rather than trying to learn everything about a topic. The paradox also helps to clarify what the problem is that needs to be solved. It is not the case, of course, that all paradoxes one uncovers indicate problems one should solve, but they do indicate problems that may be attacked expediently.

Some examples illustrate the use of paradox in identifying problems and opportunities. The existence of "stagflation" in the 1970s in the USA was a paradox: it was not supposed to be possible according to standard monetary theory to have both inflation and a recession together. Stagflation indicated an inadequacy in this theory. As a second example, the standard industrial theory over much of the last 100 years promoted economies of scale as a universal industrial law. The consistent result that medium-sized corporations outdo giants in terms of innovation (patents and new products per dollar spent), growth, and return on investment (Drucker, 1985) is a clear contradiction pointing to some type of diminishing returns with size due to internal wasted effort. If big corporations win, it is not due to efficiency, but is due to size per se. Size, for example, permits huge advertising campaigns to be launched and national chains of dealers to be supported, but these are not "economies of scale." Rather, we may call this the "bully factor." As another example, some entirely different approaches to psychological therapy (Gestalt, Adlerian, Rogerian, Rolfing, etc., etc.) were all shown to be highly effective when first presented. The paradox was that these different schools of psychology made entirely different assumptions about the mind and the emotions such that the different techniques could not possibly all be correct. It has turned out that the initial success of these techniques could in each case be attributed to the charisma of the founder. When attracted by a charismatic leader, people are much more motivated to change, and technique makes very little difference. This analysis is confirmed by the fact that the initial good results of the new therapies could not be replicated by later practitioners (Stanovich, 1992).

It is a safe bet that the conventional wisdom is often wrong. If it were not, then there would be no surprises, no massive layoffs, no business failures and no room for improvement and innovation. It is not the case, however, that the conventional wisdom is always wrong, so a pure contrarian policy is not useful and may be disastrous. Instead, contradictions provide an indication of when and where conventional wisdom is wrong, and thus an opportunity to be ahead of the game. Several examples of domains where paradox can prove useful or informative are discussed next.

Controversy and paradox

A heated debate, especially if both sides are highly polarized, is an indication that all parties involved are missing a key to the problem, such that an opportunity exists for someone who can identify what they are missing. It is useful in such cases to ask "How could both sides in this debate be wrong?" Such polarized debates often result from different parties or schools of thought viewing a problem from a different perspective or scale (see Section 8.2), or with a different objective. The different points of view are often tacit, however, which is why such debates can continue indefinitely. A typical difference of this type occurs when one person is considering an issue at a strategic level (say, what should be the outcomes of schooling) and another is viewing it from a tactical level (what methods of instruction to use). Not only does this cause confusion, but different strategic goals may require different tactical means.

Disjunctions can occur when key words are used in different ways (e.g., economy, opportunity, rights, "big government," environment). People generally assume that they are understood when they speak, but many "big" words (not those with many letters, but those full of meaning and connotation) can differ drastically in their usage. What is evident to the strategic thinker is that such different usages cause the same "facts" to lead to opposite conclusions, or similar statements to mean different things. To one person, "reducing big government" means cutting welfare and reducing paperwork for businesses, but to another it means reducing the military and lowering taxes. The strategic solution to a debate (and controversy) about such an issue may therefore not be negotiation or compromise, but first the simple (!) step of clarifying what each party means (though they may not wish to be clear).

Divergent points of view can also result from different perspectives or scales, again leading to the paradox that different parties looking at the same situation can describe it in completely different ways. For instance, if in a small town a shopping mall is proposed, the person who says it will be good for business is correct in the short term because construction money will stimulate the economy for a year or two. The person who says it will be bad for business may be taking a longer-term view about the eventual death of the old downtown and the creation of abandoned buildings. Thus, both people are correct in spite of making seemingly contradictory statements, because they are using different time-frames for assessing outcomes.

We can see that a "problem" (disagreement, debate, controversy) often exists that is at root the result of a paradox; that language is inherently ambiguous and many aspects of meaning are implicit, but we act as though we always understand what we hear and expect that others understand what we say. Attempting to solve such problems at face value is a waste of time. What must first be done is to resolve the implicit elements or disambiguate the language so that the actual issues can be laid out.

Paradox in business

In business, a paradox is often indicative of an opportunity or of a problem, or both simultaneously. Such a paradox is symptomatic of a gap between products and consumer needs, or between various portions of the economy. Let us take as an example the decline of mainframe computers and the rise of the personal computer. When the first personal computers, such as the early Apple, were introduced in the late 1970s, they were pitiful little toys compared to mainframes, with 8K memories, not much capability, and a toy programming language, BASIC. One can see that when initially introduced they allowed people to use a computer who had no access to a mainframe. But why did such toys continue to grow in popularity and eventually nearly supplant mainframes? At each step of their evolution they were slower, had less powerful software, and had less memory than a mainframe. Many of the purchasers over this period had access, even unlimited access, to mainframes, but still bought these little machines. For the big computer manufacturers this was a problem (which they still have failed to grasp) and as a situation it is a paradox: how could an "inferior" technology take over from a "superior" one?

The simple answer is that from the perspective of the user the big machines were not so great because of the use of batch and timeshare processing. The first computers were strictly batch, and used punch cards. Each job was run using the whole computer, and when it finished the next job would run. In the 1970s time-sharing became common and interactive terminals became available to allow editing of files stored on disk instead of cards. Many users were hooked up to a large central computer that would switch rapidly from user to user, giving each a small slice of computational time. This gave many people access to the big machines without their having to wait for hours for cards to be processed. For the user doing simple typing, the result was usually satisfactory, but delays were frequent when the computer got overloaded. A delay of a few seconds does not sound bad, but it means that many words can be typed without anything appearing on the screen, which is annoying and causes the person to stop. This problem was usually exacerbated by tendencies to put too many users on the system. The system managers could point to very good average response times, but to the user the delays were real. One could similarly point to very good average speeds on a freeway, but if you travel at rush hour it does not seem so fast.

Much worse, however, was that the time-sharing concept was implemented by long cable connections, usually phone lines. These lines usually had limited capacity (300 to 2400 baud). This meant that graphics and graphics-based programs (WYSIWYG (What You See Is What You Get) word processors, spreadsheets) could not run over the network. In addition, refreshing the screens of hundreds of remote graphics images would strain even a large mainframe. To make a pie chart, one had to use a command-language-based tool that would create a file that would be sent to a printer in another building. Output could be picked up two hours later. Errors were not evident until it was picked up. Repeating this process several times to get the desired graph could take several days. In contrast, on a personal computer one obtains a plot instantly and can change the options and labels many times and get a finished plot in minutes. The same holds for spreadsheets, computer-aided design (CAD) programs, fancy word processors, etc. It did not matter to the user that the big machine was faster; in real time the personal computer was faster because it did not have to be time-shared and did not have a bottleneck in the transfer of data over phone lines. In particular, the personal computer was always available. Further, key applications were simply not available on the mainframes. On a mainframe, software would be purchased that many people were likely to use. If an individual was the only one wishing to use a piece of software, the central computing department would not purchase it but it would be too expensive for the individual user. For example, a compiler for a major programming language could cost $20000 to $80000 for a large mainframe system. This constraint could be quite serious for users with various specialized needs. Thus, a revolution in computing resulted from a paradox: an inferior technology produced better response times for the user, fewer bottlenecks, and new types of application, all at a reasonable cost. After more than 15 years of this revolution, it is hard to call upper-end personal computers "inferior" anymore, but they are still less sophisticated and less powerful than a mainframe, so the paradox remains and the trend continues.

Drucker (1985) focuses on paradox as a way of recognizing business opportunities and describes seven sources of innovative opportunity. First, the unexpected success or failure should be highlighted because it indicates a missed opportunity or a change in the market or other conditions. He points out that unexpected success is not always pointed out to upper management since it is not a "problem" and is therefore often not followed up on. Second, opportunities arise from incongruities between expectations and performance (e.g., a company in a growing market that has trouble remaining profitable), or between market assumptions and market realities. Third, a type of incongruity is a missing link in a process or service. Fourth, a change in industry and market structures creates paradoxes and opportunities. Fifth, demographic changes can create economic mismatches and gaps. Finally, changes in perception and the generation of new knowledge create many discontinuities and thereby business opportunities.

Paradox in science

In science the role of paradox and contradiction is particularly notable. One use is as a form of proof or argument, particularly in mathematics and logic. If one is attempting to prove something and in the process creates a contradiction, then one has either made a mistake or the premise is wrong. This type of analysis has proven useful for testing expert systems such as those that diagnose disease. Another use is to reason by using opposites. Here, one starts by assuming the opposite of what one is trying to prove and reasoning from there. If one obtains a contradiction then this proves the original hypothesis. This is useful when it is difficult to analyze the situation one is interested in but its opposite may be simple. For example, it may be hard to prove there are no exceptions to a given generality, but easy to prove that if an exception occurs then contradictions arise.

Paradox in experimental domains is often encountered. In some cases it may mean merely that the experiments in question are just too ambiguous (Collins and Pinch, 1993), in which case the wise researcher avoids the topic or finds another way to study it. In other cases, however, a paradox indicates that something is fundamentally wrong. In recent years major paradoxes have arisen in certain fields. For example, the expected flux of neutrinos from the nuclear reactions in the sun has not been observed. Although the detection experiments are tricky (Collins and Pinch, 1993), no fault in the experiments has yet been found that would remove the paradox. For another example, the estimated age of the universe (as of 1995) is less than the estimated age of some nearby galaxies – a paradox if there ever was one. Note that in this case various assumptions and calculations underlie each estimate, so there is room for resolution of the paradox.

A major paradox has recently been uncovered in attempts to trace human origins. Ancient human fossils have been found not only in Africa, but in Europe and Asia. Fully modern humans appear to have originated about 200 000 years ago and then spread out from Africa (the single origin hypothesis). Did they mingle with or displace preexisting populations in these other regions? Or did the populations in other regions evolve in the same direction and produce modern humans from these ancient roots (the multiregional hypothesis)? Evidence from mitochondrial DNA (inherited only from the mother) seems to show a single origin for all modern humans from a fairly small population, presumably in Africa. Evidence in support of the multiregional hypothesis is that morphological features dating back a million years in these other regions appear to have continued unbroken into modern populations. An example is the shovel-shaped incisors of modern Chinese, which appear to be similar to those of ancient Peking man. These two views cannot both be right. If all human mitochondrial DNA has a common, recent origin, then regional populations cannot have ancient roots. This is a clear paradox. There are several possible solutions to this puzzle. The first is that either the DNA studies are full of holes or the morphological studies are all wet (i.e., one group or the other in this debate is incompetent). Alternatively, something may be missing. One possible explanation is that the combination of mitochondrial DNA with genomic DNA can cause incompatibilities, such that only the mitochondrial DNA of one population persists while the genomic DNA may be a mixture of the DNA from both populations (Treisman, 1995). This clever solution would resolve both types of evidence, but it remains to be confirmed.

Darwin faced a paradox that threatened his whole theory of evolution. If all organisms descended from common ancestors, how did organisms reach remote oceanic islands? If they could not travel this far then a paradox existed. The religious concept of separate creations would explain life on these remote islands but would destroy evolution as an explanation. Darwin first noted that all animals on these islands could either fly or survive long periods without food or water (e.g., snakes, lizards) and thus survive on floating mats of vegetation such as he had seen far from land on his voyages on the *Beagle*. He then did experiments which showed that many plant seeds could float for many weeks and then germinate when planted in soil. He thus conducted research specifically to remove the apparent paradox of physical barriers.

The removal of paradox was also central to Einstein's studies of space and motion that resulted in his theories of relativity (special and general). His thought experiments showed the essential paradoxes that arise when one travels at the speed of light if it is assumed that time is invariant (e.g., if one moves away from a clock at the speed of light the clock appears to stop because light cannot reach the observer from later times). He was then able to resolve these paradoxes by allowing the passage of time to be relative to the speed of the observer, thereby allowing space to be curved.

In some cases, contradiction in science can be reduced to the same kinds of linguistic tangle that bedevil normal discourse. This occurs when words are too loosely used and in particular are not defined in terms of how the object or process is to be quantified. This lack of operationalism is particularly rife in the social sciences, as discussed in Chapter 2.

Summary

It is clear that paradox is a powerful tool for both problem finding and problem solving. A paradox occurs either when people are "talking past each other" or when there is some inconsistency in a domain of knowledge. The existence of paradox represents an opportunity, whether the domain is business, political debate, or research.

The interesting thing is that there is a paradox in how successful problem solvers handle paradox. On one hand, people with no tolerance for ambiguity do not tolerate paradox and do not make good problem solvers because they seek closure too soon, thus being likely to make up their minds in favor of one side or the other in a controversy rather than looking deeper and uncovering the root of the problem. On the other hand, someone who tolerates all ambiguity without being bothered at all does not see problems to solve, is not bothered by inconsistency, and thinks things fit together when they don't. If you can read the tabloid newspapers without becoming uncomfortable then you fit into this category. The true strategic thinker simultaneously can tolerate ambiguity, but finds certain contradictions so unacceptable that they become paradoxes that call out for resolution. The art in this lies in focusing on the paradoxes that matter, that have many implications and ramifications. This is the "art" in *The Art of the Soluble* (Medawar, 1967).

8.2 PERSPECTIVE AND SCALE

Looking for perspective

For grappling with complex problems, perspective is essential. Perspective enables one to disentangle oneself from a problem that may be too close to be seen clearly – the difficulty of seeing the forest for the trees. Because things that are too close to us come to be taken for granted, it can be very difficult to conceive of them as being different. Perspective enables new conceptions.

I was visiting a state park south of Tallahassee, Florida. The central feature of the park was a clear spring, arising out of a sinkhole and forming the starting point for a river. The spring was about 150 m across and the sinkhole in the middle about 30 m across. Looking out from the bank, the view was really beautiful, and fish could be seen darting about in the shallows. There was a tower built at the edge of the spring so one could look down into the sinkhole. I climbed the tower, about 21 m high, and looked down. This was a literal change in perspective that was very revealing. Because the water was rising out of a limestone cavern, the water was extremely clear. This meant that from above every aspect of the bottom and every fish could be seen, in depth, in three dimensions, with crystal clarity. This was beautiful in itself, but of particular interest was what it revealed about the fish. Around the mouth of the sinkhole, where the water was flowing

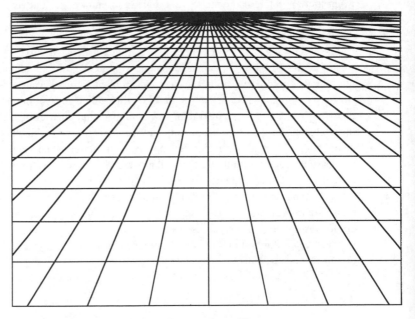

Proper perspective is essential merely to see the problem.

out, three large gar hung motionless in the water, pointing inwards. They had divided up the sinkhole and were spread evenly around it, evidently waiting for disoriented fish to emerge from the spring. One would never be able to see this phenomenon from a boat, because one would be too close and because the boat would disturb the fish. Many problems have this characteristic, that they are only visible from an appropriate distance (sometimes literally). Another example of literal perspective involves archaeology. The search for ancient cities from the ground is often frustrating, especially in the jungle. From the air, however, networks of ancient roads in the deserts of Iraq, radiating like the spokes of a wheel from vanished cities, have been easy to spot. In Mexico, networks of irrigation ditches 1000 years old have been observed from the air, though from the ground one cannot detect them.

In American business, it is assumed that the only way to deal with an economic downturn is to lay people off or encourage early retirements. It is held that layoffs are regrettable, but that there is no choice and business is business, after all. In this situation, no search for alternatives is made because it is not believed that there is any alternative. The cost of this policy, however, is very high. During layoffs, good people who may have long experience in the business are lost, those remaining are scared and demoralized, and early retirement programs can be very costly. More seriously, those remaining become reluctant to sacrifice for the company or to stick their necks out; why should they? When business picks up, staff are insufficient and opportunities may be lost. If more staff are hired, the cost of searching, interviewing, and training, and the cost resulting from the initial inefficiency of new staff can be very high. Overall, this is a very inefficient system. Further, it has a very high cost to the laid-off worker, who may use up life savings, lose his or her house, become depressed, and suffer marital difficulties. When one examines the Japanese system, one sees that they do not lay off staff except under the most extreme conditions, and yet they remain competitive. How is this possible? A large portion of the salary of the average Japanese is in the form of year-end bonuses. During a downturn, bonuses can be reduced across the board and no one need be laid off. The tradeoff is security of employment against certainty of wages. Further, during a downturn idle workers may be utilized to paint and modernize the factory, thus turning wasted time into an investment opportunity. During boom times, the American system seemed adequate because if someone was laid off they could quickly find a new job, but that is no longer the case. We may contrast a third system, in place in parts of Europe, where major industries are owned by the government. In a recession layoffs are unacceptable, but so are wage reductions, so the government subsidizes the business. This may seem to be an ideal solution but it promotes inefficiency and debt. Once we see that other systems exist that differ from the one with which we are familiar, then it becomes possible to imagine other variations and combinations.

There are other aspects of living in different parts of the world that similarly have major consequences for many aspects of how people act and do business, but that the people involved simply take for granted. For example, in certain rural parts of Europe, land ownership has been tightly held within families for dozens of generations, with each family holding on to their small plot. The consequence of this is that there is very little movement or mingling of different peoples, a situation Americans would have trouble imagining. A further consequence is that when historical events resulted in large land holdings, these have tended to be retained such that certain families maintain inherited wealth and position (related to the class system still prevalent in Britain). In complete contrast, among many American Indian tribes, land is largely held in joint ownership by the tribe, which makes such inequalities in land control impossible. In all of these cases it is only with the perspective gained by comparing different regions that we can see the consequences of various land ownership systems, whereas those within the system may take it entirely for granted and be unable to imagine any feasible alternative.

The proper focus or perspective is essential when looking at business performance. From a very close up perspective, one may examine departments within a corporation and see apparent efficiency and bustle. From a slightly larger perspective, however, one may see conflicts between departments that reduce overall effectiveness. For example, salesmen might pitch a product in ways that conflict with what the product can actually do, causing dissatisfied customers and loss of repeat business. The goal of the assembly plant to keep the lines running may pile up inventory (stock) and increase carrying charges. From a higher vantage yet, the company might be producing something that is doomed, such as a toy with a short popularity or large, fuel-guzzling cars, in which case efficiency (the close up view) is really irrelevant. A proper strategic analysis of any organization therefore depends on proper identification of the level(s) at which problems exist. To do this one must fight against the difficulty that most people tend to focus largely at a single level. The president of the company who tends to think in terms of markets and taxes and finance may completely miss the fact that the company cannot compete because it hires poorly educated people, does not train them, and provides antiquated tools and equipment. The plant manager whose focus is on productivity may have little concept of, and little or no control over, the choice of product to be manufactured.

A classic case of perspective change results from the photographs of Earth taken from space. From our human perspective, events appear very local, and boundaries appear real. One cannot cross many national boundaries without passing a big sign and showing a passport. From space, however, there are no lines, no borders, and the artificiality of our boundaries appears evident. Further, and quite dramatically, we can see from space that the whole Earth shares the same atmosphere and the same oceans. This image of a natural Earth from space has been a significant factor in influencing many people to change their perspective on issues regarding the environment.

This last example illustrates that a key to gaining perspective is recognizing boundaries and seeing that boundaries are often arbitrarily drawn. It is often the case that boundaries around academic disciplines are historical accidents, and do not necessarily correspond to the boundaries of real problems. American engineering students tend to specialize in either mechanical or electrical engineering, but Japanese students study mechano-electrical engineering, which is much more useful for problems in which mechanical and electrical components are combined, as in video recorders. Part of the difficulty facing large cities is that the jurisdictional boundaries of the city and its suburbs do not correspond to the larger system (the megacity) within which problems and potential solutions actually exist. In my neighborhood, the city, county, school district, park district, and congressional district all have different borders and each overlaps with multiple other entities. We often draw a boundary on a map and designate a certain area as a park or nature preserve, but many animals range over a far wider area than this and of course have little idea that a particular area might be safer than other areas.

Problems can often be solved by recognizing that a certain boundary is artificial and can be overcome. For example, the traditional segregation of product types into hardware, clothing, drugs and sundries, groceries, flowers, etc. represented a set of boundaries defining discrete types of store. Recognizing that these boundaries are arbitrary has led to the megagrocery store and the megaretail store (e.g., Walmart, K-Mart, Sainsbury, Géant Casino) in which several types of store are combined, which has the advantage to the consumer that several types of item can be purchased at one stop, thus saving time. It could be argued that a real solution to the race issue must involve the recognition that racial categories (boundaries) are also arbitrary, which becomes more evident as more people intermarry.

Viewpoint perspectives

A type of perspective that must always be considered in human systems is that of different viewpoints. People pay lip service to different points of view, but what they usually mean is that they recognize that people have differing agendas or goals or wants. More than this, though, the life experiences and training of an individual may influence literally how they see the world. The city person standing by the river bank sees a beautiful spot and dreams of building a house there. The naturalist observes the mud stains 2 m up on all the trees and notes that only trees that can tolerate prolonged flooding grow there, thereby concluding that the location floods for prolonged periods and at great depth. I knew an older couple in Colorado who had spent their entire lives out on the flat plains, and could not tolerate going up in the mountains. They were used to a certain landscape. After living in the Pacific Northwest for several years, where the vegetation is lush and deep green, I was struck, upon returning to the South, by the signs of nutrient deficiency (yellowed foliage, particularly). My perspective had changed. To one person, an old neighborhood just looks old and he or she wants a new house. To another, the large old homes have character and their low price suggests an opportunity for renovation at a profit. We can say that not merely do people react differently to what they see, but they actually see it differently. The recognition of how one's own perspective and that of others can be colored by viewpoint can help one to avoid personal blind spots and biases and also to understand the actions of others.

Perspectives in time

A change in perspective that can be crucial to understanding involves viewing events at different timescales. We tend to view the riverbank where we sit and fish as fixed in space. It seems like a great place to put a house. At a longer timescale (decades) we can see that floods cover that spot as deep as 6 m on a regular basis, and furthermore that the river shifts its banks at regular intervals. As another example, barrier islands in the American Southeast regularly erode at the southern end and build up at the northern end at rates that can exceed a meter per year in places. One should be very careful about where one puts a hotel under such conditions. The Mississippi Delta has lost huge amounts of land over the last 50 years due to subsidence because sediment from the Mississippi has been rerouted by levees, and the Nile Delta is likewise diminishing because sediment has been retained by dams. In these examples, what we take to be fixed and permanent is clearly not so, even on a human timescale. The converse of this is also true: although we view the landscape as fixed and permanent, we do not believe that any of the changes that humans make (dams, farming, canals) are permanent, and yet the irrigation networks of the Maya can still be seen and early Bronze Age copper mine tailings are still devoid of plant life in Britain and elsewhere.

When we take too short a time perspective, the result is often that we cannot understand what is occurring. If we observe our yard or garden for a while, we may see a bird flitting about. The motion seems random. If we observe for many hours we may observe the bird repeatedly returning to the same tree and discern that it is building a nest. Ants seem to wander at random, but with long observation we might note that, when an ant returns from a location where there is a large food supply (a dropped banana or a dead beetle), other ants begin to follow the same trail and find the food also. With a short-term perspective, the opening of a new road always seems to improve traffic. On a longer timescale, however, it happens that people begin to move farther from their jobs (particularly farther from town centers), which increases their need to drive and reduces their ability to take mass transportation. The net result can be hopeless congestion with little mass transit (think Los Angeles). In all of these cases, short-term observations provide very little information.

A matter of scale

A related type of perspective is gained by considering issues of scale. We may consider scale in terms of physical size, speed, and complexity. In any situation, if one increases the scale (bigger, faster, more complex), the nature of the system response changes in a consistent manner, and often drastically. Scale must inherently be considered in all aspects of engineering, but also enters into managing an organization, writing software, and doing any type of technical work.

The most obvious type of scale effect is that resulting from changes in size. A mouse and an elephant must inherently be built differently because an elephant with legs proportioned like those of a mouse would not be able to stand without breaking a bone. This is because, in bone, strength is proportional to cross-sectional area, but stresses are proportional to length (due to bending forces) and the mass of the elephant increases as a function of volume. Several other interesting consequences follow from changes in scale, without which elephants would not be successful. First, larger size makes elephants completely safe from predators (except human beings). Large size also increases their life span because of physiological advantages that are not yet well understood. Of particular importance is that the large size of the gut of the elephant makes it possible for them to obtain nutrition from lower quality food because they are able to retain the food for longer and achieve more complete digestion. This is very fortunate because it would not be possible for an elephant to obtain sufficient high quality food (fresh leaves, fruits, seeds, etc.), nor could it nibble at such small items very effectively. Large animals must cover more ground in search of food and water, which makes communication more difficult, but again the elephant's large size provides an advantage. The size of its vocal cords causes the sounds it produces to be very low in pitch and its larger ear bones are better able to hear such low sounds

Scaling relationships make elephants the size of insects and insects the size of elephants impossible.

than ours are. Such low pitched sounds carry much farther, up to several kilometers, compared to high pitched sounds, which helps elephants to stay in touch with each other. A further advantage of size is that a very large animal can have large fat deposits, which can help it to survive hard times. Thus, an elephant can easily go days without food whereas a shrew, with its high metabolic rate, is in danger of starvation in a matter of hours. The scale of the elephant produces a suite of new traits that cause it to live in a world very different from that of a mouse.

We may employ a formal analogy here and compare the elephant to a large corporation and the mouse to a small corner store. The metabolic intake of the corporation is the profit it makes on its products, and a large corporation can afford, just like the elephant, to subsist on low quality "food" (low profit margin items in high volume). The corporation has "fat" deposits (savings, cash, assets) that exceed that of the corner store and can afford to lose money for many months, whereas a sole proprietor might go bankrupt in a very short time. Like an elephant, a large corporation cannot move very fast, but also like an elephant it is much less subject to predators. In the area of communication, the sole proprietor can call all the employees together for a meeting, whereas the corporation must employ slower, more formal means of communication such as memos, manuals, etc. Thus, we can see many similarities that result from similar effects of physical scale.

Physical scale also affects all kinds of manufactured and engineered products, and as such must be considered by any inventor or manufacturer. As an object becomes larger it will always be necessary for it to change its proportions or materials to meet the same goal. As a truck is increased from pickup size to semi-trailer size, the weight exceeds what tires can bear, and the number of axles must be increased. Larger aircraft require different proportions as well as different materials, including far stronger materials and connections, than a single pas-senger 'plane. In manufacturing, problems always crop up when scaling up from the benchtop to full manufacturing. For example, it becomes very difficult to maintain constant conditions in a large vat where fermentation or some other microbial process is going on compared to a beaker-size scale, and failures in large vats are quite common. A grass hut will stand up with almost any type of fastening, but larger structures must be connected in a much more rigid fashion. Issues of physical scale must therefore be considered in any design or manufac-turing process. In addition, consideration of scale can throw light on various types of failure (e.g., of bridges) and on the way in which larger entities (e.g., corporations) operate.

A second type of scale problem involves speed. Any time a process is speeded up, its nature changes in ways that must be taken into account. For example, the mechanism in a video recorder must be more sophisticated than in an audio cassette player to prevent the tape from breaking at the higher speeds involved. On a highway or motorway, exits must be long compared to the right angle turns of urban streets. High throughput systems such as overnight delivery services must operate very precisely and use sophisticated information systems. In general, the consequences of a glitch in a fast system are much worse than in a slow system. A person who stops their car to look at a street sign on a suburban street causes few problems, but stopping on the highway might cause a crash. We may in general say that the higher the throughput (speed) of a system, the more likely that a glitch will cause turbulence. This is a direct analogy with flowing water in a stream, and applies to the flow of paperwork or to the flow of work on an assembly line. If you promise to fix a pair of shoes within a week it does not matter much if an employee is sick, but if you promise reading glasses in an hour it matters very much. The drive for competitiveness in modern corporations seems to be sound, but as it pushes people to ever faster paces there becomes less and less room for human weakness. The person who is out sick for two weeks may be seen as being unresponsive or lazy. There is no room for the person with a good track record who is having a temporary depression (perhaps for good reasons such as grief). There is certainly no room for thinking, daydreaming, being creative, or learning new skills (see Chapter 1). In the long run, it is impossible to perform at a maximal rate month after month and year after year anymore than one can sprint for as long as one can jog, and the consequence is the high rate of "burnout" currently observed among professionals and managers in large corporations. This is also why productivity often returns to previous levels some time after an efficiency expert increases productivity: the rapid pace of the "improved" system may be unsustainable.

Rather than cracking the whip and expecting people to work harder and faster for longer hours, true reengineering seeks out efficiencies in the system itself. In flexible manufacturing (Bylinsky, 1994) the computer shoulders the burden of keeping track of special orders and parts so that workers can concentrate on the productive work of assembly. In many industries, new product cycles have been shortened by bringing together teams from marketing, engineering, design, production, etc., rather than by merely trying to speed up the old sequential system. The changes in system behavior with increased speed and the consequences of slowdowns in fast systems must therefore always be considered in system design.

A further scale factor to consider results from the consequences of increases in complexity. An increase in complexity always increases some type of cost factor. In biology, increased complexity necessitates longer development times (longer gestation and immature stages in higher mammals, for example) and a significant expenditure of energy (the human brain uses a significant portion of the energy we expend). In an organization, complexity of function leads to an increased cost of coordination, commonly manifested in large numbers of meetings, memos, and phone calls. In computer software, complexity leads to an increased risk of "bugs" or of failure to complete the product. In computer hardware, high performance chips are very expensive to design and difficult to manufacture. From Chapter 3 we saw that this principle is general to all types of productions or systems, and in fact that failure risk goes up nonlinearly with complexity. This is why in the end the communist system in the Soviet Union failed: it is not possible to explicitly direct a complex economy from a central bureaucracy. For this reason, self-correcting mechanisms are necessary. The complexity of modern society means that legislatures will always be in the mode of fixing things and tinkering with the laws and will never finish their job. The stability of the American governmental system results from its multiple systems for correcting errors (e.g., the judicial system will void a law that is uninterpretable or unenforceable). Complexly engineered products need many rounds of tinkering to perfect them. Sophisticated scientific theories require a long period of debate and modification before they become finalized. We can in general say that complexity is not free, and may in fact have a very high cost. The benefit of complexity, of course, is that it may enable far more powerful solutions to be achieved, but the potential cost of achieving such a solution should never be forgotten.

A perspective on perspective

We are creatures of habit, and tend to take our environment for granted. If our organization has a cumbersome and slow procurement department, we assume that it is not possible to do it better. If everyone around us is becoming exhausted, we are a little scared but assume it is inevitable. Without perspective, we do not see the larger picture and even miss completely many things that are going on. Why do people build houses next to rivers that flood? Why do businesses act like they have never heard of economic cycles? It is a lack of perspective. Perspective is a key to understanding complex systems, to inventing, to scaling up, to design, to developing fruitful analogies, and to scientific investigations.

9 Analysis: Tools of thought

It is commonly known that success in any profession depends on the possession of both domain-specific knowledge (facts) and domain-specific techniques (tools). For example, a civil engineer must know about building materials, construction regulations, etc., as well as techniques for calculating buckling of columns and other factors. It is generally believed that there is an unbridgeable gulf between disciplines such that a person needs considerable retraining to change professions. While this is true for the domain-specific knowledge component of professional expertise, it is not entirely true for the techniques or tools of problem solving. Many tools of analysis are in fact quite similar across fields. A profession that shows this clearly is applied mathematics, whose practitioners apply their mathematical techniques across many different disciplines. Philosophers also may span many disciplines, but it is more difficult to verify that they do so successfully. Business leaders are similarly often able to successfully run several different types of business. In the arts, some individuals seem able to master multiple media (such as a singer/songwriter/dancer/actor).

The reason that some individuals can exhibit such versatility is that they can carry over their methods of reasoning, of problem solving, and of analysis from one field or problem to another. Even within a field, the creative and innovative professional generalizes across problems, whereas the plodder can only solve problems if they closely match problems whose solution has already been worked out. That is to say, the plodder does not apply much reasoning at all, but uses a cookbook approach. Thus, the successful problem-solving professional, innovator, or artist may be distinguished by the depth and breadth of their analysis or reasoning tools rather than just their mastery of domain knowledge or technical manipulative skills such as how to use a spreadsheet or oil paints.

The tools of successful problem solvers are presented and illustrated in this chapter. These tools include evolutionary refinement, formal analogy, the detective model, classification, scenario generation, web and network analysis, failure analysis, and the use of mental constructs such as cycles and spirals. These tools are all used in multiple domains, though they are not necessarily all universal in their scope. These tools perform multiple roles in the overall problem-solving process. In one sense they capture and formalize what were originally innovative reasoning processes. They thus represent higher-order mental processes or in some ways an automation of complex reasoning steps. In another role, a creative step may involve the recognition that a certain problem may usefully be attacked by using a certain tool. Familiarity with these tools even affects one's perception of the Medawar zone discussed earlier in this book (p. 12), because skill in applying such tools puts otherwise unsolvable problems within reach.

Evolutionary refinement

Biological evolution is a totally blind process that nevertheless builds complexity and marvelous adaptations over time. It does so by a process of incremental change of existing structures combined with ruthless elimination of inadequate designs. A similar approach has utility in certain contexts as a problem-solving strategy.

We may note several properties of the evolutionary process. First, at each stage in the evolution of a species the organisms must be functional. Second, changes are usually incremental. Third, early stages tend to be simpler. Software proto-typing provides an example of this evolutionary approach. The formal approach to software development formally specifies the user requirements and the input and output requirements, and then uses these to formally develop the software structure and algorithms. After this is all done, coding begins. When coding is finished, the software is delivered to the user. However, it often occurs that the final program developed in this way is not really what the user wanted and a massive reworking must be undertaken. An alternative is prototyping. A simple, flexible version of what the user requested is developed. Following feedback from the user, it is improved and tested again in a continuous evolutionary fashion: it starts simple, functions at each stage, and is improved incrementally.

This incremental approach is a very important strategy. A difficulty many people experience is that they think their entire creative product should be created all-of-a-piece. They think they should start the novel on page one or the software with formal specifications or the new product with a schematic. Such an approach is almost guaranteed to lead to writer's block or some type of other mental barrier. An evolutionary approach allows a crude problem solution to grow in refinement and complexity until it is adequate. We will see evolutionary refinement elements in many of the specific techniques presented next.

Formal analogy

Analogy is a very significant problem-solving strategy, but at the same time its importance is often overestimated. For instance, Koestler's (1964) theory of bisociation as the fundamental dynamic of the creative process makes over much of analogy as a central tool of thought. His insights may be most applicable to humor, where surprise caused by combining frames of reference is in fact the heart of the production process, and in modern art where bizarreness caused by merging conceptually remote images is also valued (consider the paintings of Salvador Dali). The combined image of a fish riding a bicycle can be amusing, but does not solve a problem.

It is useful first to clarify the distinction between poetic analogy and formal analogy. Poetic analogy (blowing autumn leaves are like refugees fleeing an oncoming army) is useful in the arts and is clearly related to creativity in such fields. In contrast, in formal analogies the two things being compared actually have fundamental properties or behaviors in common. Poetic analogies are useful in real problem solving only to the extent that they spur the memory to retrieve a tool, fact, or formal analogy that one can apply directly. Free association (lateral thinking) tends to generate mostly poetic analogies and is not terribly useful for practical problem solving.

Formal analogies are central to one's search through memory to retrieve a technique to solve known problem types (Langley and Jones, 1988). For example, many home repair problems involve glue or some other fastener (at least in my house). Analogy helps one to retrieve from memory a case that is similar to the one currently being faced. In a calculus class, the key solution step is recognizing that a problem is similar to one that you have solved before. Once this is recognized, then one knows what types of technique need to be applied. These examples involve first-order analogies that refer one back to directly similar cases in prior experience. Even solvers of routine problems use first-order analogies on a regular basis. Giere (1994) argues that, in science, analogies of this type (problem A is similar to example B) are based on the actual similarity of problem type in terms of the model one would use to solve the problem (e.g., in physics problems). Such analogies are therefore central to finding a method of solution.

We may next make a distinction between close and distant analogies. A close analogy is one where the things being compared have many properties in common. For example, an attacking army may be compared to a pack of wolves without stretching the comparison too far. More distant analogies are the product of primitive cognition (Arieti's (1976) paleologic). Paleologic analogies may share only one or a few features in common. Such a mode of thinking is common in dreams, in children, and in schizophrenics. When distant analogies are believed at face value, this is a symptom of mental illness, such as when a man concludes that, because he is a carpenter, he must be Jesus or that, because it is round like an eye, the moon is a big eye watching him. In the arts, distant analogies provide raw material for symbolic representations, and in this sense are directly useful, even though not to be taken literally. When they are played with, then they can become raw material for innovative thinking. This is because in problem solving one may need to emphasize only a single feature of an object or problem by which it resembles some other object or problem. For falling objects, color, shape, flavor, and texture become irrelevant; the objects are all "the same" (analogous) if their mass is the same. To find these types of similarities one must be willing to consider ways in which things are similar that differ from standard ways of viewing them. It is in this sense that de Bono's "lateral thinking" is useful; it allows distant analogies to be generated rapidly.

Distant analogies are central to innovative problem solving. Distant analogies often point to problem-solving templates that one may be only loosely familiar with. For example, a sociologist might draw the analogy that a revolutionary coup is like a boat flipping over. This analogy is more than poetic because both a government and a boat can exist in one of only two possible states but are unstable in intermediate states. Further, the transition between the two states is very rapid in both cases. This is a useful analogy for the sociologist, because the dynamics of boats are well characterized in engineering. From common experience with boats he or she can recognize an analogy, and then go to the relevant literature (engineering in this case) and learn about formal models that might carry over to the problem of characterizing a coup.

This example also illustrates another benefit of distant analogies. The boat analogy is not perfect, but rather may provide a useful template or starting structure. In this sense, the distant analogy brings the problem solver into the proper domain of related models, within which a search can be directed more efficiently (Giere, 1994). Further work on the initial template may lead to the modification of various details to better solve the goal problem. Nevertheless, a fruitful distant analogy can get one on the right track.

Some other examples of the use of distant analogies further illustrate these points. Earthquakes are critical disaster generators, but are very difficult to study. One cannot, for example, generate an earthquake experimentally. Piles of sand onto which grains are gradually added produce sand avalanches that occur on all scales, from a few grains to a collapse of the pile. The distribution of sand avalanche sizes is similar to the distribution of earthquake sizes, and probably is due to similar reasons related to friction and the dissipation of energy. The analogy between earthquakes and avalanches is more than poetic and suggests methods to study processes (such as earthquakes) that are otherwise hidden underground.

Distant formal analogies increase the breadth of models, tools, and techniques that the problem solver can bring to bear on a problem. That this has more than trivial implications can be seen from the well-established fact that outstandingly creative and productive scientists have particularly broad interests (even outside of science) compared to their more typical peers (Simonton, 1988). After being involved in making the atomic bomb during the war, the physicist Richard Feynman found himself unable to do research (because of mental fatigue from the war effort) until he began playing with models of spinning plates (experimentation performed in the cafeteria with plates spun on the end of his finger). This apparently silly activity was a productive distant analogy because it turned out that spinning plates provided a simple model of some serious phenomena at the atomic level (Feynman, 1984).

Everyone has observed tornadoes, traffic jams, static, and boats flipping over, without necessarily having studied them in any detail. Such real world phenomena may provide useful models for similar processes that occur in business, design, engineering, physics, or any other realm of endeavor. A honeycomb provides a useful design starting place for a strong but light support structure and for optimal packing of objects. Radio static might provide useful ideas for information transmission failure or random walks on the stock market. Within one's specialty there are many case studies or examples that one has read about without having learned all the details. If an analogy can be recognized between the problem at hand and cases or phenomena with which one is familiar (but not an expert on), then one can look up the well-studied cases and use these as a starting point for further work. A facility with distant analogy as a method for quickly identifying relevant models obviates the need to know everything and thus makes the strategic thinker more efficient.

While analogy is a very powerful tool, and one that can produce what appear to be flashes of insight, it is not the only tool that successful strategic thinkers bring to bear. That is to say, a flash of analogy insight is not the whole story. Other tools and techniques are presented next.

The detective model

For certain types of problem the best way to organize information and to solve the problem is to function as a detective. A detective must identify a list of possible suspects, and then compile information on each. A typical analysis looks like Table 2. This tabular analysis points to data needs and may even produce a match that implicates one of the suspects, thus solving the problem directly. One must always keep in mind, of course, that witnesses may be wrong, alibis can be faked, etc.

The detective model is the approach used by the Centers for Disease Control in the USA to identify the unknown source of an illness such as Legionnaire's disease or to trace the origin of a measles outbreak. In the original Legionnaire's disease case, the disease was fairly quickly traced back to the hotel where the Legionnaire's had been having a convention, but isolation of the disease agent proved more difficult. Initial studies implicating smoking in cancer also used this approach.

A particularly interesting example of the detective model involves the tracking down of the causes of Kaposi's sarcoma (KS). This skin cancer is common in AIDS patients and in others with suppressed immune systems. It has been known that KS is common in parts of Africa, but the etiology of the disease was unclear. A detective style approach helped to clarify the nature of this disease. Initially, it was not clear whether KS in Africa was due to a disease (such as HIV) or to some other cause. Mapping the zones of frequent occurrence showed no overlap with HIV

Table 2. *Detective model for problem solving, showing criteria versus suspects*

	Tom	Harvey	George
Motive	Y	N	Y
Alibi	N	N	Y
Opportunity	Y	Y	Y
Physical evidence	N	N	N
Witnesses	N	Y	Y
Criminal record	Y	Y	N

Y, yes; N, no.

incidence, but there is an interesting overlap with regions dominated by volcanic soils (which was a very clever observation on the part of the person who made this connection). Further, KS in these areas differs from KS in AIDS patients. In AIDS, KS results from immune system failure and can occur anywhere on the body. In Africa, KS occurs largely on the lower legs and feet. This restricted occurrence tends to rule out a systemic disease agent (a conclusion confirmed by the lack of overlap with HIV), which presents a real puzzle. A final important clue in this detective story is that the individuals in Africa exhibiting KS are generally poor farmers who farm barefoot (wealthier farmers can afford shoes). Examination of the lymph nodes of these farmers shows that by walking barefoot they get small bits of volcanic pumice under their skin. These pumice bits are mostly trapped in the lymph nodes of the lower leg, but they are persistent and difficult for the body to eliminate. They lead to a local immune suppression that can be demonstrated by comparing white cell activity in the lower leg and in the rest of the body. Thus, KS occurs in the immune suppressed areas of the lower leg and feet. The detective model, by successively eliminating suspects on the basis of facts as they are accumulated, can solve even very puzzling problems. Note that this is also an evolutionary reasoning approach.

Another example of the detective model comes from closer to home. In fact, it involves homes: the search for one, to be precise. When searching for a home, a person generally has a list of criteria: three bedrooms, family room, not too old, fenced yard, etc. These are like the evidence in the criminal investigation, and houses one looks at are the suspects. Certain of these criteria are non-negotiable, such as the number of bedrooms, and a house that fails to fit is eliminated. Others are somewhat "soft," and are subject to compromise. The approach one uses may also be very much like the techniques used to track down a disease. First, one might limit one's search to a given distance from work. Next, one might narrow down to an area where the schools are good. Next, one might identify areas close to shopping, but not too close. Then, one might begin actually inspecting houses for the detailed fit to the given criteria. When the list of suspects is exhausted (there are no homes in your desired price range with three bedrooms that are near a good school) then one or more of the criteria must be modified.

In all of these cases, the detective model involves progressively narrowing down the universe of possible suspects. In the case of Kaposi's sarcoma in Africa, this involved focusing on a geographic area characterized by a particular type of soil, and then narrowing down to a class of people (poor farmers) who did not wear shoes. In the case of house hunting, regions of the city are progressively eliminated and then individual houses looked at. Overall, this is a common and effective problem-solving technique.

Classification

For many problems, a useful strategy (or at least a starting point) is classification (which includes decomposition). One may decompose a population into sub-populations or a process into subprocesses or even causal factors into component factors. We can also sort and lump in different ways. For example, when we break the human population into smokers versus nonsmokers, the lung cancer rate obviously differs. As another example, it is usually found that incidence of various diseases and causes of death differ between men and women.

The ability to make useful class distinctions is a central function of language and shows successive refinement with maturity (Giere, 1994). To a two-year-old,

Classification difficulties. Illustration by Richard Loehle.

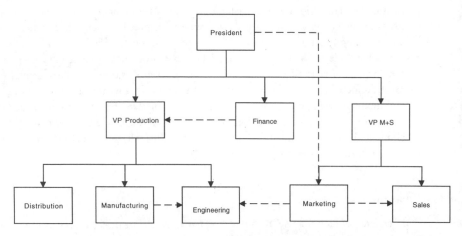

Hierarchy or tree diagram. Vertical solid arrows show lines of authority and are all that an official organization chart shows. Also important are the hidden lines of influence (dotted lines). The president of the company may pass marketing ideas directly to marketing. Marketing may try to influence engineering to develop new products and sales to try certain approaches. Manufacturing may approach engineering with technical problems. Finance may put constraints on production or impose rules. In a large organization these unofficial lines of influence may be extensive.

all animals might be "doggies," whereas an adult recognizes hundreds of kinds of animal. People generally recognize more categories of object in domains that are more important to them. A city dweller might not be able to distinguish different types of weed or grass but knows many types of cut flower and house plant, whereas a farmer distinguishes not only a whole host of weed species but also recognizes varieties of corn and soybean.

For strategic problem solving, the key point is that the solution to a problem may require a re-sorting into different classes. To the concrete-minded person, each object has a name, and that is that. But it may be useful to lump into the class "weeds" not just small plants such as dandelions, but also fast food restaurants and traveling confidence tricksters. For some purposes we might lump together all kitchen items, but for other purposes all electric appliances, both kitchen and otherwise.

A particular type of classification is a hierarchical one, also called a tree diagram. Such a classification has many applications. Hierarchies actually exist in most human organizations, and are manifested as an organizational chart. Tree classifications are used for sorting out which species evolved from which and how they are related (how closely related, how long ago they separated). There are specific mathematical tools for deriving such trees from trait data. We may use a hierarchical classification to store information in a database, of which a library cataloging system is a classic example. We may conceive of a hierarchy of needs, as in psychology, or of tasks, as in planning. Well-structured computer programs have hierarchical features. Hierarchical structures have indeed many uses in describing the real world and also for organizing our work or plans.

When working with organizational hierarchies, it is best to remember that they represent only the lines of authority, but that work may flow or be regulated in an entirely different way. Different departments at the same level may put demands on each other (e.g., marketing, engineering, manufacturing) but not have any official authority to do so. This is a frequent source of poor organizational performance, particularly if disputes between such departments must go very high up the hierarchy before being resolved. Low level individuals in accounting, safety, or procurement may have veto power or signoff authority over actions by individuals at all levels of an organization. It may sometimes happen that an individual can get work done by service components of an organization as though they were subordinate, even though they are not in an organizational sense. There are, therefore, actually two organization charts: the authority chart and the actual influence or control chart. It is the latter that one must learn in order to get things done.

The solution of real world problems frequently involves the decomposition of a process or function into its parts. For example, a dam in an arid region is useful only if it does not lose more water than it saves. Some dams in the western USA were built with the assurance that evaporation would not be excessive and promptly lost millions of gallons into the ground because the lakes were constructed in valleys with sandstone walls. In this case all of the pathways of water loss were not taken into account (a full decomposition was not performed).

The recognition of new categories can resolve paradoxes and solve puzzles in many cases. For example, the terms liberal and conservative seem to have lost their meaning in American politics. Voters are constantly voting in puzzling ways and politicians often do not seem to fit with the party they nominally belong to. A key to this puzzle is that people's attitudes on economic and social issues can vary independently. Some people are conservative on both dimensions (the classic conservative who is against big government, against social spending, etc.), but others may be economic conservatives and social liberals or vice versa. Further, some individuals take an individualistic approach to issues, rather than sticking to a party line. Once these new categories are recognized, the modern political muddle makes more sense (though the media seem to prefer the old, and simpler, two category system).

Classification and decomposition also play a role in the arts. A person with musical skills can distinguish the parts played by different instruments. This is a type of decomposition that is critical to the ability to compose music. In most art, facial features are defined with respect to each other, and are thus not independent. One of the striking things about Picasso's work is that he decomposed facial features into separate units (eyes, nose, mouth, ears) which he treated independently with respect to position, angle, and even emotional tone.

The ability to classify, reclassify, and decompose are related to the use of analogy in a deep way. In usual classifications into say trees versus grasses, we are using some concrete trait (size, form) to classify. In analogy, we are using more distant or surprising traits to classify or notice a similarity. So, if I say that the telephone is a kitchen appliance, it is not because we use it as a pounder to tenderize meat, and on first glance one might not count it as a kitchen appliance. In this analogy the connections that put the telephone into the class of kitchen appliances are less direct and one has to think to find them (e.g., it is used to order pizza, to call a friend for a recipe, to talk on while cooking, to alleviate boredom, etc.). We can say that all analogies involve classifications, but that not all classifications (or decompositions) are analogical.

Classification is similarly at the core of the retrieval of memories in the sense that one often remembers classes as higher level entities or groupings, and that similarly classed things are easy to remember together (e.g., the typical barnyard animals can almost be pictured as a group). Memories are not, of course, filed away by classes like the card catalog in the library, but related things do have stronger associations or linkages in memory.

Some people argue that mental operations are nothing but the recognition of, and operations on, classes. While at a very low level there may be some truth to this, it is like saying that music is nothing but musical notes; such a view does not help to make one a better problem solver in the first case or a better musician in the second. What is particularly useful is to move beyond the concept that categories refer only to objects, such as furniture or foods, and realize that one also uses categories for processes. For example, most people have a concept of oscillation (springs, pendulums) (Giere, 1994), and would not have trouble extending such a concept to the stock market. Giere (1994) argues that hierarchical and radial structures exist in scientific theories (e.g., from the general concept and equation of a pendulum to more specialized cases of multiple connected springs). Realizing that one may classify not just objects but processes, one may explicitly search for models and categories that exhibit similarities, and solutions may be derived from this identification of similarity. For example, growth is a process-based category, of which there are various types, from simple to complex, but all of which have certain features in common. Oscillation, chaos, conflict, and communication are other examples. Classification is not merely about naming things, but may allow one to begin taking steps toward explicit modeling of a phenomenon.

Scenarios

The creation of scenarios is a good problem-solving tool that is particularly useful for planning. A scenario is an ordered sequence of events that either necessarily happen in the stated order, are hypothesized to happen in a certain order, or represent a sequence of events toward a goal. An insect lifecycle (egg to larvae to adult and back to egg) represents a necessary scenario. We must discover it but the insect cannot deviate from it because the stages are developmentally linked. The supposedly regular cycle of the rise and fall of civilizations is a hypothetical scenario. A typical goal scenario is the plan a student makes when he or she goes to college: major in something fun, graduate with honors, make a lot of money after graduation. A scenario is not therefore an arbitrary sequence of events but rather is one that has some causal linkage structure. It has the property of representing a plausible (if not necessarily inevitable) sequence of events. A scenario may also trace out the sequence of consequences resulting from a given action. A dream or goal per se, however, may consist only of the desired end state but lack a picture of the sequence of steps that could lead to the goal. For example, millions of teenagers dream of being rock stars or actors, but do not have any idea about the sequence of steps that would lead to their goal (and usually lack even the concept that steps toward the goal are necessary).

In order to imagine outcomes of our possible plans or to construct scenarios, it is necessary to be able to trace the effects of various actions or possible changes. A well-known example concerns the ramifying effects of the automobile on the family and on the city. The car allowed easier travel to work from a distance, and thereby created the suburbs. It also made dating easier and took teenagers away from parental eyes. It clearly had an effect on breaking up extended families, as well. Let us take a little less widely known example. Can the reader trace out the consequences for China of their language being picture-word based rather than alphabet based? Such a written language is surely harder to learn, since there is no relation between the symbol for a word and the sound of the word, but there are more serious consequences as well. A bigger problem is that such a language lacks an alphabetical order for ordering lists. Without this, it is impossible to have a phone book because there is no way to order the entries; no directory assistance; no Rolodex; no card catalog at the library (actually the Chinese have an indexing system, but it is very awkward); no database of customers. If you go to the hotel front desk and ask if Mr Wu has checked in, they must look through the entire list of guests. No typewriters; only recently have the Chinese developed menu-driven software with which they can select words to go into a document. How do you file personnel records or tax returns? This one change in language makes all the difference and creates ramifying consequences that impede the modernization of China. In contrast, Hebrew and Arabic, which also look strange to Europeans, are alphabet based and have no such problems.

Scenarios are very powerful when they are effectively applied. A business plan is a scenario, as is an ideal career path. Scenarios can also be used to trace out adverse consequences. For example, in a military campaign several different scenarios are usually worked out in advance to cover different circumstances, such as what action to take in the event of a reversal or of bad weather. During World War II, tracing out the scenarios resulting from different methods of

In Chinese your Rolodex is useless because there is no alphabet to order the entries.

countering Hitler's military led to the conclusion that air attacks against industrial targets such as ball bearing plants would be the most effective. This scenario proved to be accurate, and a turning point was reached when German factories were unable to keep up the production of airplanes at the rate they were being destroyed, leading to total air superiority by the Allies.

A problem with the use of scenarios is that merely by being put in this form they may appear to be more certain than they are. Stock market forecasts, for example, are often phrased as though the prognosticator understands the causal factors affecting the market and can trace out their consequences over some months or years. In fact, many such forecasts are not much better than guesses. Scenarios generated by agencies such as the Central Intelligence Agency (CIA) to predict the consequences of certain world events or of United States policy are far less certain than they appear, and may bear no relation to reality in some cases. When the Soviet Union fell apart, no agency had such a scenario as even a remote possibility. Scenarios are often presented by political leaders to rally support for some policy or another, but such scenarios are often vague and not scientifically crafted. In fact, it is more likely that they are 80% wishful thinking or active deception.

Successful use of scenarios results from the confluence of several particular skills. First, the ability to order events in time is crucial (but is by no means universal, as can be seen by observing children and impulsive individuals).

Second, the ability to trace out consequences of actions ("if I study hard, I will get good grades") is essential. Those tending toward magical or wishful thinking do not do well in this area. Third, the ability to envision alternatives is crucial. To reach a given goal played out by a scenario (e.g., go to college) it is useful to envision things that could interfere with this scenario so that they can be guarded against. Some imagination is helpful in this respect.

From this discussion we can see that plans and scenarios are related but are not equivalent. A goal scenario (go to college) can be the spur to development of a plan (save money, take college introductory classes, etc.). A plan can include components to guard against adverse factors that may interfere with a goal scenario (e.g., the creation of backup plans for retreat in a battle). A plan can also lead to the generation of a sequence of steps, but these steps need not be related in the form of a scenario. For example, a plan to construct a factory includes finding a site, arranging financing, purchasing the land, designing the building, etc. Each of these steps does not logically cause the next, as in a battle scenario, and in fact many of the steps can be carried out in any order or in parallel. To take another example, a reorganization scenario is that a reorganization will cause reduced costs and faster customer response, which will lead to increased market share and higher stock prices. This is a (hypothetical) causal sequence. The plan to achieve the reorganization may involve many simultaneous actions as well as some sequential ones.

Given the above, it is possible to see strategic planning in a new light. Strategic planning is merely a subset of strategic thinking in general, which is why it has not been treated until now. Strategic planning is usually goal directed, and as such usually has a goal envisioned as a scenario. A goal without a scenario is usually called a corporate "vision." For the reasons stated above, such "visions" are pure fluff unless they lead to the generation of scenarios and plans to effect those scenarios. Vision statements of this type, floating high above the corporation like fluffy white clouds, actually increase cynicism in the ranks and should be avoided.

Strategic planning can be made much more effective by application of the techniques presented in this book. Many business motivational books have much to say about goals and motivation (in fact these are two of their main topics). If, however, one does not understand the system (markets, society, the engineering and manufacturability of your product, issues of efficiency and brittleness, feedbacks, bottlenecks, etc.), then goals cannot necessarily be reached. The application of the techniques presented in this book should enable one to gain a better understanding of the workings of complex systems so that one can move toward one's goals on the basis of knowledge rather than just enthusiasm. The ability to generate scenarios, including the possible role of adverse factors, is enhanced by the application of the combination of creative idea generation and structured problem solving. The verification of generated scenarios is made easier by the application of the various reality checks discussed in Chapter 4 and the assessment of the overall feasibility of a strategic plan can benefit from the critical path model presented in Chapter 3. For example, a scenario that involves a long sequence of risky or difficult steps can be seen to be highly unlikely to succeed. If these risky steps can be reworked when errors come up (they are iterative-type problems) then the overall risk goes down. An understanding of paradox, contradiction, bottlenecks, issues of scale, and other factors discussed in Chapter 8 can assist one to recognize opportunities, construct scenarios, and make effective (rather than futile) plans to reach desired goals. Thus, the techniques of strategic thinking not only provide assistance at various particular points of the strategic planning process, they also enable the larger picture of strategic planning to be grasped and utilized more effectively.

Solution construction

As part of strategic planning, generation of scenarios, and other problem-solving techniques, one must be able to generate a sequence of steps between where one is now and where one would like to be: this is the difference between the scenario and wishful thinking. Except for cases that are widely known (e.g., the steps involved in going to college), it is not always clear how to generate the step-by-step solution required. There are several specific techniques that may be used.

A very useful approach is to work backwards from the goal. To be a medical doctor, one must have a medical degree. To get a medical degree in the USA one must major in premedical studies, obtain good grades and have a great deal of money to pay for tuition. Working backwards in this way the preconditions for each succeeding step can be determined.

Many problems are not so clearly defined as the go-to-college scenario. That is to say, one cannot always lay out the full series of steps in detail. Consider taking a cross-country trip. It is easy to plan the general route and major areas to stop, but the details cannot be determined from a distance. It is more effective to leave some flexibility in the plan because many details (roads under construction, tourist sites to see) cannot be determined until one is close to a destination. Similarly, one can easily decide to go to college, but the exact courses to take must be contingent on availability, scheduling, success in prior courses, etc.

Sometimes working backwards fails because the obvious set of prerequisites to achieve a goal state are not possible. For example, the obvious requirement determined by working backwards from the goal of owning your own restaurant is to have around $500000 to buy one. The logical conclusion from this working backwards is to give up on the goal as unattainable. Another course of action is to see how one could construct a solution stepwise from the current condition. This might involve first getting a job as a restaurant manager to gain experience and credibility, meanwhile saving as much as possible. Then one might try purchasing a very small restaurant, such as a small delicatessen. This could provide leverage to combine with some other business partners and a bank to secure the necessary financing to purchase the dream restaurant.

Related to stepwise construction is the concept of prototyping. In software design, the concept of structured design seems very orderly and logical: obtain the specifications, lay out the overall design, and then code and test the full software product. In reality, it has turned out that user specifications are rarely clear enough to proceed in this manner. A prototype that demonstrates how the product will look and feel and shows the basic simplified functionality is therefore very useful because it allows rapid feedback before excessive effort has been expended. A prototype in architecture is a sketch of a design; in product design it is the mock-up. Prototypes allow one to proceed by iterative refinement from a coarse idea to a more detailed finished product with minimal chance of being on the wrong track.

What if?

Related to the scenario is the "What if?" method of analysis. In the What if? approach, you change a rule or law of operation and trace out the consequences. In the random rule change case, one just gets silly stuff that children like to make up (What if pigs had wings?). In a more sophisticated vein, impossible (or improbable) What ifs provide a basis for science fiction stories (e.g., What if we lived forever? What if some people could read minds? What if robots revolted?). Humor is profitably obtained by What if? changes in the normal rules. What if a man got pregnant? has been the basis for several movies. What if one combines sports (e.g., luge and bowling)? has been the basis for some funny commercials for beer. What ifs also provide a basis for serious problem solving. What if trains could fly? This sounds absurd, but is the basis for maglev trains. The metal wheels

A flying train is a silly idea . . . unless it becomes a maglev train! Illustration by Richard Loehle.

of a train produce terrible friction, much worse than rubber tires on a road. This friction and consequent heating and wear on the wheels limits train speed, increases fuel costs, and causes high maintenance costs for track and wheels. A maglev train eliminates this friction. Once the cost of raising the train off the ground by a magnetic field is considered, the additional cost of making it go faster is small. Thus, the silly concept of flying trains actually has led to a product. One must ask an additional question about maglev trains: what if the power fails? This is not a trivial consideration, because then one is dropping a speeding train at least a small distance. Tests of maglev trains dropped on their rubber wheels at high speed have shown problems with the tires catching fire (as of 1994). So What if? is valuable for trouble shooting as well.

Other innovations can be obtained from What ifs. One may ask what would happen to the laws of Euclid if parallel lines meet eventually instead of staying the same distance apart. The result of this change in the rules is a system of geometry (geodesy) where two lines that are parallel at the equator meet at the poles. By asking what happens if space itself is curved, one gets the curved space–time graph of Einstein. We saw above that pigs with wings is silly, but maybe bacteria that produce human insulin are not so silly.

What ifs have been instrumental in the development of new consumer products. Overnight delivery services were founded on a What if? that at the time seemed ludicrous. What if you could take your phone with you? This sounded silly in 1960, but today one may hear a phone ring from a purse or a briefcase almost anywhere. What if you could watch more than one channel at once on television? This is now available. What if you didn't have to wait for your beefburgers? Changing this one rule of restaurant operation (that cooking of food starts after the order is placed) created a whole new industry and saved people huge amounts of time.

While changing rules arbitrarily is only useful in the domains of humor and art, selective changes in the rules can lead to whole new sciences, technologies, and products. The key is to trace out carefully the implications of a change in the rules. In social engineering, legislators are often playing What if?, but their basis for making projections is rather fuzzy. It may be asserted that reducing capital gains taxation will increase investments, but one does not know for sure. One can't make a prototype. "Three strikes and you're out" prison sentencing similarly is based on an assertion of the effect of changing the rules, but without any firm guarantee. We often find out What if? only long after such a change is made.

A subset of What if? analysis is the playing of the devil's advocate. There is a strong tendency when doing any planning to assume that the best outcome will occur. In a business plan this temptation is quite strong, because otherwise investors might not be interested. It is very important to counter this tendency with a series of negative What ifs. We should always ask "What if there is a disaster?" This would point out the need for fire insurance, for a backup line of credit to get the business open quickly again, etc. We should ask "What if the

Some "What ifs" are fanciful.

product we plan to make turns out to be a stinker? What if the economy hits the skids? What if I try medical school but find out I faint at the sight of blood?" This line of reasoning leads us logically to the technique of failure analysis.

Failure analysis

It might seem paradoxical that a way to achieve success is to look for failure, but such is indeed the case. It is characteristic of a successful technical product that it does not fall down, blow up, catch fire, turn out to be incoherent, short out, or lead to lawsuits. A considerable portion of the expertise of the civil engineer is dedicated to verifying that his or her structures will remain standing. Such verification is achieved by understanding possible failure modes and demonstrating that they have been reasonably guarded against. For example, earthquakes exert several types of stress on buildings, including shaking and swaying of the upper floors. Observations of modes of building failure have led to specific construction practices to prevent these types of failure.

In general, the solution to a problem or the creation of any device, product, plan or system should include as an integral part the analysis of possible modes of failure, their likelihood, and possible means of overcoming or preventing such failures. Volvo is famous for their investigation of accidents and the consequent design of impact-resistant cars. In Japan, large sums have been spent to earthquake-proof buildings. In battle, possible modes of failure include a break in the line, insufficient munitions, being circled and attacked from the rear, and panic among the troops. These sources of failure are guarded against, respectively, by secondary lines of defense, good logistical operations, tactics and intelligence, and troop discipline and training. No army has long survived that ignored modes of failure.

It is useful to distinguish different modes of failure. A *brittle* system is one that fails abruptly outside its range of tolerance. For example, a tree snaps off when the wind exceeds a certain level. A *robust* system, in contrast, can continue to function under a range of conditions. For example, the B-17 Flying Fortress was able to return from bombing missions in World War II in spite of being shot up and having pieces of wings missing. It is questionable whether modern high performance jets are robust in this sense. In a software system, graphical user interfaces and error trapping can enhance robustness.

Another important feature is whether failure is incremental (graceful) or catastrophic. An army that is losing a battle should be able to retreat in an orderly way. This characterized the Roman legions, for example, as opposed to many of the armies they fought which lacked discipline and would scatter if bested or if their leader was killed. In fact, the Romans had a specific, highly ordered defense, the turtle, that they would implement if outnumbered or losing. With this defense the men closed ranks in small groups and presented a wall of shields with protruding spears. In this defensive posture they could regroup or retreat. A

The B-17 Flying Fortress was robustly designed. Illustration by Richard Loehle.

characteristic of modern economies compared to less developed economies is that modern economies have many mechanisms that make economic downturns more gradual and less catastrophic (savings accounts, lines of credit, unemployment insurance, etc.).

Several factors can contribute to robustness or grace under pressure. Distributed information systems can allow for incremental failure modes. For example, in World War II, American soldiers were briefed about a mission as an entire unit. This meant that if officers were killed (as was common on D-day), the next ranking soldier could take over, even if conditions changed. In contrast, the German and Japanese militaries were much more hierarchical, and only officers were trusted with mission information. When experiencing success, their armies were highly effective, but when pressed by Allied attack and under shifting battle conditions, their system caused heavy casualties and contributed to their defeat.

Another factor promoting robustness is feedback in the system. This is discussed in more detail in Section 10.3, but it is touched on briefly here. Feedback can provide information that leads to an adjustment in response to a change in conditions. Feedback that is weak or delayed can lead to a response that is too late, which may be catastrophic. In the American Civil War, the South's missing cavalry at the battle of Gettysburg is an example of this. General Lee had intended to withdraw from engagement unless the ground was of his own choosing, but at the crucial moment when his army encountered the Union troops, his cavalry was nowhere in sight, so he could not tell whether he was facing the entire Union army or just a small force. The result was a disaster for the South. Lags in feedback can contribute to industrial cycles when businesses expand without realizing that market saturation has already occurred. Feedback that is timely can help to prevent overshoot behavior. Effective feedback has been crucial in reducing inventory swings and overordering, which thereby reduces inventory carrying costs.

Analysis of failure should extend to consumer products. Such an analysis would both lead to well-designed products and allow anticipation of likely consumer complaints. Old-fashioned telephones were well designed with respect to a common likely failure mode: being dropped. In contrast, one is well advised not to drop many modern phones. Another consumer example is hair dryers. A likely failure mode for hair dryers involves dropping them into water while they are switched on. This type of event not only destroys the hair dryer, but can lead to electrocution. As a consequence (not necessarily of forward-looking failure analysis but more likely due to lawsuits) some of the better models are beginning to feature ground fault interrupt circuits (though one is still advised to keep them out of the bath). A common failure mode for a toaster is for toast to get stuck, which can cause a fire in a poorly designed model. In the mad dash to get new consumer products to market, there is a decreased tendency to check for modes of failure, even though doing so can increase consumer satisfaction, reduce returns of defective items, and reduce liability exposure.

Finally, it is noteworthy that an understanding of failure may directly solve a problem. For example, the key to understanding the operation of the AIDS virus (and consequent symptomology) was figuring out how it could cause the immune system to completely fail. Many historians have pondered the fall of the Roman Empire, which always seemed to have tremendous significance. This mega-failure has been blamed on internal corruption and other political factors, but may have been largely the result of climatic changes (drying) in North Africa and the Mediterranean region, which put pressure on the Romans' agricultural production, along with huge increases in the populations of surrounding regions such as northern Europe.

One may even observe a role for failure in the arts. It is often the case that a new musical or artistic style is a reaction to a perceived failure or deficiency in an existing style. Perceptions that realism is incapable of representing certain emotions or concepts, and that it was too confined in terms of the universe of possible visual patterns contributed to the rise of modern art. Physical failure of certain arts media to persist over time due to flaking, fading, sagging canvas, etc. has influenced how artists paint. Perceived failures in public buildings (e.g, spaces not to human scale, funneling of winds into passageways by structures, poor use of light) have influenced design in many ways.

Overall, failure analysis is an integral part of problem solving, while being at the same time a specific tool for organizing information. Failure analysis can be a useful type of reality check, as well, by helping one to take off the rose colored glasses and look specifically for what might make a product or system fail. The inventor often begins with a perception of where a product fails, and then seeks to alleviate this failure. Political opponents are motivated to probe for policy failures (though not necessarily to treat them honestly). Failure analysis has therefore multiple uses and implications in strategic problem solving.

Cycles and spirals

A useful structure for organizing information or events, particularly events that occur over time, is to use some variation on the cycle, including the spiral. In a business such as farming that is inherently tied in to the annual cycle of the seasons, planning, including financial planning, is based on this cycle. Many other cycles exist that can help one to organize information and anticipate future changes. In business, it is widely known that there are underlying cycles of prosperity and recession. It is even known that some industries are more susceptible to such cycles (e.g., steel, cars, paper). In spite of this, banks commonly loan money as though downturns cannot occur. Many business plans assume either that current conditions will continue or that things will have an upward trend. Far fewer business failures would occur (particularly in banking) if planning were based on a recognition that the economy is cyclic.

Another natural and well-known cycle is that of the establishment, aging, and renewal of neighborhoods. As homes age, they naturally require more upkeep. Expensive homes are usually not only better built, but are more worth maintaining. Lower income homes are more likely to decay into slum status. A complete cycle involves renewal of such decayed areas, which may occur by "yuppie-fication" (the moving in of the young and upwardly mobile), bulldozing, or conversion to industrial or highway sites. In ancient times, by contrast, fire frequently performed this renewal function. Rome, for example, burned on a fairly regular basis (Boorstin, 1992). In other ancient cities, it was easy to tear down old houses because of their small size and simple construction. The problem of slums in modern times may be at least partly a result from the higher cost of tearing down old housing.

It is very useful to think and plan in terms of cycles in many other areas as well. The growth of infants is loosely periodic, and therefore so are their appetites (which drives parents to distraction). Manic depression is cyclic over months or years. An individual's level of alertness varies in a cyclic way over the day. Awareness of such cycles can assist in scheduling tasks for the most appropriate part of the day. Tasks such as jogging and doing arithmetic all have optimal times. For many people, the natural cycle includes a nap after lunch, which is therefore a bad time to schedule a class if one is a student or to arrange a seminar in which the lights will be turned down. Coffee is often used to fight these natural physiological cycles, but it is perhaps better to take them into account and use them to enhance productivity (i.e., do intellectual tasks when most alert, run errands and make phone calls when sleepy) rather than to fight them.

The spiral is a thought construct that is also useful. We may visualize the spiral as like the swirl of water running down the drain. The spiral is commonly used to describe the course of alcoholism, and the down-the-drain quality is explicitly carried over. In this context, the spiraling (circular motion) represents the fact that the alcoholic is usually not uniformly drunk, but rather tends to cycle in and out of severe episodes. The downward direction represents the self-amplifying destructive trend overlaid on this cycle. During drunken episodes, the alcoholic misses work, which creates stress at work and at home, alienates family and friends, and damages his or her health. As these problems accrue, they amplify worry and depression, which leads to further drinking. The spiral narrows as drinking becomes less episodic and more continuous. The alcoholic spiral really does resemble water running down a drain. This is a classic case of runaway positive feedback, which is discussed in Section 10.3.

A spiral structure may also be discerned in the process of economic development. On top of the ups and downs of a developing economy (the loops in the spiral), successful development leads to increases in productivity, infrastructure, and education that lift overall levels of wealth. There is also a tendency for boom and bust business cycles to become less pronounced over time. This structure is thus like an upsidedown bathtub spiral. Spiral structures may also be usefully

The spiral usefully depicts the downward slide of the alcoholic.

applied to describing the maturation of a good marriage and other phenomena. Overall, cycles and spirals provide useful constructs or templates for understanding phenomena and for problem solving.

Transformations

A useful mental construct is the transformation. A transformation converts one type of thing into another type. For example, raw materials (A) enter a factory and are transformed into finished products (B), symbolized by the following:

$$A \Rightarrow B$$

Upon marriage, a single person is transformed into a married person. Upon purchase, a new house becomes a home. A transformation is generally a discrete change in state and represents a qualitatively different condition. A person can become single again by divorce, but will never be the same in legal status or in behavior as a never-married person. Note that a second transformation is required (divorce) to undo the state attained by marriage. To convert a bottle back into a raw material, a transformation via grinding is necessary.

Transformations are useful for recognizing how one enters different states. In many cultures, the transformation from youth to adult has been heralded by a rite or ceremony. This was a discrete transformation, with the new adult being expected to act as an adult in distinct ways. In contrast, in modern cultures this transformation tends to be very gradual, with obtaining a driver's license and leaving school being two of the few milestones that are widely recognized. In the absence of a clear and discrete transformation step, many young people in fact have difficulty making the transition to adulthood, and may continue to exhibit juvenile traits (irresponsibility, lack of commitment, financial dependency) well into their late twenties.

Transformation is also the key to reaching goals. If it is decided that a matrix organization (one with multiple cross-departmental lines of communication and teaming) will be better than the current hierarchical organization, it is not sufficient to proclaim that this is the goal. One must design a transformation that will convert the current organization into the desired one. Failure to specify an efficient transformation will lead to chaos and low morale, as well as reduced productivity, and even to the eventual abandonment of the goal. It is often the case that it may even be easier to start from scratch than to transform an existing organization into a new form.

Let us consider transformations involving private versus state ownership of enterprises. When a nation decides to nationalize an industry such as the railroads, it generally purchases it and makes it part of the government. This transformation (which may or may not be a good idea) is in some cases easily reversed by merely putting the enterprise up for sale if the enterprise has been run as a fairly independent entity and not overly bureaucratized. If, however, the state owns almost everything, as in the former Soviet Union, then the reverse transformation is very difficult because the state owns most of the capital so that there is no large pool of money available for making purchases of the enterprises for sale, nor businesses to act as agents or purchasers. That is to say, the bulk of assets are not liquid and are in fact owned by the seller. The first step in such a transformation must be the distribution of state-owned assets of ownership to make them liquid, which is what happened in Poland in the 1980s.

We generally think of transformations as reversible, though perhaps with difficulty (marriage is reversed by divorce), but there are many domains where this is not so. For example, the transformation called extinction is irreversible. Once a high crime slum is created, it is very difficult to undo. Once pollution is widely dispersed (e.g., as during the Chernobyl disaster) it is impossible to retrieve.

It is useful to recognize transformations because following a transformation a qualitatively different structure is created, i.e., a transformation does not just result in an incremental, additive change but in a structural change. A condemned house has an abruptly different utility. A prison sentence produces an irreversible change in one's future opportunities. A corporation must behave very differently from a sole proprietorship. Being deep in debt is a qualitatively different state in which one is in danger of losing one's house. The utility of the transformation model is also in the recognition of the nature of the transformations that produce a given change. Understanding transformations can enable one to utilize these transformations for achieving one's goals, or to avoid the occurrence of undesirable transformations.

Nets and webs

When we are faced with multiple factors in a problem context, it is particularly important that we possess tools for relating these factors. In the absence of such tools, there is a tendency to focus on single factors (Stanovich, 1992). For example, slums may be blamed on prejudice alone, when in fact slums have existed (and do exist) in racially uniform societies. However, merely making a list of factors that are related to a given problem is more likely to cause frustration than to lead quickly to a solution. Network and web diagrams and constructs provide powerful tools for dealing with such complex systems. We may consider as a simple case a spoke diagram. In this diagram, the item being affected is at the center and the factors impinging on it radiate out as spokes. This might apply to the factors impinging on an individual's health, each being independent and focusing on the individual.

When there are multiple entities involved, a web diagram can be used. In this diagram, the different entities or variables are connected by arrows showing what affects what. This can be used to illustrate the multiple interactions in an economy or social system. A similar diagram, a loop analysis, focuses on the elucidation of feedback loops (discussed in Section 10.3). For instance, if economic development enhances educational opportunities in a country, which in turn enhances

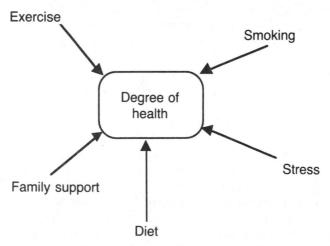

Spoke diagram illustrating influences that converge at a focal point.

economic development, this would be a positive feedback loop. Economic development could simultaneously reduce the birth rate (a negative feedback loop) which would increase the chances of success for each child (a positive feedback), and so on. Each of these factors can be diagrammed with arrows with pluses and minuses to show their effects and interactions. Such a diagram is a powerful tool for understanding the causal structure of a system. In the face of multiple loops, it is often the case that the timing and magnitude of the feedbacks determines the ultimate level and relative prominence of the different loops. In such a case, it may be necessary to resort to explicit calculations to determine the outcome, often using simulation. Computer simulation is a powerful tool for analyzing such complex interactions, although care must be taken because of the simplifying assumptions that are often introduced.

Workers and their tools: Summary

One of the chief characteristics of experienced craftspeople is that they know their tools, what they are capable of, when to use them, and how to get maximum performance from them. While no one doubts this for hand tools or for the artist, the role of tools in conceptual work seems completely overlooked. In school, for the most part only subject-specific analysis tools (how to do a return on investment calculation) are taught. Of far more importance for strategic thinking is the mastery of general tools of thought and analysis. In this chapter general constructs were discussed for organizing information, for tracing causation, for classifying, and for generating analogies. In Chapter 10, further tools and techniques are described in the context of general principles of system organization.

10 Solutions: Getting a grip

If, in a rural corner of the world, we observe a small boy leading a large ox or water buffalo, we may wonder at his fearlessness. Closer examination, however, may reveal a rope passing through a ring in the animal's nose. This is an example of getting a grip on the problem (in this case, literally). The boy has found an effective control point for the system.

The strategic problem solver also seeks to get a grip on the system, either to learn more about it or to manipulate and control it. It is not very useful simply to know trivia about a system if one cannot use these facts to some end. On the contrary, if one understands the key aspects of a problem such that one can solve the puzzle or manipulate the system, then the details are perhaps not so important. There are certain key dimensions of system behavior that are indicative of control points. For example, a tradeoff highlights a constraint and is inherently a control point for determining outcomes. A bottleneck is a control point governing throughput and is a critical point for system control. Information flow can also be manipulated to control a system. The feedback structure of a system can point to effective control strategies as well as illuminating fruitless ones. This section addresses these aspects of the overall process of problem finding and problem analysis, discussed above, and problem solution.

10.1 CONSTRAINTS AND TRADEOFFS

A very effective strategy for controlling a system or solving a problem is to look for constraints. Constraints feature prominently in any design problem, such as inventing a new device or improving a product such as a computer. They are also central to understanding how things work, whether it is an economic system, a medical problem, or a social dysfunction. Tradeoffs are the usual consequence of constraints. A tradeoff occurs when one can have more of something only by giving up something else. Tradeoffs are not always obvious, and in their personal lives people often fool themselves that they can have it all, that there are no tradeoffs. An understanding of the constraints operative in any given setting provides a powerful tool for analysis. It can prevent one from wasting time trying to create something that cannot exist or do something that is impossible. For complex problems, the constraints operative in a system can provide real insight into how the system works, where it has weak points, and even may explain its dynamic behaviors.

The way in which constraints are typically overcome is either with information or with new technology. Information, by allowing one to organize, track, and sequence objects and actions, can help one to overcome many constraints. Information itself, of course, has a cost, and can therefore also act as a constraint, a factor we will also explore. New technology may incorporate information, such as in computer-controlled fuel injection in cars, or may result from the substitution of new materials or processes (which of course is also the result of new information produced by experimentation). In the sections that follow, the role of constraints in different domains is explored in the context of the roles of information and new technology in overcoming these constraints. This interplay applies generally to all types of innovation, discovery, and problem solving.

Technological constraints and tradeoffs

Nothing illustrates the role of constraints and tradeoffs as much as technical innovation in industrial design. We observe repeatedly that improvement of some product or device continues until some constraint is reached that causes further innovation to become increasingly difficult, at which point a new technology is needed to allow further improvements. New technology is inherently also about information. It is useful to explore several examples here.

When it became clear in the late 1970s that the days of cheap fuel were over, there was a push toward (and legislation mandating) better fuel economy for cars. For many people, smaller cars provided a quick answer, but many vehicles must be larger to fulfill their purpose, such as family cars, utility trucks, pickups, vans, and limousines. For these vehicles, high fuel prices were deadly. The process of change in the quest for better mileage from fuel is instructive for what it shows about constraints and technology. At the time, some automobile industry representatives claimed that not much improvement in mileage was possible because of limits in the energy contained in the fuel, but it has turned out that a whole series of improvements (DeCicco and Ross, 1994) has led to substantial improvement. One of the most obvious ways to improve mileage was to reduce the weight of the car (besides just building a small car). Older models featured heavy frames, thick sheet metal exteriors, huge engines, and heavy interior construction. A considerable improvement in mileage was realized by reducing the excessive robustness of the body and frame. After a certain point, however, a constraint was reached because the body became too fragile to support ordinary use and to protect the passenger. Other sources of savings were necessary. The use of novel lightweight materials for bumpers represented an application of new technology that produced substantial weight reductions. Improvements in mileage at the point of combustion were also sought. Traditional carburetors did not allow for much improvement in mileage, but a new technology based on information, the computer-controlled ignition system, did lead to substantial savings. Thus, the modern car incorporates several information-processing systems and high tech materials. To obtain further savings, it was clear that engine weight needed to be reduced, but the use of aluminum blocks was not entirely satisfactory due to their tendency to warp at high temperatures. A potential solution to this that is currently being explored is the use of ceramic and ceramic/metal combinations for the engine, which represents the use of a novel material. It has also been found that new types of tires improve fuel mileage, as well as lasting longer. The combined result of all of these innovations is cars that routinely get over 10.5 kilometers per litre (30 miles per gallon), and sometimes over 14 kilometers per litre (40 miles per gallon), figures that were regarded as impossible two decades ago. In the process of achieving these results, a number of constraints due to materials or technology had to be overcome by substituting materials, by introducing new technologies, and by utilizing information-processing capabilities (in the ignition system). This entire process of innovation hinged on recognizing successive constraints and realizing that they could be overcome.

Computer technology provides another excellent example of the problem of constraints. For certain types of problem, speed is essential. For example, it will not suffice to take three weeks to run a computer algorithm to predict tomorrow's weather. Straightforward improvements in computers have led to a steady increase in central processor unit (CPU) speed, but for the truly large problems special purpose computers have traditionally been used, the so-called super-computers, such as those produced by Cray Research in Minnesota. These computers are very sophisticated and complicated. In particular, the CPU, which does the actual number crunching, is very complicated, which makes its design difficult and expensive. Manufacturing such complicated devices has also been expensive, with quality control being critical. In spite of improvements in this technology with each passing year, the expense prevented these machines from becoming accessible to most users. There were in fact constraints in this problem that most people did not recognize. The result of these constraints was that foreseeable increases in CPU speed did not seem likely to be adequate for the new demands being put on computers. A completely new technology was therefore developed that did not depend on superfast CPUs – the massively parallel computer. It was noticed that most of the problems for which supercomputers were being used involved the repetition of the same computations for multiple sets of data. For example, in weather forecasting, the same computations are performed at thousands of points in space, and then repeated at the next time interval. For fluid dynamics problems, a grid of points defines where the flow of fluid must be computed. In parallel computing, many of these spatial points are fed to a grid of CPUs simultaneously and the set of computations is performed on them all at once (up to hundreds or thousands at a time). In this type of computer, the individual CPUs need not be complicated, and in fact need not even be blindingly fast. Their sheer numbers mean that even reasonably fast processors (which can be manufactured quite cheaply) can perform computations on large data sets at a speed comparable to that of a supercomputer, but at an overall cost that is much less. Clearly, in this case the constraints due to the bottleneck at the CPU were much more efficiently solved by using a totally different approach than by simply pushing the limits of silicon and miniaturization.

Biological constraints and tradeoffs

In biology, constraints are central to the design of organisms, although this fact has taken many years to uncover. Because organisms cannot change their shape at will, there are necessary tradeoffs that cause an organism that is good at solving one problem to be bad at other problems. For example, the hollow stem of many weeds allows them to grow fast (cheap construction), but it does not permit them to become the size of trees because of insufficient strength. The chitinous exoskeleton of insects provides strength and protection, but at larger sizes (such as that of a horse) the weight would be prohibitive, transmission of oxygen via diffusion would not be adequate, the internal attachment of muscles would be problematic, etc. Thus, the huge organisms so popular in horror movies, such as giant spiders, can be clearly seen to be ludicrous because they violate physical constraints.

For other examples, we can examine the form an animal takes. The optimal foot for running is either padded or hoofed. Such a foot cannot be used for grasping and is not very good for digging or swimming. To be efficient at digesting grass, ruminants must have very large digestive systems, which limits how small they can be. In this way the physical form of an animal constrains what it is good at, where it can live, and how it can obtain food.

Humans must endure such constraints as well. For example, in track and field sports competition, it has been found that the same individual can only rarely be competitive in both sprinting and distance events. This results from the fact that there are two types of muscle fiber, long and short. The short fibers have a quick response and are good for explosive action such as sprinting or boxing punches but they tire quickly. The long fibers can not respond as quickly but have much greater endurance. When a runner trains for long distance races, the long fibers develop preferentially. With a sprinter the converse occurs. To be best at a particular type of race, short or long, one needs the most of the short or long fibers, respectively, and it is impossible to maximize both at the same time. Other constraints exist as well. For example, the type of response that allows us to respond to emergencies (the fight or flight response) is damaging to the body if maintained constantly. Thus, the hard-driving person who seems to be getting so much done is not doing so without a cost.

We can see the role of "technology" in the way in which different metabolic systems or the construction of different biological structures has played an important role in the evolution of life. For example, early ocean creatures were soft bodied or had external shells or bony structures. When bony fish evolved, they quickly became dominant. When woody plants evolved, they quickly dominated the earlier ferns and soft stemmed plants. New structures that evolve such as shells, bony skeletons, jaws, or woody stems may be compared to new technologies that humans invent, with similar consequences.

Information also plays a very significant role. All life forms respond in some way to information by pursuing food, avoiding predators, seeking shelter, etc. But in particular, there are many cases where organisms use information to circumvent the limitations inherent in the physical structures of the organism. As a simple case, many plants respond to weather information that indicates the coming of freezing temperatures or drought by becoming temporarily inactive (dropping their leaves, etc.). Plants are typically also plastic in their growth responses, and will slow down their growth if resources are limited in order to persist with the resources available. This ability is what accounts for the existence of bonsai plants. If animals had this capability, then we would see elephants the size of dogs in adverse habitats, but we do not, though reptiles and fish are somewhat plastic in their growth. Plants can even adapt their morphology. In many species, the leaves produced in the shade on the lower branches are more adapted to shaded conditions (thin, unlobed) whereas those produced in full sun are shaped differently (thicker, deeply lobed). In this way information is used to adjust the morphology of the plant to enable it to survive in a wider range of conditions.

Economic constraints and tradeoffs

In any economic system there are constraints and tradeoffs. Failure to remember this is a constant source of comfort to confidence tricksters and get-rich-quick schemers. One of the most fundamental is the tradeoff between risk and yield for investments. Stock market investors are often encouraged to take on more risk to get a higher yield. If the person plans to hold on to an investment for 20 years, this may be good advice, but otherwise "more risk" may mean in practice that their life savings could drop in value by 30%. When put in these terms many people are not willing to take any risk at all, and prefer an insured financial instrument such as a treasury bill or government savings bond.

A second economic constraint is that every action has a cost. This is an unhappy constraint for many people. The cost of meetings is rarely counted, for example, but can be quite high. New government rules and regulations (animal welfare, human subjects, accounting, safety, nondiscrimination) have caused, over the last few decades, a doubling of the percentage of university staff devoted to generating the paperwork required to document compliance. This has increased overhead costs on grants, which has caused other government agencies (those providing research grants) to complain about excessive overheads. The same thing has occurred in the case of unfunded federal mandates in the USA (rules from the national government that cause expenses at the state or local level, with no funds provided to comply with these rules), such as many environmental regulations. In each case, no accounting has been made of the costs of the requirements and whether the benefit justifies the cost. If personal life followed the same stringent requirements as dictated by the United States Occupational Safety and Health Administration (OSHA) and the Environmental Protection Agency (EPA) in the USA or the Health and Safety Executive in the UK, one would need to don a space suit to use ammonia floor cleaner or paint a bedroom, and all sports would be banned as too dangerous. Gilbert (1978) brilliantly characterizes the nature of the problem: the focus has been on regulating behavior and documenting behavior rather than on regulating outcomes. Regulating behavior always has a very high cost because one must be able to document compliance at the level of hundreds of individual actions. Regulating outcomes does not necessarily have a high cost and only aggregate statistics (e.g., injury rates) need be compiled. For example, OSHA regulates safety railing height, ladder construction, training requirements for ladder use, and a thousand other minutia, and compliance must be documented, even for factories that are inherently safe or that have a well-trained and careful workforce. The outcome (lack of injuries) is what is important, not the record keeping. Good outcomes are not necessarily expensive whereas mandated record keeping has proven to be very expensive. From 1988 to 1994, new United States Department of Energy (DOE) orders for safety accountability led to more than a doubling of safety department budgets at the DOE national laboratories (not counting huge expenditures for increased personnel training and safety meetings) with no improvement in actual safety (accidents and radiation exposure), according to the Galvin Commission Report to the DOE (February 1995).

The general tendency when faced with an economic constraint is either to spend someone else's money, or to gloss over the hidden costs. In the examples above, regulators were shown spending other people's money. In a corporate reorganization or downsizing, the costs of disruption and lowered morale do not appear as columns in the accounting ledger and are thus often ignored. When shopping, most people do not take into account fuel, car mileage, and the cost of eating lunch out in the savings resulting from going all over town to save $10 on a dress or bowling ball. Because it is a necessary constraint, it is useful to ask how much any action really costs and to be suspicious when someone acts as though an action is free.

Personal living constraints and tradeoffs

In personal living there are also constraints and tradeoffs that must be recognized. For example, because there are a limited number of hours in the day, people who try to "have it all" (a high powered job, a family, housework, hobbies, recreation, gourmet cooking, sports) find that they are exhausted all the time, and in fact are not giving fully in one or more areas (ignoring the children or spouse, for example, or skimping on sleep and therefore cheating their future health). Only the individual with extreme physical stamina can endure such a schedule. The same is true of the entrepreneur who puts in 70 hours per week at work on a regular basis. People make up all kinds of rationalizations to cover the gaps in their obligations, such as the myth of "quality time" and using smoking to help them cope with nervousness.

In other areas of life also there are such tradeoffs. In romance one can have a number of casual dates or one can develop an intense relationship, but one cannot do both at the same time. When driving, going too fast is dangerous, but exceedingly cautious drivers also are dangerous because they do not act decisively. In the realm of careers, those who try to keep their options open too long end up without any marketable skill.

Unwillingness to recognize that such tradeoffs exist is a constant source of problems for people. A woman falls in love with an extroverted, athletic man and then resents the fact that he loves to be away from the house playing sports and that he is not sensitive and responsive. A young couple will buy a huge house while both are working, and then when they start a family they will lament that they "have to" put the child in day care so the wife can work. When house hunting, people often want a combination of features that does not exist, such as a suburban style yard or garden and neighborhood near the centre of town. Politicians hate to admit tradeoffs and typically end up "having it all" by borrowing and making the deficit larger. The simple reason for this is that each member of Congress sees the tradeoffs differently. One is willing to trade a smaller military for more education, another is willing to reduce entitlements in exchange for more medical research, but no one is in charge who can make them agree on what is being traded off for what; thus, the default tradeoff is against the future by borrowing.

Although the opportunities are not as great as in technological innovation, in personal living also new technologies and information can help to overcome constraints. For example, as much as personal organizers and being penciled in on the calendar are laughed about, being organized (utilizing information) can help to reduce the chaos inherent in a busy schedule. Information on nutrition and vitamins can help one to maintain stamina. Information technologies such as car phones, answering machines, etc., can help in this area as well. New technologies help one to circumvent scheduling problems. For example, with a video recorder one can tape a television show when one is busy and then watch it when one is free. This overcomes the constraint that one cannot be in more than one place at one time. Answering machines perform this same function (though they only annoy your friends if you don't reply to a message). Portable computers help to make otherwise wasted time on an airplane into useful time, thereby helping to overcome the hours-in-a-day constraint. And so on. We can see that strategic thinking applies directly in everyday life just as it does in one's profession.

Summary

There are always constraints and tradeoffs in any problem or system. Ignoring them is called wishful thinking. Strategic thinking requires a clear awareness of constraints. New processes, systems, materials, or information may allow constraints to be overcome, as in the fuel mileage example. Awareness of constraints can tip one off to efforts to deceive, as when one is promised something for nothing. For some problems one actually works directly with the constraints to find a solution. In mathematical optimization, for example, one uses the constraints to bound the problem and to find a solution. When searching for an oil pipeline leak, one can be certain that the oil entering must eventually exit somewhere and thus flow rate changes can be used to localize the leak. Overall, an understanding of constraints is critical to strategic thinking.

10.2 COMPLEXITY

In real world problems, one is usually faced with extreme complexity. Whether it is predicting the weather or understanding the causes of urban decay, whether tracing the causes of divorce or puzzling over the spread of AIDS, there are multiple pathways of causation, multiple actors, and various kinds of heterogeneity. The common response to complexity is to focus on a single cause. Some insist that homelessness is strictly a function of poverty and resist any evidence that a large number of the homeless are alcoholics who will not take a job if one is offered. Divorce is sometimes blamed entirely on the feminist movement, when in reality other social factors contribute to it. Such single cause analysis makes it easy for one to write letters to the editor of a newspaper, but is not really useful for solving the problems at hand. For this one must be able to disentangle complexity and be able to analyze it. This section addresses these issues.

Detecting patterns

A clue to the nature of complex behavior is the creation of patterns. These patterns can elucidate the nature of the web of causation involved. Patterns can occur in space, in time, or in categories. For example, decades before it was understood that malaria and other diseases are transmitted by mosquitoes, it was noted that these diseases were most prominent during the summer. It was also noted that those living near swamps were most affected. The existence of a pattern in space and one in time helped to point the way to the solution of the mystery of the source of these diseases, which until this century had not only killed millions but had made certain regions barely habitable.

The existence of patterns was crucial to untangling the causation of AIDS. This disease was particularly hard to comprehend because of its unusual difficulty of transmission and because of its long latency period. Disease experts have only to trace back a few months to a year at most in the case of the usual sexually transmitted diseases to discover how contagion has spread, but AIDS takes many years to manifest itself. The fact that the initial occurrence in the USA was within a restricted population of gay men in San Francisco was what made it possible to track down its origin and method of spread.

The existence of spatial patterns can also lead to the uncovering of scientific principles. For example, the regular hexagonal pattern of cracks in dried mud flats indicates that there is a least energy principle at work, as does the regular configuration of soap bubbles on wire frames. The pattern of ripples in the sand below the shallow water at the beach also appears to be the result of some simple regular process, but surprisingly the mechanism has not yet been worked out. In biology, it has been noted that certain types of plant are found only in certain habitats (e.g., cacti in deserts, mosses in moist areas). These patterns have led to the discovery of how different habits of growth and physiological responses allow plants to live in different habitats (i.e., the patterns hinted at relationships between form and function).

Tracing the threads of causation

In many cases, causation does not lead to simple patterns in time or space or of discrete groupings. Rather, one must trace out the threads of causation, like tracking the course of a root through the soil. This is particularly so for distributed causation. A distributed effect is one where the causal agent acts at many points or through many individuals. In such a case there is no single place where one can stand and observe an effect. For example, one can stand and observe a person hit a ball or directly observe hurricane damage, but the overfishing of a lake happens one fisherman at a time, gradually, so that it cannot be directly observed. The difficulty with such processes is that we tend to ignore such little, incremental, or distributed effects and they thus become invisible. There are some general principles, however, that can be applied to help trace such effects and causes.

☛ Nothing is free

Whereas it is obvious that nothing is free at the store, in other realms we treat certain goods as if they were free because the costs do not have to be paid directly. The realization that nothing is free provides a tool for tracing out consequences.

Within organizations, there is a tendency to view meetings and requests for information as free. Clearly managers need information in order to manage, but the cost of obtaining this information is rarely accounted for. Even more costly is the time spent in meetings, not only in direct cost of time spent by all parties (up to $30–$100/per hour per person for senior people), but in space required for meeting rooms, in the costs of setting up a meeting, and in the costs of disrupted schedules, for a total of up to $2000 for a one hour staff meeting for a 20 person department. If meetings had to be purchased and approved the way equipment is, it is doubtful whether they would be taken so lightly or whether so many of them would be a waste of time.

A corollary of this principle is that virtue is also not free. Let us take as an example the Americans With Disabilities Act (1994). This is certainly a virtuous law. At the level of requiring access, we can clearly afford to have a few handicap spots reserved at the supermarket and to have sidewalks and doors that allow wheelchairs to be admitted. These costs are negligible. But when carried to extremes, the law allows absurdities that interfere with the practice of every profession. A woman sued a movie theater because she was too fat to fit in the regular seats and wanted to bring her own chair, but her chair blocked the aisles so the theater would not let her in. A blind student sued a medical school because they would not allow her in as a student, but they argued that it is impossible to examine patients without sight and certainly impossible to do surgical procedures without sight. People have successfully claimed alcoholism as a disability, or extreme weight. When such suits become common (as they are beginning to) then they become a hidden, distributed cost of a virtuous law that is too vague.

A major area where goods are assumed to be free is in the realm of pollution control. The pollution control laws of the USA as now written do not take much, if any, account of the cost of reducing various pollutants or cleaning up waste sites. If half a hectare of land costs $10000, does it make sense to mandate spending $1000000 cleaning it up if there is no risk that the contamination will spread? There is an absolutist trend among some in the environmental movement who insist on reducing pesticides in food and pollutants in the environment to zero, even though the cost of doing so is infinite because it is impossible to perform any action without creating some type of waste. The literal interpretation of the laws regulating food safety (no harmful pesticide residues allowed in food taken to mean zero rather than very low and safe levels) becomes ludicrous when one can measure chemical residues to parts per trillion; such an interpretation would cost the economy untold amounts in lost agricultural production.

In general, it is easy for those in authority to request or order actions that are expensive if the costs are distributed and must be borne by someone else. Congress is the ultimate example of this tendency in the USA. This has led state governments to react against unfunded mandates. Corporate reorganizations, for another example, are also not free but are often treated as if they were, and in fact can be disastrously expensive.

☞ Everything goes someplace

This seemingly obvious principle has significant consequences for tracing out causation in various realms. Let us examine pets. All pets in a pet store that are sold go someplace, usually to a home. What then? Many pets are kept until they die (which is sometimes a brief time!), but what about the rest? Some escape and some are let loose. For these, what then? Where do they go? If it is a pet bunny, it probably gets eaten but may join the other wild rabbits. However, if it is a walking catfish that escapes, it may become the founder of a wild population. The consequence of ignoring the principle that everything goes someplace is that dozens of species from other parts of the world now make their home in Florida, including monkeys, poison toads, tilapia (cichlid fish), pythons, and catfish. Wildlife officials are now much more cautious about imports that have the potential to escape.

Let us take as another example tires. All tires wear down eventually. On heavily traveled roads one can calculate that the amount of tire dust is so great that the sides of roads should be centimeters deep in the stuff. Since they are not, we can ask where did it go? A little investigation reveals that bacteria break tire dust down gradually. Without asking where did it go, we would never know this fact because the phenomenon is not visible.

This principle is most particularly relevant when tracing out the fate of pollutants. It is easy to assume, as was the wont in the old days, that once pollution blows away, it is gone. For bad smells, dust, and pollen, this is certainly true, because dust settles back as dirt and pollen decays after it hits the ground. For other pollutants, however, we must remember that it all has to go somewhere. For pollutants such as lead that do not decay, this means that eventually they will become a problem wherever they go, as has turned out to be the case.

☞ Entropy is a pain

We may summarize this principle as: you cannot unscramble an egg. In the realm of pollution control this means that it is impossibly expensive to go out and collect the pollution once it has been spread all over the landscape. In the realm of governance, this means that it is much harder to get good morale back than it is to lose it, and much easier to create anarchy than to undo anarchy (witness the political situations in Bosnia, Haiti, and Somalia). Overall, entropy is the tendency for disorder to enter any system or structure. Metal rusts; books get dirty and faded; paint peels.

An understanding of entropy is very useful for tracing out causation. Entropy indicates that little glitches and imperfections are likely to accrue every time there is a transaction or a communication and also that there will be a cost to maintaining anything. What this means is that many types of problem result purely from the structure of a system. For example, negotiations between multiple

Entropy happens, even to the Parthenon.

parties are far more likely to be problematic when each speaks a different language and comes from a different culture purely because of translation and interpretation errors. One need not necessarily look for a "reason" that problems occur in this setting or ask who was the bad guy who scuttled the dialogue, because noise alone may be to blame.

We may ask how some laws come to be interpreted in such strange ways and find again that entropy has much to do with it. Consider that in a legal system that gives strong weight to precedent, noise (e.g., a particularly persuasive lawyer, a judge with strong personal opinions) can gradually distort the intent of the law. Once a ruling is made in a certain direction, there is a tendency to cite this as precedent. Since no one tallies up all the rulings and summarizes the predominant interpretation of the law, unusual rulings can carry disproportionate weight. These distortions ("noise") can build up and either change how the law is applied or create hopeless confusion and uneven application of the law. Such is the case in product liability trials, in the treatment of drug violations, and in cases involving the criminally insane: very inconsistent, almost random application of the law. The fault lies in a system that amplifies noise by relying heavily on precedent.

As another example, the more arcane a system, the more sensitive it is, and the more steps are involved, the more likely it is that entropy (noise) will be a problem. This follows directly from the multistep problem-solving model in Chapter 3. When I worked for an organization with a loose procurement system, entropy was not a problem. If there was a mistake on a procurement form, the procurement officer would fix it or maybe give me a call for clarification. Later, under a new set of strict rules, even trivial mistakes would send the whole thing back to be redone. When this occurred I had to start over with the entire chain of signatures. Since the system had simultaneously become more complex (new rules, more rules, new forms), which caused more errors, and more sensitive (less tolerant of minor mistakes), noise in the system was not smoothed out but was amplified. The consequence was that the wait for purchasing a computer or even software became extended to 12 months, and service contracts could take 18 months.

We can see from these examples that entropy is not merely something that happens to ancient pottery, but inserts itself into every process. If a system becomes hypersensitive to noise, then it can overreact or become swamped with delays (as in the example above). The Swedish navy in 1995 sheepishly admitted that their accusations of near shore approaches by Russian submarines were really misinterpretations of the sounds of swimming minks. Their acoustic system was hypersensitive, but had inadequate protection against false signals. Entropy can also lead to a gradual divergence between a system and its intent, as in the legal system example. In these and other cases, one must understand noise to understand how the system works.

Degrees of complexity

A very important type of pattern results from different types and degrees of complexity. If only a few objects or forces are involved in an interaction one can often predict the result. In the simple system one can trace out the effects at the level of the details (e.g., the paths of two billiard balls). Similarly, if very large numbers of objects are involved, the behavior may again appear simple or regular (e.g., the rate of popping of popcorn at a movie). A very large complex system can become simple because one observes the average or ensemble behavior, and not the details. In a gas, therefore, one does not try to trace out all the collisions or measure the speed of every molecule, but rather takes the temperature, which is a measure of the average energy across all the molecules.

A totally different effect occurs when complexity is at an intermediate level (tens to 100 interactions). Such middle number systems are likely to produce complex and unexpected behaviors. For example, natural ecosystems are very complex and behave like large number systems, producing fairly predictable behaviors at an aggregate level (average plant mass, average number of species). If, however, one is interested in the dynamics of an individual species within this system, it may be subject to many forces and limitations such that it becomes almost impossible to predict the population changes over time. In very simplified systems such as are created in the laboratory, one again achieves predicability. This is why the Biosphere colony had such trouble with their natural ecosystem replicas: they were too complex to be predictable but too small to exhibit ensemble behavior and higher order regularity.

We may extend this analysis to national economies. Modern industrial economies are so complex (so many different industries, sources of capital, outlets for
trade, resource bases, interactions) that no single economic problem affects the
whole economy. In contrast, a nation that is just beginning to industrialize is more
like a middle number system: complex, but not extremely complex. The result is
much more unpredictability, more complex dynamics, and more volatility. This
leads to more extreme economic crashes such as the Great Depression of the
1930s in America and Britain and the depressions of the late 1800s in Europe and
America.

It can be very helpful to know the type of complexity one is dealing with. For
simple systems, observations or simple experiments may provide insight. Control
is easy. For large number systems, ensemble behaviors are more useful measures
and again control may be possible. For middle number systems one should be
aware that predictability is more problematic and control nearly impossible. One
should be particularly concerned if the system one is trying to create turns into a
middle number system. Sophisticated systems analysis (simulation) may be
needed in these cases. With such an analysis, one should seek to uncover modes of
response (cycles, instabilities, chaotic dynamics or attractors, thresholds of
response, buffering, etc.) rather than expecting to make precise predictions. In
this way, the characteristic modes of behavior of the El Niño weather system have
become understood, even though we cannot make precise predictions about it.

Summary

When attempting to understand or manipulate complex systems, it is imperative
that one does not allow the desire for simplicity to rule. Single factor explanations
or policies are simply inadequate for such situations. Patterns can provide clues to
underlying processes. Tracing out causation and deciphering behavior can be
usefully achieved by understanding conservation laws (nothing is free, everything
goes someplace) and the effects of entropy. An understanding of complexity per
se is also essential.

10.3 FEEDBACK AND INFORMATION

An understanding of the roles of feedback and information in complex problem
domains is essential for effective problem solving. Feedback is a critical determi-
nant of the behavior of complex systems. The way in which information is
transmitted in a system must be understood because of the ways in which
information is biased, blocked, and distorted. Finally, proper utilization of
information feedback is crucial to enhancing personal performance as a professional. These issues are explored here in turn.

Feedback and system behavior

For any social, biological, or mechanical system, we must consider feedback to grasp how it functions. Without feedback to regulate such a system, it will fall into disorder and lose the ability to function. A person is hungry and eats. If the feedback to hunger is destroyed (e.g., by a brain injury), the person will starve and die. This is a symptom of anorexia. During driving, one must constantly correct the course of the car to stay on the road, using feedback from the location of the car. In many types of system, the feedback is not conscious as it is during driving, but results from the interplay of forces. For example, wolves are generally unable to reduce deer to too low a level because the deer become too hard to find. If deer get too common, they become malnourished, which makes them easier to catch, which causes the wolf population to increase, which reduces the deer population. This is a classic population interaction in ecology. The feedback here is not designed and therefore does not achieve a perfect balance. It is loosely governed between too few and too many deer and tends to cycle over this range. If wolves are removed (and human hunters are also removed), then deer increase to the point where they damage the vegetation and are at risk of massive starvation. Again there is feedback limiting the deer, but they are limited by starvation and not by predators.

In the wolf–deer system we can recognize several typical components of feedback systems. Positive feedback is the tendency of deer to increase more rapidly when they are low in number (because food is more abundant). This tends to help them to avoid extinction. Negative feedback by either predation or starvation limits the maximum population size. A lag may be recognized in the time it takes the wolf population to increase when the deer become very abundant. If positive feedback is too strong or lags are too great, then there will be a tendency

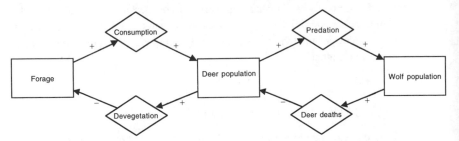

Negative feedback loops that govern a deer population. Increased forage availability increases consumption which allows the deer population to increase, but increased deer cause removal of vegetation, which decreases forage availability in the future. This is a negative loop. A similar negative loop occurs with more deer allowing the wolf population to increase which then causes a decrease in the deer. Other loops involving disease and other factors are also involved. Diagrams of such causal loops can help to clarify the causal structure of a problem.

to overshoot and for the numbers to collapse. This can be observed in many insect populations whose natural rate of increase is so great (with each adult female laying hundreds to thousands of eggs, they can increase very fast). In such populations, boom and bust cycles are observed (e.g., locusts, gypsy moths, aphids).

The examination of another natural system, the ant colony, provides an example of how even a collection of seemingly stupid actors can achieve results when guided by feedback. Colonial ants are not too bright, do not see too well, and wander around, yet they are very successful in every imaginable habitat except the Arctic. How is this possible? The answer lies in pheromones the ants give off that coordinate their behavior. When an ant is out foraging, it wanders around quite a bit. If it finds a good source of food (a fruit or dropped sweet) it heads back to the nest and lays down a special trail that alerts other ants that good food is out there. It does not make a beeline back to the nest, however, but follows its original trail back. This makes quite a crooked path for other ants to follow, but it may be observed that over time the path gets straightened as other ants come and go to the food. The reason is that the new ants gradually cut off parts of the trail that wander, and those that make a more direct path leave a stronger scent trail (because it is fresher); thus more ants are recruited to the straighter path. When the food is used up, the ants do not leave a scent trail when they return, and activity diminishes as the scent evaporates. Similarly, when an ant is attacked or killed, it gives off a special scent that attracts help. Each ant is a free agent, but is able to recruit others to help to dig, fight, or forage if it encounters special conditions. Similarly, it may be recruited by others. These feedbacks governed by pheromones create concerted, though rather chaotic, action to serve the goals of the colony.

These same elements of feedback operate in any human system. They lie behind the laws of supply and demand, for example. If an item becomes scarce or demand increases, this calls forth higher prices, which stimulates more production of that good or service. This is a classic negative feedback. A lag can introduce economic dislocations. For example, if demand increases for copper, this stimulates mining efforts. However, mine expansion is typically a prolonged process, usually requiring several years. This introduces a lag, such that production of metals such as copper tends to be out of phase with demand, causing strongly cyclic price levels and periodic large layoffs among miners.

We may take as another example the governance of factory production rates. In some settings, inventory has governed the production rate on the factory floor. The production line would go full steam until inventories (stock) built up to an intolerable level, at which point production would be cut back. Using inventories to regulate production therefore causes a lag to be introduced between when there is a change in the sales rate and when this becomes noticeable as a change in inventory. The consequence can be a cranking up (paying overtime) and down (layoffs) of the assembly line. Most modern manufacturing does not base production rates solely on inventory, for this very reason, but instead uses information on sales rates and historical data on how sales change with season (e.g., the intentional build up of inventory for the Christmas rush).

When we attempt to solve problems or understand social systems, discerning the role of feedback and lags is crucial. A run on a bank and a stock market freefall are both positive feedback responses. Once a panic sets in, it breeds further panic, causing a run on a bank. The response in the USA during the 1930s of declaring a bank holiday was the proper one because it broke the feedback cycle by allowing people time to cool off. The same has now been introduced on the New York stock exchange by automatically shutting down the exchange for a period of time if prices fall too much too fast, which again allows a cooling off and breaks the positive feedback cycle. Positive feedback can also be implicated in the acceleration of hostilities leading up to some wars and the tendency of the media to focus on the same few issues at any one time; once a few newspapers cover it, others do not want to be left out, which makes it a bigger story.

The invisible hand of economics is basically the operation of negative feedback and positive feedback working in conjuction. Supply and demand are kept in balance by these opposing forces (at least in an ideal market). When these forces are prevented from operating, then distortions become evident. Thus in communist Russia in the past, lines at stores were long for many goods because prices and production were fixed and did not reflect demand. When a good is subsidized, it will appear cheap and may be overexploited (such as grazing lands in the western USA at the turn of the century). In the case of the public grazing lands, there was no feedback about the increasing scarcity of grass (and thus of overgrazing) because it was not priced according to scarcity but was virtually given away. This caused large-scale degradation of the land and conversion to shrubs or weeds. In the Soviet Union, bread was subsidized to such an extent that it was actually fed to pigs as a substitute for grain.

Lags in social systems can also cause odd behaviors. One example concerns the movement of people in the USA to different cities or regions. For many years rumor had it that Los Angeles was the land of opportunity. Millions moved there. However, when the Los Angeles highways became gridlocked and the air became unbreathable and the jobs dried up, the word did not immediately get out. For at least another decade people kept moving there. It was not until the early 1990s, when large numbers of Angelenos began to move away looking for work that the word began to spread that maybe it was not the best place to go. The lag involved in negative perceptions can be even more persistent. Cities that acquire a reputation as ugly or terrible to live in become the widespread butt of jokes, which continue long after the city has improved (Cleveland, Ohio, being a case in point).

Positive feedback can lead to seemingly inexplicable results in social systems. We may take as an example the economic phenomenon of increasing returns proposed by Brian Arthur (Waldrop, 1992). It has been observed that the product that comes to dominate a market is not necessarily superior in either price or functionality. This is quite contrary to standard economic theory, which holds that consumers should make rational choices between competing products. Increasing returns explains this phenomenon. If a product is judged not just on its attributes but on how abundant it is, then a product with an initial market share advantage may come to dominate even if it is inferior. When holiday-makers shop, they may prefer to go to the mall even though the stores are the same chain as those at home, precisely because when the stores are in the same chain the tourists can return the items later if there is a problem or the clothes do not fit. Thus more prolific chain stores have an advantage.

We may take the personal computer as another example. When IBM introduced its personal computer, it was considered inferior to the Apple Macintosh in many ways. However, because IBM could afford to advertise on a large scale, they captured a significant share of the market. Once this occurred, software companies flocked to the IBM because it represented a larger market. Any new purchaser of a personal computer could then easily see that more software was available for the IBM-type machine than for the Apple Macintosh. This, plus issues of compatibility, gave the more abundant machine the advantage. The same scenario has been played out for the Betamax versus VHS video recorder technologies. Such dominance by an inferior technology is not necessarily permanent; if a new technology is vastly superior to an old but more abundant one it will still catch on. Increasing returns can also be observed in politics, where people are reluctant to join a small splinter party, and in ecology where a species that is rare may have an excessive disadvantage due to difficulty in forming flocks or in finding mates. Positive feedback can thus explain outcomes that otherwise seem to be exceptions.

In general, then, when solving a problem involving a social, biological, or engineered system, it is advisable to look for the feedback loops and lags that govern the system. These provide the greatest potential for understanding and control. In the case of the stock market a pause in trading (a lag) has proven sufficient to break the positive feedback of freefall. In the case of ghetto poverty, there is a strong positive feedback loop of widespread poverty causing conditions for children that discourage their success in later life. Attempts to alleviate this suffering in the short term (welfare) do nothing to break this strong positive feedback cycle. Likewise, when low income housing is built as a helpful measure, it actually amplifies the positive feedback cycle if the housing is large scale because this creates a large poor neighborhood that isolates children in this setting from the greater part of society. In arid grasslands, once overgrazing passes a certain point, the conversion to shrub lands (with low grazing value) is self-accelerating because of strong positive feedbacks in the system. Understanding this is the key to preventing such conversion because reclamation is prohibitively expensive. When managing any such social or biological system, the key is to use the strong feedback loops in the system to one's advantage, rather than to try to fight them head on. In managing deer, therefore, it is not useful to try to fight the positive feedback of population growth, but rather to manage hunting pressure, the negative feedback component. Those who oppose all hunting have no grasp of the fact that deer can strip every bit of vegetation from an area and then starve to death if there is no negative feedback (since wolves and large cats are missing from the system). Lags may be particularly good control points because they can often be overcome with information, as in the factory inventory example above.

It is also good to be aware that there are multiple feedback loops in many systems such that simple control points may not exist. In the deer example, there are several types of negative feedback that limit the population as it increases: increased predation, disease due to poor nutrition, disease due to crowding (easier transmission), and lack of shelter. In the economy there are also multiple pathways of feedback that can make the success or failure of a company far from predictable. This is also why there are seemingly inexplicable differences between countries such as the difference in extent of computerization of businesses between the USA and Europe such as the far greater use of automated bank teller machines in the USA. In such complex systems of multiple feedback loops, it is necessary to think a little more carefully and probably to diagram the causal feedbacks to get a grasp of the problem (see Nets and webs in Chapter 9).

Information transmission and distortion

Above, feedback was discussed in terms largely of processes, but information was also mentioned as a type of feedback. In human systems information is usually a key component of feedback systems, and thus the nature of information and its transmission needs to be clarified next. In addition, many problems result largely from failures of communication, and so information also needs to be considered from this angle.

Information transmission is a far from perfect process with many opportunities for communication foul-ups. The basic steps are concept, encoding, transmission, and decoding. The concept step is not usually included but I wish to distinguish it here to point out that the original concept someone has may be quite fuzzy. It is not safe to assume that just because a person speaks they know what they mean. This is the first danger in taking a legalistic or journalistic view of communication: that words actually represent the person's meaning. Many politicians have been pilloried for statements that may have really been only partially thought through or even incoherent. Lawyers try to corner people with exact word phrasings, when actually they may not know what they are thinking. The encoding step represents the conversion from a concept into some form of communication (speech, handsignals, flag waving, symbols). People have varying degrees of skill in this area. Most people have great difficulty expressing their thoughts, even if you give them time to sit and compose a letter. Extemporaneously, they may do very poorly. It is only the rare person who speaks in complete sentences and paragraphs. Often a verbal communication is quite garbled. Many politicians have this problem. Such garbling of course becomes worse when one is under pressure (such as when answering questions from the press on television) and distracted. This represents the second danger in interpreting a communication: assuming that the person was successful in expressing what he or she meant (if the person even knew what was meant). This danger is constantly present when people talk about emotions (as in spousal "discussions") because (1) the person is likely confused in the first place, and (2) our vocabulary for expressing emotional states is highly inadequate. When a legalistic approach is taken to discussions of emotion, and a person is strictly held to something he or she has said, then problems are only going to escalate. In such situations it is safe to assume only that people don't know what they feel and also that they don't know how to express it. These problems are particularly acute in politics where people are held to the literal meaning of sound bites out of context. In legal settings the legalistic approach assumes that witnesses know what they mean to say, and say what they mean, with the consequence that if a witness can be tricked into a certain phrasing he or she may be held to it.

The third stage of communication is transmission of a message. In one-on-one conversation, transmission is not an issue. But for public communication it becomes a serious issue. The greatest difficulty is usually that complex issues must be summarized as items, sound bites, or 30 second summaries. It is very difficult to summarize complex issues such as international trade or a treaty on space exploration in a short item, and this leads to a serious loss of information that creates difficulties for public discourse. The second difficulty is that issues are often filtered through journalists, who introduce a bias, a point of view, that distorts the message in subtle or not so subtle ways. Finally, a message as it is transmitted may be inherently ambiguous. This is particularly so for messages encoded as symbols (a flag, a graphic sign, etc.) because such symbols, though compact, carry multiple meanings or only very vague meanings.

The final stage, decoding, is also a source of hidden trouble, and causes many problems. People usually assume that they understand correctly something they hear (i.e., that their interpretation is the correct one). There are many causes of decoding failures. A common problem is that the person does not have background knowledge in the area under discussion. A sports fanatic talking to his wife may encounter this problem. Cultural differences are a common cause of different interpretations of what one hears. If an American hears that a 30-year-old man lives with his parents, they will interpret this as immature behavior, whereas in many other cultures this is the definition of a good son. There are also differences in perspective, discussed in Chapter 8, that cause a message to be given a different slant (e.g., the difference in how an optimist and a pessimist interpret what they hear). As a protection against such decoding failures, one should be aware both of the risk that one is misinterpreting a message and also, as a speaker, of differences in viewpoint on the part of one's listeners that may affect how they interpret what you say. In fact, it can be startling how badly people can misinterpret what they hear or read, even in the case of a scientist reading the work of colleagues.

Information feedback may also result from the compilation and analysis of measures of events in the world (consumer price index, sales figures, interest rates). Such information is abstracted from data that may be measured from various signs and symbols. For example, there is no one place, no dipstick, to obtain a measure of inflation that may be used as feedback for designing economic policies. Rather, inflation is measured as a composite of the changes in prices of many items. This example illustrates several problems with abstract information. First, just because you measure something and call it by a name, that does not mean that you are actually measuring something real or what you think you are measuring. In the case of consumer prices, many aspects of what is measured are misleading. If tires double in price over a period of time, we say that they have contributed to inflation. If, however, new tires now last 100 000 kilometers compared to 50 000 kilometers for tires from the earlier period, then they have actually not changed in price at all when measured as dollars per kilometer of wear. If, further, the new tires give better mileage and do not cause accidents by blowing out and causing a loss of control on the road, then one actually gets more tire for less money than before. The same may be said for personal computers, new cars, video recorders, double glazed windows, longer life roof tiles, longer life stain resistant carpet, and so on. Some new cars now can go 106 000 kilometers before the first engine tuning. Airbags, which represent a real increase in value, are now standard on many new cars. There is a particular problem with comparing average house prices when people want bigger homes today, and comparing car prices because modern cars have more functionality (air bags, antilock brakes, sound-proofing, etc.) and get better mileage. So there may be serious biases in the consumer price index that cause it to be misleading, particularly when it is used as a feedback to set interest rates. As an example, if people feel prosperous and buy bigger homes, this pushes up the consumer price index (CPI) and leads to higher interest rates to "control" inflation, which may not exist.

Second, the idea that one is actually measuring something real with an index is not necessarily supported by closer examination. For example, the concept that there is "an economy" is very misleading. During the 1960s through late 1980s there was ridiculous inflation of house prices in much of California, particularly along the coast. For those who bought a house early and stayed, there was no problem. For those who hoped to move in from other parts of the country it soon became an insurmountable barrier. These two groups experienced entirely different "inflation." As another example, once one has bought a house and is getting older, the main components of inflation that are noticeable are college costs for the children and medical costs. During the United States recession of 1992–4, it was even found that different regions of the country experienced recession at different times and to different degrees; so in what sense is there a national economy?

When using information as feedback to guide institutions and organizations, one must take care that the measures are real and not biased or late. For example, one can have high customer satisfaction but still lose market share if no younger consumers pick up the item (i.e., all business is repeats). As another example, if what is rewarded is working hard, then people will appear to work hard even if they produce little or nothing of value. This fallacy of rewarding behaviors rather than results (Gilbert, 1978) leads to inefficiency. It has recently been pointed out that many of the statistics that the government uses to guide policy are either biased (such as the CPI) or inadequate (Richman, 1993), which has significant ramifications for how government allocates resources and manages the economy.

Another example of how information is not derived in a straightforward way from data and may not mean what we think it does is the poverty rate. We often hear statistics about the poverty rate ($x\%$ of children live in poverty) that are used to drive government policy. The figures used to derive this statistic are rarely discussed but include certain simplifications that make them less than obvious in their meaning. For example, the fact that almost everyone starts out with a low salary and works their way up is not factored into these figures. Let us see what the consequence of this is. Consider members of a population that finish school at 17, work until they are 67 without ever being unemployed, and are guaranteed a 5% raise every year (without inflation). They begin work at the minimum wage of about $10 000 per year, which we all agree is not a living wage, and work up to $71 067, with an average national income of $30 533. Under this not totally unrealistic scenario, it takes nine years of annual raises before the entry level worker exceeds the poverty level of $15 000 per annum. Under these conditions of guaranteed work and guaranteed raises, we still have 18% of the population living under the poverty line. At the same time, these young workers who are just starting out do not consider themselves poor (most college students, for example). They do not need much to live on because they are not yet trying to buy a house, do not mind having a room mate, are not yet trying to save for their children's college fees, and may have been given a car and used furniture by their parents. Conversely, couples starting a family often find themselves in financial straits because they have medical bills and must get a larger house, bigger car, and furniture for the new baby all at once. Older people on a low income are not necessarily in financial distress because they have paid off their mortgage, have investments, and are not trying to save for college fees or for retirement. Therefore choosing a dollar cutoff line and declaring that those below it are in poverty is really meaningless and does not measure who is really in financial distress. The 40-year-old who makes $28 000 per year is in much more serious shape than the 18-year-old making $17 000 per year because he or she will be unable to support a family or save for retirement. The use of the numbers below the poverty line as information feedback on the state of the economy to guide policy is virtually an exercise in throwing dice when such a simplistic measure is used.

In summary, information has a significant role to play in problem solving. In trying to understand a problem, it is not always best to assume that the problem is merely a function of concrete things or actions. It may well be that the way information is exchanged or the way data are converted into information actually is the cause of the problem. For example, much of the bad news about the environment, such as the rate of desertification in Africa, is reported uncritically by the media, when actually such news is often unsupported by the facts (Simon, 1980), and as such is a misleading guide to what actions governments should take (i.e., the "information" is actually part of the problem). What if the major portion of the "inflation" in recent decades resulted from trends toward buying bigger houses and nicer cars and fancier clothes? These signs of prosperity (or at least of choices) would then have caused efforts to choke down the economy to prevent "overheating." I am not arguing that this has occurred (though Richman (1993) argues along these lines), but that potential biases in relevant indices could indeed have led to this result. In this type of setting, what may be most needed is not better control or fancy policies, but better information. Options here include provision of more realistic conversion of data to information, faster feedback of information, reduction of noise in the signal, removal of blocks to information flow, providing assistance in information encoding or decoding, and disambiguating symbols.

Feedback and performance

If you were blindfolded and told to walk in a straight line, you would not be able to tell whether you were going straight or not. In fact very few people can go straight when blindfolded. Clearly we need feedback on our performance, but in the world of work professionals may get very little feedback. Gilbert (1978) documents that for average performers in many settings (sales, factory work, etc.) the simple provision of information on what performance (in terms of products) is expected and of rapid feedback on how one is doing at any given time can substantially increase performance. Critical here is that feedback should include information on what specific aspects of output (defects, timeliness, numbers, quality, innovativeness) are deficient. An annual performance review is totally incapable of providing this type of feedback. With such feedback, one can continually learn and improve. Gilbert contrasts this approach with the more common one of rewarding behavior. Managers typically reward two types of behavior: hard work and loyalty. But hard work, manifested as long hours, rushing around, staying at the desk, and taking work home, may have little relation to performance as measured by value added or return on investment, as Gilbert suggests. Such excessive displays of hard work may actually be indicative of inefficiency, disorder, and problems with the system itself. A "hard worker" certainly has no time for creativity or learning. A hard worker, however, does demonstrate to the boss an eagerness to please and a subservience to company goals. Loyalty is manifested as enthusiastic support for the company, for the corporate culture, and for one's boss. Loyalty is valuable to a boss because it enhances his or her power base. Again, loyalty has nothing to do with performance and may even hurt it if loyalty prevents disagreeable things such as innovation and needed changes in policy. The result of rewarding hard work and loyalty is that people find things to do to look busy and make a show of being loyal, because they respond to what they are rewarded for and what they obtain feedback about, but this type of feedback does not increase their performance or their value to the company.

We may compare several professions to observe the effects of performance feedback. When American automobile makers in the 1970s were faced with Japanese cars with better fuel mileage and higher quality, at first they fumbled and lost market share, but subsequently they recovered and have gone after quality. There are now a number of measures of performance by which they can demonstrate that their skill at making cars has gone up: mileage is up, exhaust emissions are down, consumer complaints and recalls are down, sales are up compared to Japanese cars, and the cars last long enough that some offer 106 000 kilometer (60 000 mile) or longer power train warranties.

Particularly interesting is a contrast between surgeons and general practitioners. A surgeon faces several types of feedback that keep his or her skills sharp and prompt continued improvement in technique. During surgery, he or she immediately sees if the diagnosis is wrong (the spot on the lung in the X-ray turns out to be nothing) and must with some chagrin sew the patient up without doing anything. People complain bitterly about being cut open for no reason. A mistake in surgery results in immediate problems such as spurting blood, loss of blood pressure, or damage to some other organ. In the case of a mistake, there are various people in the operating room who will notice and point it out. If the mistake is serious, the patient dies, which is pretty strong feedback. Following the surgery, the doctor visits the patient and obtains feedback about recovery, whether a fever has developed, whether symptoms have been alleviated, etc. It is often the case that an autopsy is done on any patient who dies during or following surgery, which provides further information (did they have a weak heart or did the doctor sew them up with a cut blood vessel?). If a doctor loses too many patients, the hospital may revoke his or her privileges. Thus surgeons receive rapid, frequent, and emphatic feedback about the outcomes of their work, which enables them to improve performance by finding out what works and what does not. Surgeons are sometimes held to be a little arrogant, but it is also true that a surgeon can obtain proof that he or she is a great performer. However, surgeons do not obtain very good feedback on the long-term effectiveness of their procedures. They generally work on the basis of their own experience, which is largely anecdotal and does not control for the rate at which patients would get well on their own or for how long they would have lived without the surgery. Many surgical procedures have never been tested (performance feedback) in a controlled study, and when they are they often turn out to be ineffective, such as tonsilectomies, which are now rarely performed (Friend, 1995).

We may contrast this situation with that of the general practitioner. The GP generally faces people with only moderately serious illness. If the person is really sick the GP will refer them to a specialist, but they need not know what is wrong with the person they refer, a guess will do (I think you have an ulcer, go and see a gastroenterologist). In the USA, they will only rarely hear back about the true diagnosis of a person they refer to a specialist, so there is no feedback to improve their diagnostic skill. For less serious illness, GPs generally prescribe something and send the person away. For many types of illness (colds, influenza), the person will get better even if the doctor provided no help, and thus will not return. The doctor then thinks his actions were helpful when the person does not return, when in fact the person may not return because he or she got better independently. If the doctor was way off the mark, the patient may look for another doctor or seek out a specialist. The doctor does not enquire about the fate of patients who do not return (are they just healthy? moved away? died?) and thus never learns about patients who leave to find another doctor. There is no apparent effort to follow up on patients or to see how a sample of medicine performed. Overall, there is very little information at all fed back to a GP to help to hone his or her skills or learn about his deficiencies.

We may note another aspect of the feedback process with respect to performance in the domain of medicine. In a system with some measures of performance, the consumer can improve the system by making choices. In the case of cars, buyer's guides provide information on recall statistics, fuel mileage, consumer satisfaction, resale value, and repair expenses for various models. After a while, an unsuccessful model will be either fixed or withdrawn from the market because sales fall. But for doctors, almost no information is available to the patient. With some difficulty you can find out where your doctor went to university and what his or her specialty is, but it is almost impossible to find out about death rates during surgery or even the number of malpractice suits filed against the doctor, much less his or her accuracy in diagnosis. When malpractice suits are settled there is usually a clause of nondisclosure. If patients could find out more about their doctors, there would be an incentive for doctors to improve performance, and the overall system would improve as poorly performing doctors lost patients or quit practice altogether.

Let us look at some other professions. In sports, there is instant feedback every time an event is run or a game played. There is further feedback in the form of videotape playbacks. In this way the athlete can see exactly what went wrong, with the help of the coach ("You held your head up there son. Keep it down."). A consequence is that even the average professional athlete can achieve performances quite close to the best in the world. An active scientist receives feedback every time he or she writes an article or proposal, with detailed (even brutal) critiques from reviewers. These critiques often point out the specific things (laboratory technique, statistical analysis, etc.) that were incorrect, and thus help to improve the scientist's skill. In teaching, in contrast, it is much easier to tell whether one is keeping order and the student's interest than to tell whether they are learning more than last year's class did. Gilbert (1978) discusses systems that could provide such feedback in education, but these systems are currently not much utilized.

We can see that tremendous potential exists for improving performance in any field with feedback. In manufacturing tasks, output can double or better when feedback is provided (Gilbert, 1978), but in more intellectual professions the potential is even greater. For example, the average academic may publish from a few to 24 papers over a career, in contrast to the most prolific with 1000 or so publications (see Table 1, p. 51; Shockley, 1957; Price, 1963), a ratio of 50 to 100. The same applies in the area of inventing. Without feedback, it is very difficult to tell what actions lead to improvement and it is far too easy to drift. Feedback on work quality and status is particularly critical for highly iterative tasks, such as writing, software development, and design work. In all of these domains, one must almost always start with a rough product and successively refine it. Good feedback (testing, self-evaluation, peer review, etc.) can greatly enhance the iterative refinement process and make it more efficient.

Information and discovery

There are cases where the role of information can itself be an object of study that leads to new discoveries. This is particularly so in scientific research but is also true in business. If an actor takes some action that indicates awareness of information to which the actor does not have access, this indicates a mystery or a hoax. We can find examples from economics, extrasensory perception (ESP), animal behavior, and scientific fraud. The tracing of information flow can be useful both for discovering new facts and for disproving false ideas.

In economics, a long-standing simplification has been the omniscient optimizer as fundamental economic actor. This ideal actor would always buy the cheapest good or take the most efficient action. The body of economic theory built on this assumption was truly impressive, and was quite mathematical. However, a nagging suspicion developed over time that real people were not like this ideal economic agent. If you go to the department store and find the $4 steak knife you were looking for, you do not know for sure that this is the lowest price, but you are not likely to go all over town comparing prices to save 30 cents on this knife. You must guess, from general rules of thumb about prices of goods, whether this price is low enough. That is to say, you do not have perfect information. It is not the case that this is a trivial flaw in the ideal agent theories, because it leads to significant economic behaviors. For example, the success of major chains results from the fact that on average their thousands of items are priced low enough that it is not

worth comparison shopping: you can go in and buy dozens of items and be pretty
sure it would not have been worth shopping at a bunch of specialty stores, since
this would take much more time. The fact that the shopper is not an ideal agent
also explains aspects of brand loyalty (too much trouble to check out all competing
brands) and the occasional success of inferior products when advertising provides
the dominant information about a product and it is not worth testing all the
available products to find the best.

Animal behavior provides some interesting examples of information playing a
central role in discovery. It was mentioned above that colonial ants show
organized behavior in spite of not being too intelligent. This fact led to the
discovery of the first pheromones, because it seemed logically impossible that ants
knew what they were doing and came together in little committees to plan their
foraging expeditions. It was simple to show that crushing a few ants could start a
panic (pheromones released), whereas the removal of some ants was blithely
ignored (no pheromones). Take another example: bird migration has long been a
puzzle. How in the world can birds migrate such long distances without a map?
Further, they even do it over open water and in the dark and with cloudy skies.
Since there must be some information they utilize, many studies were done to
uncover how they do it. One hypothesis, that birds can utilize the Earth's magnetic
field, were at first met with incredulity, since of course it was thought magnetic

Birds seem to know north from south, and vice versa but how? Illustration by Richard
Loehle.

fields cannot be detected by animals. Studies have shown, however, that even bacteria have magnetite bodies in their cells that allow them to orient to the magnetic field of the Earth, and that animals have bodies of cells in their brains that serve a similar purpose. Other studies appeared to show orientation by the light from stars that indicate true north or by other mechanisms. The contradictions between these results have been resolved by studies showing that birds probably use several mechanisms and intercalibrate them. Thus, the migration of birds provided a puzzle that led to the discovery of new sensory mechanisms. It is worth noting that this is also an example of where either/or debate is not useful, because in this case the correct answer was that all of the proposed mechanisms are probably used, and not just one.

A similar problem has arisen in the study of altruism in animals. Social animals are known to exhibit behaviors, such as standing guard or grooming each other, that are inexplicable from a purely selfish point of view. The theory of kin selection argues that if the others that an individual helps are related to it, then the individual can increase its fitness in an inclusive sense even if its action has a cost to itself. This theory works out genetically in a very convincing manner, and applies quite clearly in social groups such as a pride of lions. However, the behaviors in question also seem to occur in cases where the individuals do not appear to have access to information about who is related to them. This is reminiscent of the omniscient economic agent discussed above. The solution (Pfennig and Sherman, 1995) appears to be that there are biochemical and other signals of relatedness, such as scents transmitted in urine, that animals can use to assess degree of relatedness. Once again, a paradox of information provided an open question that led to the discovery of a new mode of information transmission.

ESP is a case where information transmission still remains problematical. Here again, the putative phenomena involve transmission of information by an unknown vehicle. We might argue that if birds can detect magnetic fields to migrate in the dark, why could not humans transmit information across space to one another. The difference here, of course, is that no one can deny that birds migrate at night by quite straight paths, whereas concrete proof of ESP is not so universally accepted.

Summary

In summary, information and feedback are critical components of any dynamic system. Positive and negative feedback cycles actively govern dynamic systems and prevent collapse. Lags in feedback make achievement of optimal performance much more difficult, and generally result in oscillatory behavior. Information is a critical type of feedback, but unlike feedback in physical systems, information is not necessarily unambiguous. Information may be garbled, biased, abbreviated, or inadequate. The most cost-effective strategy for improving system performance may simply be the improvement of information quality and flow, particularly for individual performance.

10.4 BOTTLENECKS

Every complex system has bottlenecks. Identifying them can be very useful for solving problems. An obvious bottleneck occurs in a road system under repair. The bottleneck can be particularly acute when system design is such that no alternative routes have been provided. Highway systems may even create their own bottlenecks by cutting off side streets, thereby making traffic more dependent on the major roads. Transportation networks also are subject to paradoxes, such that attempts to fix traffic jams by adding capacity have no effect or actually make things worse (Arnott and Small, 1994). For example, various forms of mass transportation are generally more efficient and faster for each individual if more people take them (with more traffic, trains can run more often, reducing waiting time). The paradoxical effect of adding more road capacity can be that overall average commuter times can go up as those using mass transit experience increased delays and switch to driving because there are insufficient passenger numbers to allow trains or buses to run frequently (Arnott and Small, 1994). Road capacity increases can also paradoxically encourage people to take jobs farther from their homes and thereby become dependent on major arteries (highways) to commute to work, where before they worked near home and took side streets.

It is a human tendency to hate limits and to try to push them back, but sometimes bottlenecks are useful. For example, in San Francisco, traffic flow in and out of the city is very limited by the bridges, especially during rush hour. This means that it is difficult to live outside the city and commute. The consequence is that there is much less "suburbanization" than in other cities. The central business district of San Francisco has thus not been abandoned. A city or district that is confined by such geographic circumstances is much more able to sustain mass transit, with San Francisco and Manhattan being good examples. A traffic bottleneck can thus have a positive effect.

In a business context bottlenecks can be expensive and are often associated with control points. Any attempt to exercise oversight has the potential to create a bottleneck. If a manager must sign for every purchase then he or she must be very certain to review them quickly to prevent a delay, because delays in purchasing can cause production to stop or activities to be curtailed. If procurement decides to order items in bulk to save money and holds orders until enough accumulate, then one may have to wait six months to obtain a computer for a new employee, thereby causing a very expensive loss of productivity. Clearly this is foolish because if it is known that about x computers are being ordered per month then a bulk order can be placed in advance, and waiting times can be reduced to weeks with the same cost.

Decision making often represents the most serious bottleneck. If too many signoffs are required for a new product, for example, then the delays introduced can be disastrous. This was the case with the old Xerox company, which had so many signoffs required that some potentially major products never made it to market. We may contrast this with the culture at 3M, where an individual engineer can take initiative and develop a new product with no external delays. Decision points after a new product is developed are specific and involve limited numbers of decision makers. It is characteristic of 3M's product line that many of their individual products do not require huge start-up capital (e.g., Post-it notes, Scotch tape), so a decision bottleneck is not useful. In contrast, a decision to develop a new model of an automobile should not be taken lightly, and bottlenecks should actually be introduced if not present to cause delay so that actions can be considered carefully.

It is characteristic of some bottlenecks that when their capacity is exceeded they create delays in a nonlinear fashion. We clearly observe this on a freeway or motorway, where traffic is either moving at the speed limit or crawling, but rarely can be observed moving smoothly at 50 kilometers per hour (35 miles per hour). The same phenomenon can be observed when managers become overloaded, because then they feel overwhelmed and are reluctant to make major decisions. Under these conditions, additional time is spent shuffling papers and reprioritizing tasks, and so even less throughput is achieved than normal, causing even more work back-up.

Bottlenecks need not be physical, but can be abstract. For example, in a study of a region of East Africa where there are both pastoralists and farmers, it was found that economic development was limited not by the lack of wealth but by the lack of money. That is, there was no reliable banking system. Without currency, it is not possible to save profits when one has an excess. For pastoralists, this means that wealth can be saved only in the form of live cattle, but live cattle must continually eat to be maintained. This means that the profitability of the system is much lower than if excess cattle could be sold and the money put in the bank. For the farmers, excess food that cannot be eaten is simply waste. The lack of currency also does not allow anyone to borrow to try to improve efficiency or productivity. Thus currency in this system represents a bottleneck, but one that depends on social stability and institutional infrastructures.

For understanding a complex system, it is very useful to first identify the bottlenecks. These represent points where control may be exercised. It is not, however, sufficient to eliminate a bottleneck, because this is likely to merely create a bottleneck somewhere else. Without knowledge of the entire system, the elimination of single bottlenecks can have unforeseen consequences and puts the manager in the position of the mole whacker game at the carnival where one tries to whack the moles that pop out of the holes. Such a game has no resolution and commonly goes by the name of "fire fighting" in business. A properly designed system does not have any critical major bottlenecks that can cause production or work flow to back up, but may have many little ones that cause only minor delays. A key to such design is to avoid flows of materials or decisions that are too centrally focused. In the 3M example, there is no central place for new products, rather new products originate in a distributed fashion by the initiative of engineers. This ensures a continuous flow of new products, which has made 3M so successful. In distinct contrast, when a chief executive officer is a micromanager, he or she creates a severe bottleneck that can quickly stifle a corporation. On an assembly line, care must be taken that a single local problem with one car does not create a bottleneck. One notes that efficient assembly line procedures are set up such that one is never left waiting for parts. In other types of operation, it does not always occur to people that engineers without computers and workers without tools (orders placed months ago) are "waiting for parts" just as on an assembly line, which has a cost. Every effort should be put into eliminating bottlenecks that involve parts, supplies, purchasing, etc. because these inexpensive items can cause large hidden expenses and such bottlenecks do not represent useful control points. A useful control point is one that provides oversight and so prevents the hasty or uncontrolled procurement of buildings or start-up of new factories. A distributed, flexible, matrix organization has the advantage that there are many small bottlenecks but few large ones. One does not obtain economies of scale in such an organization but delays and losses due to bottlenecks are reduced.

In design problems, bottlenecks are a constant source of problems and solutions. In computers, for example, bottlenecks in data flow can make or break a system design. A fast CPU is not much use with a slow bus, because the user will perceive it as a slow computer. As mentioned previously, road design is often motivated by efforts to eliminate bottlenecks, though quite often the initiative comes from the public or politicians, and the counterintuitive aspect of network properties (increased throughput on major roads creating the potential for more serious bottlenecks) may not be appreciated.

It is often the case that bottlenecks exist in information flow. Let us consider media reporting on complex issues such as the North American Free Trade Agreement or a tax bill. Such a bill or treaty is a complex document with many ramifications, but the only way that most people find out about it is from newspapers. This is a bottleneck of information flow. The reader rarely gets an objective brief summary of the document, much less the document itself, but rather is presented with reactions to it by commentators. This makes it very difficult to assess what the document actually says. There is movement toward putting all bills before the United States Congress on the Internet so that they may be accessed by anyone. This clearly removes a bottleneck and could have important consequences. It would allow many people with an interest and expertise in the area touched on by the bill to get a look at it before it is too late and is signed into law.

Another area where information bottlenecks are important is in military operations. In the Vietnam war, the use of the jungle for concealment and tunnels for hiding troops prevented any information on enemy activity from being obtained by the United States army. It provided an insurmountable information bottleneck that contributed to the eventual withdrawal of American troops.

It is notable that the deliberate creation of information bottlenecks is a central strategy of most oppressive governments. Literature from outside the country is prohibited. Media are tightly controlled. Even fiction is restricted to certain themes. These actions show how an information bottleneck can be a control point.

Overall, bottlenecks are very important control points. Manipulating a system often involves the creation of control points in the form of bottlenecks. If bottlenecks already exist, manipulating them or relieving them can change system behavior. It is not the case, however, that it is always wise to eliminate bottlenecks, though the natural tendency is to do so.

Summary: The strategic thinker

Strategic thinking is an overall technology for problem solving with the potential for increasing both the quantity and the quality of work in fields where creation of novel solutions is critical, for example design, invention, institutional innovation, research, software development, and engineering. It is based on an understanding of both outward processes (actions) and inner operations (cognition, attitudes). It takes particular care to be alert to the inherent flaws in all aspects of the problem-solving process, and builds in checks and balances against these flaws.

There are four factors involved in the successful development of an innovative creation: creative mental functioning, an understanding of the discovery process, an appreciation of the structure of multistep problems, and the utilization of reality checks. Creative mental functioning is necessary for one to be able to recognize problems, overcome intimidation by the status quo, overcome barriers to thought, and avoid stagnation. Various attitudes and work habits such as topic surfing and overcoming writer's block, contemplative walking and not becoming an expert, may allow one to increase innovative capacity and to recognize good ideas when they come along. Creative functioning alone, however, produces only bright ideas not finished products. Discovery is the next key step that represents the development of the germ of an innovative idea. The key point in the context of strategic thinking is the recognition that discoveries are almost always initially amorphous and in need of elaboration before they can be communicated, tested, or formally documented. Elaboration is a fundamental but usually overlooked part of the innovation process. During the elaboration of an idea or invention, prototypes or models must be built, definitions or metrics developed, vague ideas made more concrete, and the idea must be communicated. It is necessary next to keep in mind that there are always opportunities for mistakes that may destroy a new discovery or bright idea, or that may require one to rework a theory. It was shown by a systems analysis of the problem-solving process (Chapter 3) that multistep problems are particlarly susceptible to the effects of mistakes, which waste effort in an exponential manner with increasing problem complexity. An understanding of the structure of multistep problems can help one to avoid catastrophic waste of time, particularly by looking for ways to convert sequential into iterative problems. Finally, all of this work may be for naught if the product or idea is not effectively tested against reality. It is particularly important to use reality tests because the human mind does not function very logically and is prone to self-delusion. For this reason, internal reality checks are useful. We may check for the coherence of an idea or theory, examine the premises behind an idea or product, and use if . . . then conditional reasoning to verify the implications of our idea or product. It is also the case that various types of reasoning are suspect, such as arguments by opposition (exclusionary logic), reasoning from inadequate data, faulty generalization, and deductions that do not follow from the data. These flaws in reasoning should be checked for and corrected if they affect a product or idea. It is also necessary to test a product or idea on its merits. The first thing an inventor or creator should do is try to break the creative product, either physically or by finding conditions under which it is not valid or fails. It is also imperative to test a creation against some type of external data or standard. Techniques such as experiments, prototypes, scale models, peer review, opinion polls, market testing, etc. can be crucial in this regard.

Style and attitude affect performance at all four of the above stages. It was shown (Chapter 5) that different styles of attacking problems prove more successful for certain types of problem than for others. For example, one may contrast the tinkerer with the visionary. The tinkerer prefers to improve an existing product or process whereas the visionary prefers to start from scratch and create something new and better. It is critical that people with a defined style seek out work environments or problem domains that are amenable to their style of working or else they will not be very successful no matter how hard they work and no matter how smart they are. A visionary in an entry level job is not likely to be given the latitude to apply that vision in practice. Style can interact with the different stages of problem solving and affect productivity in a direct way. For example, on one hand the visionary may neglect elaboration and reality testing and leap right into declaring that an idea is a finished product. On the other hand, the tinkerer may fiddle forever with the details and never ship out a completed product. Attitude also interacts with these four stages. For example, we saw (Chapter 6) that the person who lacks a little detachment may be so afraid of failure that they never dare to look into a passing wild idea. The person who lacks humility may ignore all feedback from reality checks that might help them to correct an erroneous idea. Most pernicious of all, a person who is dishonest may ignore hints that the product is dangerous or the idea flawed. Aspects of personal style and attitude can therefore aid one to be more effective or lead one astray if there is a mismatch between style and task or if one's attitude is flawed.

It is useful to examine the question of what tasks might provide useful training in strategic thinking. Tasks that promote intense concentration such as chess promote the intensity necessary to carry out long chains of reasoning. Tasks that teach hierarchical organizational skills, such as computer programming, can help one to learn to master complex sets of information. Familiarity with maps, charts, diagrams, and blueprints also provides mental tools that can be applied in other domains. Familiarity with odds and chance is also quite useful. Surprisingly, skill in team sports is not particularly helpful, because in real life the rules change too much and the opponent is not identified by a different colored jersey. Finally, the practice of building things can provide invaluable experience for strategic problem solving.

On the basis of these ideas, it is possible to be a more effective problem solver. There are three components of this: problem finding, the use of specific tools of thought, and generating solutions.

Problem finding utilizes the fact that problems worth solving usually generate certain symptoms, including paradox and contradiction, or may be found by considering changes in perspective and scale. Paradox is a particular configuration of facts that points to an opportunity. A paradox means either that the general understanding of a phenomenon is faulty, or that our picture is incomplete. In either case, if one can recognize a paradox that others miss then there is an opportunity for discovery, for innovation, or for profit. Bottlenecks in systems can cause paradoxes, and represent possible control points for a system.

Consideration of perspective and scale provides a number of insights. Many times the nature of a problem can only be discerned with the proper perspective, which may simultaneously provide a solution. Perspective also provides insights into the causes of misunderstandings that arise in human systems. Changes in perspective (e.g., of a corporation) will show different aspects of functioning, and may show a system to be performing well in some ways and poorly in other ways. One may recognize viewpoint and time perspectives. Scale problems arise in many contexts, from growing organizations to the scaling up of architectural models or production processes. Changes of scale occur with changes in size, speed, and complexity, and general laws of scaling exist.

There are a number of general tools of thought that are generally useful, including evolutionary refinement, analogy, classification, the detective model, failure analysis, and models of cycles, spirals, nets, and webs. Evolutionary refinement is directly analogous to the evolutionary process. It begins with a functional, but crude, solution, and then successively refines it. Software prototyping is a good example. Analogy is a powerful problem-solving tool, though it is not the whole picture, as some maintain. Analogy helps one to locate in memory past problems similar to the one at hand, which may help to generate a solution. It can also provide models, comparisons, and bridges across disciplinary gulfs. The detective model is useful for narrowing down lists of candidates (causes of a disease, suitable homes to purchase, etc.) on the basis of sets of criteria. Classification is an essential problem-solving tool. Classifications organize information, models, or theories so that they can be applied more effectively. Problem solving in many cases involves a reclassification into new categories. Decomposition into component parts is an important type of classification. The generation of scenarios is a useful type of problem-solving strategy. It allows plans to be constructed so that their feasibility may be examined. The What if? type of scenario is useful for testing out the implications of some action that has never previously occurred. This represents the tracing out of the consequences of a change in the normal rules. In failure analysis, one examines what could possibly go wrong, and tries to design against such failures. Failure analysis is common in building design and in warfare, but can profitably be applied in other areas as well. We may characterize systems that fail catastrophically as brittle, and those that fail gracefully as robust. When human lives are at stake, it is best to avoid brittle designs. It is argued that many natural processes may be modeled with cycles or spirals (e.g., seasonal cycles of the economy linked to agriculture). These models may allow such systems to be better understood. A transformation occurs when something moves from one state to a qualitatively different one (e.g., by marriage or incorporation). Recognition of transformations and the acts by which they are brought about allows them to be understood and manipulated to advantage. Finally, nets and webs are useful constructs for depicting complex relationships.

Generating a solution involves getting a grip on the problem, like the small boy leading the water buffalo by a ring in its nose. It is not sufficient to know many facts about something. New knowledge is only generated or systems controlled by those who apply leverage to control points. The key is knowing where to push and how. An understanding of constraints, complexity, feedbacks, information, and bottlenecks provides this knowledge.

Constraints and tradeoffs prove to be present in most design, engineering, and systems problems. They provide insight into the structure of a system and provide avenues of attack for understanding or controlling the system. A major focus of industrial activity is the overcoming of constraints with new designs, materials, and processes. New lightweight materials, for example, have improved the fuel mileage of cars. New production processes and new silicon chip designs continually improve the performance of computers. Constraints and tradeoffs can be recognized as critical to the design of biological systems. Considerable progress has been made in biology by examining the tradeoffs resulting from physical and metabolic constraints. We can clearly recognize constraints in economic systems. For example, there is the well-known tradeoff between risk and yield in the stock market. The constraint that enforcing rules must have a cost is often overlooked. Attempts to circumvent constraints often lead to deficit financing. Finally, one may recognize constraints in the context of personal living. It is difficult, for example, to be in two places at once. Information and new technologies can help to alleviate constraints in these varied domains, but constraints will always exist and acting like they do not will always lead to trouble.

Complexity is an important attribute of many problems. Single causes are rarely at the root of phenomena. Various tools can help to tease out complex relationships. Tracing the threads of causation is useful, particularly for distributed causation. One may trace out causation by noting that nothing is free (which helps to account for all costs), by observing that everything goes someplace (which focuses attention on ultimate destinations or outcomes), and by realizing that entropy is always involved (which draws attention to the disorder produced by a process). Complexity per se is an important attribute of many systems. Complex economies appear to be more stable than simple ones because there are more industrial sectors that are less likely to be syncronized in their cycles and because there are mechanisms such as savings accounts and lines of credit that buffer against adverse periods.

Feedback exists in any dynamic system and can lead to stable or unstable behavior. An understanding of positive and negative feedback and of lags can provide insights into the dynamics and control points in a system. Information is a particular type of feedback that is important for improving professional performance and in the managing of organizations. Errors of communication and of converting data into more complex information lie at the root of many problems. Merely correcting how information is processed can often lead to improved system or personal performance.

Bottlenecks represent very useful control points. In a business setting, a bottleneck in production represents an opportunity to improve productivity. It must be cautioned that removal of one bottleneck will certainly create a bottleneck elsewhere, since something is always limiting to production, but the new bottleneck may be distributed and not necessarily easy to find. To exercise control, it is often necessary to create a bottleneck, such as a central point for financial control or for clearance of public statements by an organization. High throughput systems are particularly prone to bottlenecks. It is useful to eliminate bottlenecks that are not actual control points, such as hold-ups in the procurement of supplies that do not actually serve a control purpose (it serves no purpose to hold up operations because paper is on back order).

The strategic thinking process thus represents a synthesis of knowledge on how to generate novel ideas more effectively, how to convert ideas into products, how to utilize conceptual tools, and how complex systems function. This synthesis puts the solution of complex problems within reach and can increase the leverage that the individual problem solver can exert.

Literature cited

Adler, M. J. 1985. *Ten Philosophical Mistakes*. Collier Books, New York.

Albert, R. S. 1975. Toward a behavioral definition of genius. *American Psychologist*, **30**: 140–51.

Anderson, C. 1992. Writer's cramp. *Nature*, **355**: 101.

Arieti, S. 1976. *Creativity: The Magic Synthesis*. Basic Books, New York.

Arnott, R. and K. Small. 1994. The economics of traffic congestion. *American Scientist*, **82**: 446–55.

Bailey, J. 1995. The recycling myth. *Wall Street Journal*, 19 January.

Bauer, H. H. 1992. *Scientific Literacy and the Myth of the Scientific Method*. University of Illinois Press, Chicago.

Biondi, A. M. 1980. About the small cage habit. *Journal of Creative Behavior*, **14**: 75–6.

Boorstin, D. J. 1983. *The Discoverers*. Random House, New York.

Boorstin, D. J. 1992. *The Creators*. Random House, New York.

Boxenbaum, H., F. Pivinski, and S. J. Ruberg. 1987. Publication rates of pharmaceutical scientists: application of the Waring distribution. *Drug Metabolism. Reviews*, **18**: 553–71.

Bylinsky, G. 1994. The digital factory. *Fortune*, 14 November, pp. 92–110.

Cairns, J. 1988. Through a magic casement. *Nature*, **336**: 368–9.

Collins, H. and T. Pinch. 1993. *The Golem*. Cambridge University Press, Cambridge.

Crease, R. P. 1992. The trajectory of techniques: lessons from the past. *Science*, 257: 350–3.

Darwin, C. 1881. *The Formation of Vegetable Mould, Through the Action of Worms, With Observations on Their Habits*. John Murray, London.

Darwin, F. (ed.) 1958. *The Autobiography Of Charles Darwin And Selected Letters*, First published 1892. Dover, New York.

DeCicco, J. and M. Ross. 1994. Improving automotive efficiency. *Scientific American*, December, pp. 52–7.

Drucker, P. F. 1985. *Innovation and Entrepreneurship*. Harper & Row, New York.

Feynman, R. P. 1984. *Surely You're Joking Mr. Feynman*. Norton Publ., New York.

Friend, T. 1995. That operation you're getting may be experimental. *USA Today*, 13 September.

Gardner, H. 1983. *Frames of Mind: The Theory of Multiple Intelligences*. Basic Books, New York.

Gibbs, W. W. 1994. Software's chronic crisis. *Scientific American*, September pp. 86–95.

Giere, R. N. 1994. The cognitive structure of scientific theories. *Philosophy of Science*, **61**: 276–96.

Gilbert, T. F. 1978. *Human Competence*. McGraw-Hill, New York.

Gleick, J. 1987a. *Chaos: Making A New Science*. Penguin Books, New York.

Gleick, J. 1987b. New images of chaos that are stirring a science revolution. *Smithsonian* December, pp. 122–35.

Hadamard, J. 1949. *The Psychology Of Invention In The Mathematical Field*. Princeton University Press, Princeton, NJ.

Hall, S. S. 1992. How technique is changing science. *Science*, 257: 344–9.

Hunter, M. S. 1978. Exiting creative researchers from graduate education. *Journal Of Creative Behavior*, 12: 209–13.

Jamison, K. R. 1995. Manic-depressive illness and creativity. *Scientific American*, February, pp. 62–7.

Johnson, P. 1988. *Intellectuals*. Harper & Row, New York.

Jones, G. and K. Douglas. 1994. The quiet genius who decoded life. *New Scientist*, 8 October, pp. 33–5.

Koestler, A. 1964. *The Act of Creation*. Macmillan, New York.

Kuhn, T. S. 1970. *The Structure of Scientific Revolutions*. University of Chicago Press, Chicago.

Langley, P. and R. Jones. 1988. A computational model of scientific insight. In R. J. Sternberg (ed.), *The Nature of Creativity*, pp. 177–201. Cambridge University Press, Cambridge.

Lightman, A. and O. Gingerich. 1992. When do anomalies begin? *Science*, 255: 690–5.

Loehle, C. 1987. Hypothesis testing in ecology: psychological aspects and the importance of theory maturation. *Quarterly Review of Biology*, 62: 397–409.

Loehle, C. 1988a. Philosophical tools: potential applications to ecology. *Oikos*, 51: 97–104.

Loehle, C. 1988b. Tree life history theory: the role of defenses. *Canadian Journal of Forest Research*, 18: 209–22.

Loehle, C. 1990. A guide to increased creativity in research: inspiration or perspiration? *Bioscience*, 40: 123–9.

Mann, C. 1990. Meta-analysis in the breach. *Science*, 249: 476–80.

Margolis, H. 1987. *Patterns, Thinking, and Cognition*. University of Chicago Press, Chicago.

McDonald, K. A. 1990. Researchers increasingly worried about unreliability of big-science projects. *Chronicle Higher Education*, 36: 1, A8-A9.

McManus, P. F. 1979. *Never Sniff a Gift Fish*. Henry Holt, New York.

Medawar, P. B. 1967. *The Art of the Soluble*. Oxford University Press, Oxford.

Parker, G. 1989. Predicting the productive research psychiatrist. *British Journal of Psychiatry*, 154: 109–12.

Peters, T. and N. Austin. 1985. *A Passion For Excellence*. Warner Books, New York.

Petroski, H. 1992. *The Evolution of Useful Things*. Vintage Books, New York.

Pfennig, D. W. and P. W. Sherman. 1995. Kin recognition. *Scientific American*, June, pp. 98–103.

Popper, K. R. 1963. *Conjectures And Refutations: The Growth Of Scientific Knowledge*. Harper & Row, New York.

Price, D. 1963. *Little Science, Big Science*. Columbia University Press, New York.

Richman, L. S. 1993. Why the economic data mislead us. *Fortune*, 8 March, 1993 pp. 108–14.

Root-Bernstein, R. S. 1989. *Discovering*. Harvard University Press, Cambridge, MA.

Shockley, W. 1957. On the statistics of individual variations of productivity in research laboratories. *Proceedings of the Institute of Radio Engineers*, **45**: 279–90.

Sidorowich, J. J. 1992. Repellors attract attention. *Nature*, **355**: 584–5.

Simon, J. L. 1980. Resources, population, environment: An oversupply of false bad news. *Science*, **208**: 1431–7.

Simonton, D. K. 1988. *Scientific Genius*. Cambridge University Press, New York.

Skinner, B. F. 1959. A case study in scientific method. In S. Koch (ed.). *Psychology: A Study of a Science*, pp. 359–79. McGraw-Hill, New York.

Stanovich, K. E. 1992. *How to Think Straight About Psychology*. Harper Collins, New York.

Sternberg, R. J. 1988. *The Nature of Creativity*. Cambridge University Press, Cambridge.

Thelan, H. A. 1972. *Education And The Human Guest*. University of Chicago Press, Chicago.

Treisman, M. 1995. The multiregional and single origin hypotheses of the evolution of modern man – A reconciliation. *Journal of Theoretical Biology* **173**: 23–9.

Tsonis, A. A. and J. B. Elsner. 1992. Nonlinear prediction as a way of distinguishing chaos from random fractal sequences. *Nature*, **358**: 217–20.

Waldrop, M. M. 1992. *Complexity*. Simon & Schuster, New York.

Watson, J. D. 1968. *The Double Helix*. New American Library, New York.

Weisberg, R. 1986. *Creativity, Genius, and Other Myths*. W. H. Freeman and Co., New York.

Whimbey, A. and L. S. Whimbey. 1976. *Intelligence Can Be Taught*. Bantam, New York.

Index